Edexcel AS English Language

Alison Ross

7 Day Loan

STUDENT BOOK

Consultant: Jen Greatrex

Skills Coverage Map

Skill / Specification Coverage	Unit 1	Unit 2
Studying spoken texts	13, 15–19, 57–59	117–118, 129–133, 143–149
Studying written texts	13, 56	96–103, 112–117
Studying electronic texts	14, 16, 33	
Studying multi-modal texts	20–21, 33	128–141
Writing for a reading audience		93, 95–127
Writing for a listening audience	18	94, 128–155
How speakers/writers present an identity to their audiences	25, 27, 66, 68–70, 87–88	142–145
The effect of the way speakers/writers present themselves on real or constructed identity (the ability of most speakers and writers to project a persona)	65–91	142–145
Analysing conversation	57–60	98–103
Exploring the techniques of a variety of genres		96–103, 112–117, 129–133, 143–149
Preparation for writing, including research, recording and interviewing		104–105, 119–121, 134–135
The craft of writing/creating own texts		95, 106–109, 122–125, 136–140, 150–153
Commenting on your language choices		95, 103, 110–111, 121, 126–127, 140–141, 151, 154–155
The differences between planned and spontaneous communication	14–15	
Knowledge/understanding of the key constituents of language:	11, 31, 61	
• Characteristic speech sounds and intonation patterns (phonetics and phonology)	11, 35–40	
• Vocabulary of English, including: origins, meanings and usage of words (lexis and semantics)	11, 16–18, 22, 45–48, 76	
• The forms and structures of words (morphology)	11, 41–44	
• Phrases, clauses, sentences (grammar)	11, 19, 23, 29, 49–55, 76, 82	100–102
• Texts in speech and writing (discourse)	11, 56–61	
Understanding key concepts from semantics and pragmatics	12, 84–88	146–147
Graphology – the writing system and its presentation	11, 31–34	
Understanding mode	10, 13–21	
Understanding field	10, 22–23	
Understanding function	10, 24–26	
Understanding tenor	10, 27–30	
The influence of contextual factors:	10	
• Geographical variation and attitudes to different varieties of English	38, 67, 77–80	
• Occupation and the use of subject-specific jargon	22, 81, 82	
• Gender and the age of the speaker/writer	71–77	
• Social context, such as location, occasion	12	
• Cultural issues, e.g. the impact of modern technology, the influence of youth culture, multiculturalism	83	
• Power issues, e.g. political correctness	27, 82–83	
• Class/social status and language	38, 66–67, 80	
Contemporary language change (electronic forms and conventions)	14, 33	
Topical issues in language	38	

Contents

GCE AS English Language
Introduction

Welcome to English Language at advanced level. In this course you will explore a wide variety of written, spoken and electronic texts, including literary, non-fiction and media texts. You will be asking the question, 'How do these texts use language to construct their meaning?' You will also create your own texts.

How can I make English Language most rewarding ?

1. Approach language with an enquiring and open mind. Listen to how people talk (and listen to how you talk). Don't judge what is being said, but try to describe it, and ask questions about it. Challenge simple assumptions that you or others may have, such as that written language is always formal and spoken language always informal.

2. Draw on the experience and understanding of language use that you already have. Think about all the different situations in which you use language effectively – not just writing essays but texting your friends, using MSN and chat forums, talking at home at and school or college, in contexts across the spectrum of detail, complexity and formality.

3. Enjoy reading and listening to all sorts of texts – even when the text may seem unfamiliar and strange. The more you stick with it, the more you will learn and be able to say something about it.

4. Practise using the toolkit provided to respond to texts. During the course you will need to do this sometimes concisely by providing short answer responses, sometimes in essays and sometimes creatively.

What will I learn?

Unit 1 – Language Today. Language is used in a huge variety of ways, so you will be studying a huge range of texts, all of them contemporary. You will explore how people use language to reflect many different aspects of their situation or identity – how they 'present' themselves in the world through words. You will learn to be something of a detective taking a forensic approach – looking out for the smallest clues in a text as to its purpose and meaning, perhaps even at the level of handwriting, grammar or spelling. But, again like a detective, you will also be stepping back from the individual words to assess the wider context.

Unit 2 – Exploring the Writing Process. The central focus of unit 2 is on two pieces of your own creative writing. One of these will be something that the audience will read – a journalism interview or a piece of narrative writing. The other piece will be something that an audience will listen to – a spoken presentation or a dramatic monologue for radio or stage. You will show your understanding of the writing process by writing a commentary on each piece.

In this unit, therefore, you will develop your skills as a writer for different audiences and purposes. In the world of work this will be a rewarding and valuable skill – whether you are writing reports, giving presentations or using digital communication.

Your creative writing will grow out of your understanding of how language is used in a wide variety of texts. The emphasis is on your development as an independent reader, writer and thinker, and on building up your skills to research, plan, select and shape materials.

How will I be assessed?

Unit 1 is assessed by an external exam. Unit 2 is assessed by coursework.

Unit 1

30% of your A level course is assessed by a 2 hour 15 minute exam. You have to comment on texts selected from examples of spoken, written and electronic language.

Unit 2

20% of your A level course is assessed by your teacher. You have to write/create your own texts for a reading and a listening audience. In consultation with your teacher you will choose your own topics for writing and then add a commentary explaining your purposes and how you achieved them.

How does this book help you?

The Student Book is designed to support you with each unit of AS Language by providing:

- clear explanations of what is required of you, what you need to do, and how you will be assessed
- a wide range of different kinds of texts, along with activities to build the skills you need in understanding and writing them
- guidance in approaching both the examination and coursework tasks, so that you understand what the examiners will be looking for and how to achieve your full potential

Throughout the course you will build on the skills you already possess about language. The world of language is a fascinating one – especially in today's fast-changing world. We wish you success as you build your confidence and skills in using language, responding to it, and enjoying it.

Jen Greatrex, Edexcel

How to use this book

This **Student Book** is divided into Unit 1 and Unit 2. **Unit 1** supports your work for the AS exam 'Language Today'. **Unit 2** supports your work for the AS coursework

component, 'Exploring the Writing Process'.

The Teaching and Assessment Guide provides additional support, including commentaries, explanations of linguistic concepts and further texts and exemplar responses. It can be used alongside this book.

Unit 1. Language Today: an outline

Unit 1 in the **Student Book** is divided into two sections, reflecting the two sections of the exam. They are:

Section A: Language and Context (pages 10-64). In this section you will develop the skills that you need to tackle the short answer questions in Section A of the exam. You will learn how to identify and comment on the key features of spoken, written and electronic language. You will also explore how language use varies depending on the context. The final part helps you prepare for Section A of the exam by giving you a sample paper and analysing the questions and their requirements.

Section B: Presenting Self (pages 65-91). In this section you study the ways language varies according to the user: their age, gender, geographical background, ethnicity, occupation or status. You explore some theories about attitudes to language use, as well as some ideas about ways that meanings are implied by language use in a specific context. The final part helps you prepare for Section B of the exam by giving you a sample paper and analysing the questions and their requirements.

Unit 2. Exploring the Writing Process: an outline

Unit 2 in the Student Book focuses on your coursework. It is divided into four main sections, dealing with each task in turn. Each section is free standing: you can begin with the task of your choice or even work on two tasks in parallel.

Each section takes you through the process of writing in clear stages. It begins with researching style models and analysing key techniques, before moving on to the early stages of planning and drafting the text. The later steps develop the skills of constructive criticism and redrafting. There are suggestions for commentary writing throughout each section, and each ends with a summary of advice for writing up your final version.

The sections are:

Section A, Writing for a Reading Audience: Journalism interview

Section B, Writing for a Reading Audience: Narratives

Section C, Writing for a Listening Audience: Scripted presentation

Section D, Writing for a Listening Audience: Dramatic monologues

---

Section A of the exam is based on a group of short texts. You have one hour to answer a series of short answer questions on them.

Section B of the exam gives you two longer texts. The question will ask you to analyse and compare the ways that the speakers/writers present themselves. It will also ask you to refer to relevant research and theories.

For the coursework unit you will hand in a folder containing two pieces of your own writing. One is for a reading audience – either a journalism interview or a narrative. The other is for a listening audience – either a scripted presentation or a dramatic monologue. You also have to write a short commentary on each piece of writing.

Unit 1
Language Today

What you will do in the course

In Unit 1 of Edexcel AS English Language, you will:

- learn how to analyse and compare spoken, electronic and written texts
- develop your understanding of the contextual factors – subject, purpose, audience and genre
- create a 'toolkit' of key terms for describing language use at various levels (phonology, graphology, lexis, grammar, discourse)
- explore some theories about the ways meanings are conveyed in language use (semantics and pragmatics)
- consider some theories and research about attitudes to language use.

What the examiners are looking for

Examiners use three Assessment objectives (AOs) to mark your answers.

Assessment objective		What this means in practice
AO1	Select and apply a range of linguistic methods to communicate relevant knowledge using appropriate terminology and coherent, accurate written expression.	You should use: • relevant concepts from linguistic study • precise linguistic terms • a clear style of writing.
AO2	Demonstrate critical understanding of a range of concepts and issues related to the construction of meanings in spoken and written language, using knowledge of linguistic approaches.	You should apply: • ideas from semantics and pragmatics to explain how language conveys meaning • knowledge of theories and research about varieties of language use • awareness of social attitudes to such varieties.
AO3	Analyse and evaluate the influence of contextual factors on the production and reception of spoken and written language, showing knowledge of the key constituents of language.	You should show: • knowledge of significant aspects of the situation, eg function or mode • understanding of their influence on the language use • ability to analyse language at various levels, eg grammar and discourse as well as lexis.

In the exam

- There is one exam (2 hours 15 minutes)
- In **Section A** you are given a number of short texts from *one* of the modes: spoken, written or electronic language. There are some questions, which require very brief responses, such as:
  - provide the precise terminology to describe language features
  - find further examples of these language features
  - identify the context.
  There are two questions that require longer responses, explaining the links between language use and context. (50 marks in total)
- In **Section B** you are given two texts (from different modes) to compare. You write one longer response, where you analyse the 'presentation of self' for each speaker/writer. You will relate your own ideas to any relevant theories about language. (50 marks)

Section A Language and context

Section A gives you a number of short texts from one mode – spoken, written or electronic. Within this single mode, there will be some variation, for example, the texts will be produced in different situations, for different purposes or different audiences. The questions ask you to identify some language features typical of that mode and relate them to the context. Section A is worth 50 marks.

What you will learn

- the concept of register and formality – the ways language use varies according to the situation
- characteristics of speech and writing, the differences and the overlaps
- features of new electronic modes of communication
- a 'forensic' approach to texts – the ability to use evidence in the text to find out who produced it, where, why, when, and for whom
- ways of analysing context: mode, field, function, tenor
- a 'toolkit' for analysing the key constituents of language: graphology, phonology, lexis, grammar, discourse
- important concepts in semantics.

How you will be assessed

- Some questions require brief responses. You will need to use precise linguistic terminology to describe characteristic features of the mode and then find similar examples. You will use your analysis of the language of the texts to make informed judgements about their context: who wrote them, where, why, for whom.
- Other questions ask for a longer analysis of the language and context of one group of texts. The examiners are looking for evidence that you can make links between textual features and their context. (50 marks: AO1, AO2 and AO3 apply.)

Section A shows you how you can use your own intuitive response to language as the basis. You can use the linguistic terms and concepts to produce a more thoughtfully considered and argued explanation of the ways meanings are constructed.

How this book will help you

Section A begins with context and develops the terms and concepts used at GCSE: subject, purpose, audience and genre. The first part provides a useful framework for analysis of mode: spoken, written or electronic. The following three parts explore the other variables of field, function and tenor. As you apply these concepts to texts, some language analysis is included.

The rest of Section A focuses on text analysis, providing a 'toolkit' of terms and concepts for each of the key constituents of language: graphology, phonology, morphology, lexis, semantics, grammar, discourse. You will use these linguistic methods to explain the ways meanings are constructed in a range of language use. Your awareness of contextual factors and textual features will provide a useful foundation for the coursework unit and in the A2 course.

Section B Presenting self

Section B asks you to analyse and compare two longer texts, taken from the modes not tested in Section A (speech, writing or electronic). The focus of the question will be on the ways that speakers or writers present themselves through their use of language. Section B is worth 50 marks.

What you will learn

- the concept of idiolect – the distinctive characteristics of an individual's language use
- theories about wider social influences on language variation, for example, region, gender, age, status, occupation
- pragmatic theories about the ways meaning can be implied in a particular situation
- how to use this knowledge and understanding to analyse and compare two texts in an effective exam response.

Section B is an opportunity to examine some of the media debates about language. You will study some of the important linguistic research into topics, such as language and gender, and assess whether the findings accord with your own experience of language use. You will learn to take a critical approach to popular 'myths' about language.

How you will be assessed

There is one question on two texts, taken from different modes of language use. It asks you to analyse and compare the ways the writers or speakers present themselves. You will need to show understanding of the different contexts for each text, as well as some precise analysis of language features at more than one level. The examiners are looking for a thoughtful, tentative approach, as you include discussion of the wider social context and reference to any relevant theories or research. (50 marks: AO1, AO2 and AO3 apply.)

How this book will help you

Section B extends your ability to analyse texts and context by looking at the wider social context of language use. It introduces some important theoretical areas of language study. Your knowledge of particular theories and research studies is an initial step. A critical approach is the most important aspect of your studies at AS/A2 level. You should always bear in mind the distinction between theories and facts. So, ask probing questions and weigh up the evidence against competing theories or your own experience. This section guides you towards relevant reading and encourages an independent, questioning approach.

How to succeed in Unit 1

- Trust your own intuitions – you have been a language user for nearly two decades.
- Gradually build up a toolkit for each aspect of linguistic study – keep an orderly folder.
- Be selective – only use a term or concept if it reveals something relevant.
- Ask questions – as Einstein said, 'I am not very clever, only very, very curious.'
- Gain the confidence to challenge others' theories.
- Acknowledge doubts – it is often better to express ideas in a tentative way.
- Keep your eyes and ears open – there is a wealth of language around you all the time.

A Language and context

In this section you study the ways language varies according to the user: their age, gender, geographical background, ethnicity, occupation or status. You explore some theories about attitudes to language use, as well as some ideas about ways that meanings are implied by language use in a specific context. The final part helps you prepare for Section B of the exam by giving you a sample paper and analysing the questions and their requirements.

1 Introduction

Writing about language

If the short answer question focuses on context, ask yourself the questions 'What? Who? and Why?', then use the linguistic terms 'mode', 'field', 'tenor' and 'function' in your answer.

This section begins with **context** as it is – almost always – the best way to approach any **text** and the way you should plan to analyse texts in the exam. The meaning of the term 'context' may be a bit fuzzy for you, but try imagining language (the 'text') completely out of context – disembodied words appearing out of nowhere, like this:

> Hey there

Suppose you had no idea whether these words were spoken or written, let alone who they were addressed to or the situation. It would be impossible to know what this language text means. It could be a friendly greeting, an aggressive challenge, a cry for help, or have many other meanings. Not all examples are as extreme as this. You generally know a lot about the context of language use; this section tells you how to make the most of this knowledge.

Exploring the context

How do you analyse a text as an English Language student? (A text is any example of spoken, written or electronic language.) You begin by asking all sorts of questions about it.

Activity 1

Read the following text. It was found one morning just inside the doorway of a bed and breakfast bedroom.

1   Answer the questions around the text.

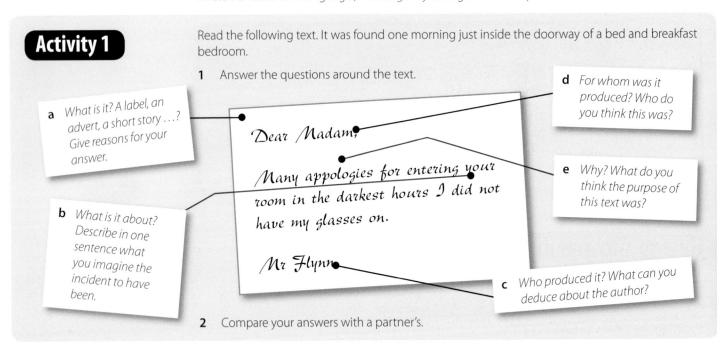

a What is it? A label, an advert, a short story . . .? Give reasons for your answer.

b What is it about? Describe in one sentence what you imagine the incident to have been.

d For whom was it produced? Who do you think this was?

e Why? What do you think the purpose of this text was?

c Who produced it? What can you deduce about the author?

> Dear Madam,
>
> Many appologies for entering your room in the darkest hours I did not have my glasses on.
>
> Mr Flynn

2   Compare your answers with a partner's.

These relatively simple 'What? Who? and Why?' questions all relate to the circumstances of the text – what we call its context. The questions relate to some important linguistic concepts – **mode**, **field**, **function** and **tenor** – which you will learn more about in Part 2 (pages 13–30).

Key terms
text
context
mode
field
tenor
function

- **WHAT** is it? ──────────→ mode (text type)

- **WHAT** is it about? ──────→ field (topic)

- **WHO** produced it? ⎫
- For **WHOM**? ⎬──────→ tenor (relationship between writer and audience)

- **WHY**? ──────────────→ function (purpose)

Focusing on the style

Once you have explored the context, you need to turn your attention to the detail of the words themselves. Ask yourself this question:

How does the style of language reflect this particular situation?

Close examination of text might bring some individual words, letters or punctuation marks to your attention. You may notice the appearance of the text. If you step back, you should be able to see whole sentence structures. A panoramic view would show you the shape of the whole text, including the way it begins and ends.

These key constituents are given special terms in language study, which you will explore in Section A, Part 3 on pages 31–62.

- **Phonology**   the sounds of language
- **Graphology**   visual marks on the pages
- **Lexis**   choice of words
- **Morphology**   word structure
- **Grammar**   sentence structure
- **Discourse**   structure of the whole text

One way of understanding language study is to use the idea of 'levels', as if language were a physical structure. The smallest elements build up into larger structures, which then combine to form even larger structures, and so on:

Key terms

phonology   lexis

graphology   grammar

morphology   discourse

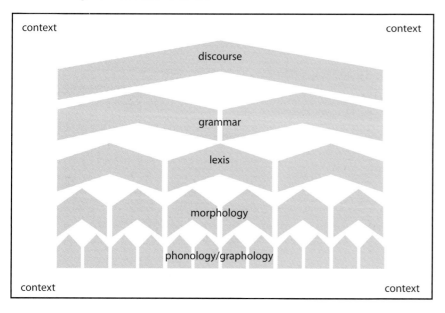

Activity 2

Discuss these questions on the style of Mr Flynn's note. Each question relates to one of the areas of language study listed above.

1. What does the choice of address ('Dear Madam') and sign off ('Mr Flynn') suggest? (This is a question on discourse.)

2. Why do you think the writer chose 'entering' rather than 'coming in'? (This is a question on lexis.)

3. Why do you think the writer says 'darkest' rather than 'dark'? (This is a question on morphology.)

4. What do you notice about spelling and punctuation? Does the handwriting tell you anything about the writer? (This is a question on graphology.)

5. Is the sentence structure in the note standard? In other words, is it appropriate for formal written English? (This is a question on grammar.)

Constructing meaning

Language analysis is not just a way of dissecting a text and labelling the parts. Language is essentially a means of communication, so the aim of language study should be to shed light on meanings and explain how they are conveyed.

Activity 3

Look at Mr Flynn's note again. How sincere do you rate the apology on a scale of 1–10? Some opinions about the note are given below – use your responses to these to argue for your view.

A His use of 'Mr' rather than a first name isn't really a mark of respect. It keeps his identity anonymous so makes him rather distant.

B Some of his word choices show he is respecting the person he is writing to, eg 'Madam' and 'entering'.

C The style sounds almost poetic in the phrase 'in the darkest hours', which is odd in this situation.

D The note is very brief, so overall it's not a heartfelt apology.

E The casual grammar in places makes me think he doesn't really care about what he is writing.

F He makes spelling and punctuation mistakes, but these are probably unintentional.

G The writer avoids saying the words 'I' or 'you', which would make the apology more direct and personal.

Writing about language

When you identify language features, always explain why they are significant to the whole context. For example: **There is a mixture of formality and informality in Mr Flynn's note. This is because an apology to a stranger usually involves a high degree of formality, but a handwritten note tends to be more informal.**

Two areas of language explore the ways meanings are constructed: semantics and pragmatics.

- When you talk about the associations of the phrase 'in the darkest hours', you are dealing with **semantics** (the relationship between words and meanings). You will learn more about semantics on pages 45–48.
- When you try to work out what Mr Flynn really means by 'many apologies', you are discussing **pragmatics** (the ways meanings are implied in a social context). You will learn more about pragmatics on pages 84–88.

Formality

One key concept in language study is formality: the way people adjust the tone of their language to suit the situation they are in.

Many people would think Mr Flynn's situation requires a fairly high degree of formality, as a stranger is writing to apologise for being in a woman's room late at night. Mr Flynn makes some effort to be formal, but the note remains quite casual in tone. Perhaps we need to know more about the social context – messing about at night might be common for Mr Flynn.

Activity 4

Role-play these scenarios in pairs. Be aware of the formality of the language you use. Then rank the situations according to their level of *formality/register*.

a F is interviewing M for a job.

b M and F are friends having coffee.

c F is a waiter serving M with coffee.

d M is complaining to neighbour F about his children.

2 Looking at context

In this part you will explore the important concepts for analysing context – mode, field, function and tenor – in more detail. As you look at examples of texts, you will begin to use some precise terms to describe language features. Part 3 will deal with each of the key constituents of language – graphology, phonology, morphology, lexis, grammar and discourse – in more detail.

Mode

What does mode mean in language study? In its broadest sense, it refers to the way that language is transmitted from person to person.

Writing about language

You use either the term 'mode' or 'genre' to identify types of language use. For example, you could describe a text as 'essay-writing mode', 'lecture mode' or 'the genre of a written story'.

Activity 5

Look at the following examples of language use. They are all different language modes. Which of the five senses – sight, hearing, touch, smell and taste – is used for each?

a	Braille notice	**d**	morse code message	**g**	TV programme
b	telephone call	**e**	smoke signals/semaphore	**h**	sign language accompaniment
c	letter	**f**	text message	**i**	MySpace site

Although smell can communicate feelings and the sense of touch is used in the Braille, human language uses hearing and sight as the main channels of communication. So spoken and written language are two important modes to study.

Spoken and written modes

Within the overall categories of spoken and written language, there are various sub-types, for example:

Spoken language		Written language	
• conversation	• interview	• letter	• essay
• lecture	• anecdote	• article	• novel

Activity 6

1 List further examples of sub-types under each main heading, as above.

2 Note any overlaps. For example, a story could be spoken or written. Some lectures include written language, in the form of handouts. Draw a Venn diagram like the one begun below to show this.

conversation
anecdote

story
play

letter
novel

Is one mode more important than the other? In the history of language development, spoken language evolved first, with written language coming much later. This order of priority is also true for child language development: we all learned to speak before we could write. If you think about the amount of spoken versus written language, you use far more spoken language in a typical day. But, in terms of status, written language seems to have the upper hand. Perhaps this is because the ability to read and write is limited to people with access to education, which is the privileged minority in some societies. Written language also attained a higher status because it used to be the only way of leaving a permanent record, which was essential for government and law, although this situation has changed in recent times.

Electronic modes

Developments in technology have introduced new ways of transmitting and receiving language, apart from face-to-face speaking or writing on paper. This, in turn, creates new modes of language.

Activity 7

1   List modern technology (eg telephone, radio) for transmitting and receiving language. Which sense(s) does each use?

2   What new modes (eg radio phone-in, chatroom) do you use? For each, say whether it is interactive or one-way communication.

Writing about language

- In your study of English Language, you will be able to experience a range of modes: *hearing* actual speech, *listening* to audio, *watching* visual recordings, *following* hyperlinks on computer, etc. But in this book and on your exam paper you will only be able to see written versions of spoken and electronic language. This means that you can only imagine body language and tone of voice. Your analysis must focus on the words used.

- When you use these terms and concepts, show that you are aware of subtle degrees, connections and overlaps. For example, a public text is usually carefully planned and message-oriented, but may appear to be spontaneous and include some social, context-dependent language use in order to create a sense of an 'in-group'. For example, a poster advertising a cable TV company listed all the advantages as bullet points, finishing with a final bullet: 'Um, that's all.'

These electronic modes of language use are significant because they are often a fusion of spoken and written language. For example, a website can combine written text on the screen with access to audio clips of speech. Even where there is not a combination of speech and writing, there are interesting overlaps. A text message uses only writing on a screen, but operates like a spoken conversation in many ways because it is interactive. A radio broadcast uses only spoken language, but it may be read from a written script. Some media broadcasts are interactive, inviting phone calls, emails or text messages from the listeners.

In order to analyse the way language is used in electronic modes, you need to be aware of the distinctive features of spoken and written language.

Contexts of spoken and written language

Before you consider all the interesting areas of overlap, think of the differences between the typical situations for speaking and writing.

Speaking tends to be more immediate. There is generally little time for planning what to say, as the other person is there waiting for a response. Except in a few public situations, there is no permanent record of speech. These are all features associated with **informality** in the style of language use.

Writing, on the other hand, is often produced over a period of time, without the reader present. There are chances to plan and revise what you want to communicate, which is just as well, as writing is permanent. Written language often has a large, public audience. These are all features associated with formality in the style of language use.

It is useful to think of these aspects as a sliding scale from one extreme to another, often connected to the degree of formality.

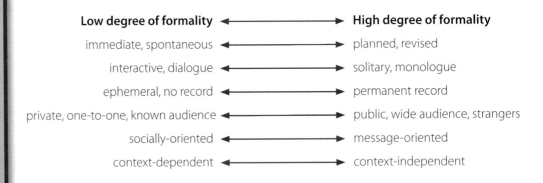

Low degree of formality	High degree of formality
immediate, spontaneous	planned, revised
interactive, dialogue	solitary, monologue
ephemeral, no record	permanent record
private, one-to-one, known audience	public, wide audience, strangers
socially-oriented	message-oriented
context-dependent	context-independent

At one extreme, we use language to maintain social relationships. At the other end of the scale, the purpose is to communicate facts and information. If the message needs to reach a wide range of people, the language use should be as clear and explicit as possible (context-independent).

Look at the following email as an example of context-dependent language use:

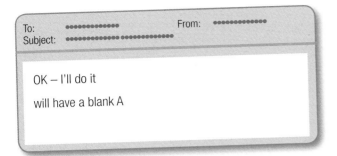

No one outside the situation could know what 'a blank A' means or what 'it' refers to. The term '**deixis**' (from Greek, meaning 'pointing') describes words that refer (point) to something. All pronouns (I, you, he, she, it, we, they) refer to a person or thing. Sometimes it is clear in the text what they refer to, but in this case there is no information about the identity of 'I'.

It would be too simple to say that all speaking is casual, social interaction and all writing is carefully planned, formal information. So now you will consider all the subtle variations in people's use of language.

Activity 8

Choose one of the scales listed above, for example, ephemeral ←——→ permanent and draw a line to represent it.

a   Place examples of spoken and written language along the line. For example:

spoken language

| chat at bus stop | excuse for being late | class presentation | TV drama |

spontaneous •————————————————————————————• **planned**

| note | diary entry | letter | essay | application form | novel |

written language

b   Compare your scale with others' and comment on any similarities or differences.

The degree of planning is often connected to the type of audience, rather than the mode. Whether writing or speaking, a large group of strangers generally causes more planning. However, if you have a very sensitive message to convey to a loved one, you may well rehearse your words carefully.

Similarly, people tend to plan more carefully if the speaking or writing is going to leave a permanent record. Many public figures publish their diaries, which are much more polished and self-aware than those intended to remain private.

Context of electronic language

Where does the electronic mode fit into this framework? Let's start with the most widely used form of electronic communication – email messages.

Emails are generally interactive, as the response can follow within minutes. They can be carefully planned (depending on the audience and purpose), but are usually addressed to and read by a single person. Emails are permanent and, even if deleted, can be retrieved from a hard drive. Text messages, on the other hand, are always private, whereas websites like MySpace have more public access than emails.

1 Read the following emails.

Email A

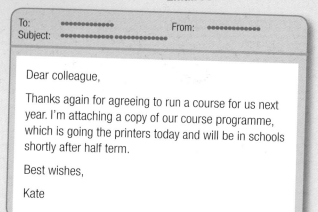

To: ●●●●●●●●●●●●● From: ●●●●●●●●●●●●
Subject: ●●●●●●●●●●●●● ●●●●●●●●●●●●●●

Dear colleague,

Thanks again for agreeing to run a course for us next year. I'm attaching a copy of our course programme, which is going the printers today and will be in schools shortly after half term.

Best wishes,

Kate

Email B

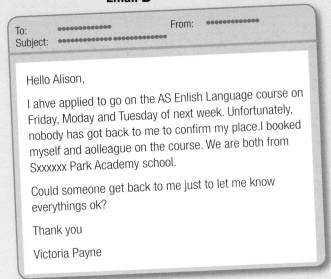

To: ●●●●●●●●●●●●● From: ●●●●●●●●●●●●
Subject: ●●●●●●●●●●●●● ●●●●●●●●●●●●●●

Hello Alison,

I ahve applied to go on the AS Enlish Language course on Friday, Moday and Tuesday of next week. Unfortunately, nobody has got back to me to confirm my place.I booked myself and aolleague on the course. We are both from Sxxxxxx Park Academy school.

Could someone get back to me just to let me know everythings ok?

Thank you

Victoria Payne

2 Place each email at a point on each of the formality scales below.

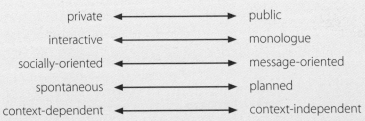

private ←————————→ public

interactive ←————————→ monologue

socially-oriented ←————————→ message-oriented

spontaneous ←————————→ planned

context-dependent ←————————→ context-independent

Comment on any significant language features, including **terms of address**: the way each person addresses and names themselves and the other.

This type of analysis of mode is beginning to focus on the language, for example, the discourse (terms of address) and graphology (typing errors). The next part looks in more detail at the lexis of spoken language, in comparison to written language.

Lexis of spoken language

Of course, people can use any words they choose, whether speaking or writing. But the lexis tends to differ slightly, with writing often being more formal and impersonal in tone and speaking using more colloquial language. The term '**colloquial**' literally means 'speaking together'. These general assumptions about the style of written and spoken language are supported by research.

The CANCODE project is a collaboration between Cambridge and Nottingham Universities. They collected 5 million words of spontaneous spoken English to create a **corpus** (from the Latin, literally meaning 'body'). It was funded by Cambridge University Press, who own the copyright. This collection of data can be analysed by computers to observe statistical evidence. For example, what is the most commonly used word in the English language? Is it the same word for both speaking and writing?

Independent research

Find a range of examples from your electronic language use (emails, text messages, MySpace, etc) and analyse them using the scales above. Is there anything unusual or surprising about the language use? Can you explain it? Read *The Language of ICT* (Shortis, 2000).

Activity 10

Key terms

colloquial   filler/filled
pause
corpus

lexical item   backchannel
behaviour
terms of
address

1   Look at the statistical results below from the CANCODE research.

Rank	Spoken language	Written language	Rank	Spoken language	Written language	Rank	Spoken language	Written language
Top 40 words								
1	the	the	15	mm	her	29	what	by
2	I	to	16	is	you	30	do	this
3	and	and	17	er	is	31	right	are
4	you	of	18	but	with	32	just	were
5	it	a	19	so	his	33	he	all
6	to	in	20	they	had	34	for	him
7	a	was	21	on	as	35	erm	up
8	yeah	it	22	oh	at	36	be	an
9	that	I	23	we	but	37	this	said
10	of	he	24	have	be	38	all	there
11	in	that	25	no	have	39	there	one
12	was	she	26	(laugh)	from	40	got	been
13	it's	for	27	well	not			
14	know	on	28	like	they			

Note: The word 'Ok' came in at number 52 and 'Okay' at number 84. They should have been counted as a single **lexical item** (word) and together would have made the top 40.

2   List all the words that are commonly used in spoken language, but are not so frequent in written language.

3   You might wonder why some of the spoken language was counted as words, rather than noises or sounds. The decision was based on whether they convey an identifiable meaning. With a partner, discuss the following questions. Use the comments in the box below as a starting point for your ideas.

   a   Why is a laugh included, but not a cough?

   b   Why is 'mm' listed as a separate item to 'er' and 'erm'? (The technical term for these is '**filler**' or '**filled pause**'.)

   c   Why is 'yeah' counted as a separate word to 'yes'?

Meaning of noises and sounds

- The term '**backchannel behaviour**' refers to noises the listener makes in the background as response to what the speaker is saying.
- A laugh is more deliberate than a cough. A short laugh can show that you are agreeing or sympathising with the speaker.
- The filled pause, 'mm', often occurs as the listener signals that they are listening, but wants the speaker to carry on.
- 'Er' is used by the speaker to fill a pause between words, perhaps because silence is uncomfortable.
- 'Erm' usually fills a pause between the boundary of complete sentences to indicate that the speaker has not finished their turn and wants to keep talking.
- The word 'yes' is a clear affirmative, usually in response to a question.
- The word 'yeah' can be used for the affirmative in informal situations, but it is often used as backchannel behaviour as the listener shows support for the speaker.

Independent research

Keep a notebook record (if you cannot make audio recordings), and note when laughs, filled pauses or 'yeah' occur in spoken language. Why do speakers use these sounds? If it is fair to call them 'words', what do you think they mean? There is little published research, but you could type 'yeah backchannel' into a search engine to find articles on the internet. The University of Pennsylvania, for example, provides a lot of useful notes for students.

Activity 11

Investigate the frequent occurrence of these words in spoken, but not written language:

so   well   like   right   know   just   OK

1   Provide examples of each word in spoken language use, for example:

- Are you <u>well</u>?
- That was <u>well</u> good.
- <u>Well</u>, what are you waiting for?
- It was not … <u>well</u> … not really suitable.

2   Comment on the function of the word (the way it is used), in addition to its literal meaning, for example:

- 'Well' literally means the opposite of 'ill'.
- It is used as an **intensifier** (similar in meaning to 'very' or 'extremely').
- It is used to mark, or signal, the beginning of a new topic.
- It is used to fill a pause, as the speaker hesitates and thinks what to say.

You will notice that all these words are used in different ways in spoken language. They often have an interactive function, indicating that the speaker is involved in a dialogue and is willing for the other person to join in. In spoken language, the word 'know' usually occurs in a phrase, 'you know what I mean' or 'don't you know?' The term '**marker of sympathetic circularity**' refers to its function of checking the other person is still 'with you'. **Tag questions**, such as 'aren't you?' or 'didn't she?', have a similar interactive function.

Your study of features of spoken language may provide you with interesting material to use in a spoken presentation for your Unit 2 coursework.

The linguist Professor Ron Carter suggests that it is more revealing to use the term 'purposefully vague language' for certain features of spoken language, such as 'sort of', 'kind of', 'stuff like that', 'and so on', etc. Although there are situations that require absolutely precise information, social talk between equals is not one of them. In examples such as, 'about ten-ish', 'slim-ish', Carter describes '-ish' as a 'democratic morpheme'!

Take it further

1   Use a search engine to research uses of the word 'like' in contemporary spoken language and attitudes towards its use. Type the words 'like quotative' or 'like discourse marker' into a search engine to find relevant articles on the internet. Wikipedia can often be a good place to start. BBC Voices website is also an excellent forum – go to 'Your voice', then 'The art of conversation'.

   a   List the various functions of the word 'like'.

   b   Why do you think its use is both common among younger people and stigmatised (criticised as non-standard)?

2   Use a search engine to find out about increasing use of 'innit' as a tag question. Try Wikipedia and BBC Voices websites as a first stop. Do you agree with the points made in the online article 'It's Hinglish, innit?' at http://news.bbc.co.uk/l/hi/magazine/default.stm

3   Add to your research into the features that are characteristic of spoken language. Look in the bibliography for suggestions of books on the topic. You might begin with *The Language of Speech and Writing* or *Language and Creativity: The Art of Common Talk*, both by Ron Carter. Is it enough to say that spoken language is informal, whereas written language is formal?

Grammar of spoken language

Spoken language uses some structures that are not so common in formal written language. You have already come across the terms 'deixis' (page 15) and 'intensifier' (page 18). Here are more useful terms to describe grammatical structures.

Discourse markers are particular words (often adverbs) and phrases used to mark boundaries in conversation between one topic and the next. They function rather like a new paragraph in writing. For example:

> <u>Anyway</u>, give Jean a ring and see what she says.
> <u>Right, okay</u>, we'd better try to phone and see what they have to report.

Interrogative and **imperative** sentence structures are used more in spoken language because it is often a two-way communication, with the possibility to ask questions, make requests and give instructions. Interrogatives are easy to spot as they are followed by a question mark. Imperatives use the verb in its simple form, or add 'do' or 'don't'.

> <u>Can you help</u> me with this?
> Which one <u>do you mean</u>?
> You <u>don't</u> mind, do you? (tag question)
> Quick, <u>grab</u> hold of the end.
> <u>Do give</u> it a rest.
> <u>Don't touch</u> that.

Ellipsis happens when speakers leave out some parts of the full structure because they assume the listener already understands this information. An alternative term for abbreviated structures is minor sentence.

> Coming to mine this evening? (Are you …)
> Amazing party! (It was an …)
> No idea. (I have … what you are talking about.)

Modal expressions are words and phrases that indicate the attitude of the speaker towards the situation they are describing.

> I <u>suppose</u> it <u>must be sort of</u> difficult to phone or <u>whatever</u>.
> I <u>feel</u> they <u>maybe should</u> resign <u>really</u>.
> We <u>maybe ought to perhaps</u> have a word with him about it.

Writing about language

- Avoid making negative comments about spoken language, such as it is 'lazy', 'sloppy', 'not proper English'. Instead, think positively about the reasons for, and effects of, using language in an informal, apparently spontaneous way.

- In the short-answer questions, you need to show your knowledge and understanding in three ways:

1   Use accurate *terminology* to describe the language use in the texts and context.

2   Explain the *effects*.

3   Analyse the *connections* between the language and the *context* of its use.

Here is a short example of a teacher addressing a Year 11 class: 'Um, OK, can we have a bit of quiet now?'

The speaker uses a filled pause (**terminology**), 'um' and the discourse marker 'OK' to indicate she is about to say something. Her style seems quite relaxed and informal (**overall effect**), perhaps because she has a good relationship (**context**) with her class. She uses an interrogative (**terminology**) structure, but it functions (**effect**) as an instruction. It is less assertive (**effect**) than saying bluntly 'Be quiet!' and maintains (**link to context**) the cooperative relationship with the class.

Multi-modal texts

So far, you have looked at some distinctive features of spoken language: the words most commonly used and a few common grammatical structures. We are assuming a contrast here with written language; in other words, these types of features are *not* commonly found in written language. At the two opposite ends of the scale, the stereotypical style of writing is a carefully constructed monologue addressed to a large, unknown audience; the stereotypical style of speaking is a spontaneous conversation with one or two familiar people.

But, of course, language use is more complex and interesting than that. If we think of the image of a spectrum like a rainbow, styles of language shade into and overlap with each other. For example, people sometimes write as if they were speaking to a friend or they speak from a carefully planned script to a large audience. Nowadays, we have the fascinating phenomenon of electronic language use, which really does blur the boundaries between speech and writing. Although often written, it tends to be done without much pre-planning and is an interactive dialogue. The resulting style might be called, like new genres of music, 'crossover' or 'fusion'.

The next activity lets you practise your skills of analysis on three texts, while giving you examples of multi-modal texts and crossover in styles.

Activity 12

1   Read and compare the three examples of language use on page 21.

   a Identify the mode of each text – spoken, written or electronic.

   b Rank the texts according to the degree of formality.

   c Identify some of the lexis and grammar of spoken language in each.

   d Comment on the effects of these features.

   e Explain how this links to the context. (You might use the concepts from the formality scales on pages 14–16, planning, interactivity, etc.)

You can read a sample response to the first text, before writing your own response to the other two texts.

Sample response to example A

a   The mode of this text is written, as it is an extract from a printed book, but it uses many features of spoken language.

b   It is much less formal in style than the extract from Tony Blair's speech, but not as informal as the extract from the chatroom conversation (both below). Although Derren Brown uses some noticeably formal lexis (machinations, incontinent, tantamount), it is mixed with some informal (Tom-noddy). His grammar has many features of spoken language, in particular the use of interrogatives (Am I mad?) and imperatives (bear with me). He uses direct address with the first and second person pronouns (I, you), spoken discourse markers (Now) and adverbs (simply, merely, just) as hedges to alter the force of the statement.

c   These features of spoken language create a lively, personal style to engage the reader's interest as if they are having a conversation (What's that?) with Derren Brown, rather than simply reading a book. The tone is quite arrogant, but humorous with his exaggerated formality (Cease all activities that are not entirely tantamount to bearing with me.)

d   This style suits Derren Brown's purposes, as his persona is a blend of extreme intelligence with likeability. His popularity is based on TV and live shows, so he needs to create an impression of spontaneous interaction in his writing.

Example A from *Tricks of the Mind* by Derren Brown

Now, although it is vital that these two cards stay together, you are now very bravely going to ask the Tom-noddy to shuffle the cards. What's that? Won't that undo all our clever machinations? Have
5 I separated myself from my senses? How could such a thing work? Am I simply mad? Perhaps at this point you are ripping these pages from their binding in blood-red boiling anger, incontinent with rage at the wasted effort you have put into
10 learning this so far; already dialling the ladies and gentlemen at both the Fourth Channel and the *Daily Mail* to insist that this volume is torn from the shelves of WHSmith and simply never aired on Radio One. I merely say: bear with me. Cease all
15 activities that are not entirely tantamount to bearing with me, and let me explain. It is for this reason alone, if you will just simmer down for a second, that you have chosen a poor shuffler.

Example B Tony Blair speaking at conference on education, 4 September 1997

Thank you all very much indeed for coming to Downing Street this morning for this Education Summit. I suppose we meet in rather sombre times and I think there is a tremendous sense of national grief at the moment and,
5 indeed, something I think more profound than anything I can remember in the entirety of my life time. Something that isn't just our grief as a nation – it is personal to each one of us. I know there are people around this table that will have met and known Princess Diana, and work that
10 she has done. And I suppose of all the subjects that it is important to take forward, it is the education of our children and the future of our children, and this is a meeting that has been arranged for a considerable period of time and we thought it right that we continued to have it and have
15 the discussion about how we can improve the system of our schools and the education of our children for the future. And what I would like to do, if this is agreeable to you is to try and divide our discussion into four different parts.

Example C from Chatroom of the week, Tim Dowling, *The Guardian*, 7 January 2003

Current topic: Another great year has come and gone here at the NewsRoom. Which do you think were the most important news events of the last 12 months? Who were the major newsmakers of 2002? Nominate your favourites here.

Pashmina:	any new years resalutions Bronco
capitalistpiglet:	It's got to be Saddam
5 Bronco:	yes next year im gonna remember to put a bucket by me bed
jenni@boughtledger:	I'm still jenni from the block
Host_Chris2:	Saddam Hussein is an obvious choice of course, but what about people from earlier this year?
Bronco:	like michael jackson throwin his baby out the window
Pashmina:	I forgot about that!!
10 *LadeezMan	has entered the NewsRoom*
capitalistpiglet:	what about the launch of the euro?
LadeezMan:	hi
Host_Chris2:	I was thinking of Stephen Byers
Bronco:	who
15 Pashmina:	your just sayin that cos u look like him chris2. Hi ladeezman hows u
jenni@boughtledger:	I'm still jenni from the block
LadeezMan:	I just woke up. What day is it

What you have learned

✓ Mode refers to the three main channels for communicating language: speech, writing, electronic communication
✓ There are some key differences between spoken and written language.
✓ It is helpful to think of a scale, or continuum, between two extremes.
✓ Electronic language shares features of both speech and writing.
✓ Multi-modal texts also merge the typical features of speech and writing.

Field

The field of a text is its topic or subject matter. This will clearly influence the choice of lexis. For example, a leaflet about training dogs will contain many words relating to dog breeds, equipment, etc. The term for such a group of words is **subject-specific lexis**. Such an obvious point might not be worth making, but you might notice an underlying **semantic field** – other groups of words related by meaning – that is not so directly linked to the main topic. Menus, for example, tend to connect food with comfort, by using words like 'nestling on a bed of …' The presenter Jeremy Kyle was quoted in an article in the *Daily Mirror*, defending his TV confrontational show: 'Some people will always think I've got the eyes of Satan. Others will think I'm a TV God.' His choice of the words 'Satan' and 'God' suggest that he considers himself of a similar status. You might think of alternative words to express his point that some people dislike him and others approve.

Activity 13

Read the extract below from a sports report in the *Sunday Mirror*.

a   Apart from 'football' and 'sport', what other related words do you notice?

b   What effect does this have?

Take it further

Look at the work of the Campaign for Plain English on www.plainenglish.co.uk. Which people and organisations do they target? Do you agree that it is important to write in a clear and simple style?

Southampton 1   Crystal Palace 4

Peter White at St Mary's

JAMES SCOWCROFT plundered a hat-trick as Palace got their season off to a right royal start at St Mary's.

Saints were simply ripped apart by Palace, who finished six places and 10 points below George Burley's side last season.

…

But Saints were suddenly in tatters as Scowcroft pounced twice inside a minute.

After Clinton Morrison's angled shot was pushed away for a corner, Stuart Green swung the cross in from the left and Scowcroft sneaked in front of Bennett to power home a 30-minute header.

Then Scowcroft chased a long clearance from Julian Speroni, easily shrugged off Bennett's challenge and calmly lifted the ball over the stranded Bartosz Bialkowski in the home goal.

But in stoppage time of the first half, Saints gave themselves a much-needed lifeline when Palace failed to clear Youssef Safri's pass and Marek Saganowski pounced.

Speroni then helped set up Scowcroft's hat-trick, when his long punt was misjudged by Bialkowski, who could only knock the ball into the air and Scowcroft darted in to head home.

And just two minutes later Saints' defence was in total disarray as Morrison turned to rifle in Palace's fourth.

Saint's manager Burley said: 'Some of the goals we conceded were horrendous. I know there's a lot of work to be done and we've got to show character to bounce back, but I am sure we will.'

'We have just got to battle on and get some more bodies into our squad.'

Independent research

Find examples of the 'World's Worst Writing' from *The Philosophy and Literature Journal* on www.putlearningfirst. com/language/21plain/ wwwrite. In what was the effect on you as a reader? In what type of publication were these texts originally produced? Do you think the intended audience would react in a different way? Is there an example of writing that you would nominate for this prize?

Jargon – to impress and oppress?

The term **jargon** (which derives from an Old French word meaning 'warbling of birds') is often used in a negative sense for unnecessarily complicated words. Sometimes people involved in a particular occupation or hobby do seem to delight in using words that no one else can understand. The Campaign for Plain English promotes clarity in public documents and makes an award each year for the worst example of 'gobbledygook'. In 1994, the politician Gordon Brown provided one example:

new theories of economic sovereignty across a wide range of areas … the growth of post-neo-classical endogenous growth theory and the symbiotic relationships between growth and investment in people and infrastructure.

Often, however, specialised technical jargon helps precise communication. Medicine is one area where specialised vocabulary is an advantage (if not a necessity). Linguistics is another! This type of language is called **field-related jargon**. It is still important to use jargon carefully, with the aim to be precise and clear, not for the pleasure of using big, obscure words.

Activity 14

1 Which of these are names of figure-skating moves, rather than phonetic (the study of the sounds of language) symbols?*

2 Choose a topic you are familiar with – a hobby, interest, occupation, etc.

3 List 10 examples of field-related jargon. Include two that you have invented.

4 Exchange lists with another student and see if you can identify the fake jargon.

- Crossed Lambda
- Inverted Omega
- Inside Ina Bauer
- Long-Leg Turned Iota
- Closed Reverse Epsilon
- Yogh
- Bullseye Polish Hook
- Back-Tail Gamma

Use of appropriate sentence structures

Although the field of a text has most impact on the use of lexis, you may want to comment on the grammar, if it affects the tone or degree of formality. Some topics, such as death or religion, are very sensitive and require an appropriate style of sentence structure, as well as vocabulary. Some topics like pop music and fashion are less serious and so a more informal style is fine.

Activity 15

1 Read the extract text to the right. The mode is a leaflet, left in each room in a chain of hotels.

   a Identify the two contrasting semantic fields.

   b What do you notice about the grammar of the text?

2 Comment on the effect of these language choices.

Remember it is important to develop your initial general impression of the register of a text, by:

P – making a more specific point

E – providing evidence from the text

E – explaining the relevance (the ways the language choices suit the context)

1
FIVE MINUTES
To breathe:
Sit in the lotus position, close your eyes, relax and breathe in deeply.

2
FIVE MINUTES
To tone up:
Sit with a straight back, stretch out your arms and bend your body forward as far as you can go.

3
FIVE MINUTES
To relax:
Pull your knees up against your chest, put your chin on your knees, then rock forward and backwards and from side to side.

This leaflet uses the semantic fields of work and leisure. The list does not use complete sentences, such as 'to breathe'. There are imperatives telling the reader what to do, for example 'bend your body forward'. It is very informal for a hotel leaflet.

- Needs to be specific about the filed and provide examples
- Negative point — needs to explain why this is relevant
- Explanation misunderstands primary function of leaflet
- Too general — what type of register is it? How does this language use suit the context?

Notice how this response just skates the surface at first, then digs out a few random examples. Can you improve on this example? (Note the examiner's comments.)

You can see from this example that it is difficult to comment on the field of a text, without discussing its function.

What you have learned

✓ Field refers to the subject matter of the text as shown in the choice of lexis.

✓ You can use these terms: subject-specific lexis, field-related jargon, semantic field.

✓ It is not particularly interesting to notice that there are words from the field of sailing in a handbook about sailing, but it would be interesting if there was an underlying semantic field connecting sailing with flying or freedom.

[*Inside Ina Bauer is the only skating move.]

Function

You may be familiar with the purpose of texts being described in a limited number of ways as to inform, persuade, entertain, and so on. However, it is important to develop the concept of purpose further. The related term 'function' encourages you to see that language has many more than the few purposes mentioned at GCSE. People use language for all sorts of communicative functions, some specific (eg weather forecasting, exchanging faulty goods) and others more broad (eg interacting, expressing feelings). An example of language use with a very specific function would be:

> I name this ship Queen Mary II.

Multi-functional texts

Most language functions are more complex and cannot be described in a single phrase. Often people are trying to achieve several things at once. It is important to understand as much as possible about the situation, before reading the text.

Activity 16

The exam paper will always give you any significant details about the text. For example, here are the significant details about the text in Activity 17:

> It is the 'Health and Safety' paragraph from the information section of a leaflet given out at the 2007 Cornbury Music Festival.

1   Before you read the text itself, think about what you expect from the context, for example:

mode	– leaflet	– suggests clear and simple style
	– public, message-oriented	– ditto
field	– health & safety	– suggests serious tone, legal jargon
function	– information	– suggests clear style
	– advice	– suggests use of imperatives

2   Then think about the whole situation and any underlying purposes. At a music festival, it's unlikely that anyone will read the whole leaflet carefully. In that case, why would the organisers print the information and advice?

Activity 17

Read the text with these thoughts about the context in mind.

a   What are the field and function (the sort of information and advice the text gives)?

b   Identify the language features that convey this.

  • **Lexis** – Can you group vocabulary into related fields? To what extent is the vocabulary formal or informal?

  • **Grammar** – What sentence structures are used? Does it include interrogatives or imperatives? Is the reader addressed directly as 'you'?

c   What effect does this style have?

An outdoor music festival

Health & Safety

In the interests of Health and Safety, please observe the signs and stay behind barriers and fencing when directed to do so by the festival stewards. The festival takes place on uneven farmland so take care, especially at night. Please do not climb any trees on site. Give site traffic
5   plenty of space to pass and don't ride on vehicles. Drugs are illegal and anybody caught with/using them will be handed over to the police. It is possible that exposure to loud music may cause damage to hearing. Please be aware that strobe lighting may be used during the festival.

Writing about language

Remember to consider all the aspects of context to get a full picture. So far you have mode, field and function. For example, you might begin an exam response like this:

This leaflet has been designed to give out to everyone attending a music festival. The heading indicates its function to provide information and advice about health and safety. The layout of any leaflet allows the reader to skip sections and find topics of interest, so few people would read this section carefully when they are enjoying a weekend festival of music. Its primary function may be to satisfy legal requirements. I expect the lexis to be in the field of health, safety and law, with some references to leisure and fun. I expect the sentence structures to be clear, but not simple, as the organisers need to explain precisely. There may be imperatives to express warnings and instructions ...

Cross purposes?

The text above was public and message-oriented, so it used **declarative** sentences. This term refers to the following structure, often used to make statements about facts:

>   The festival takes place on uneven farmland.

The term '**transactional**' also refers to language used to pass on information. In personal and interactive situations, the language use is often more socially-oriented. Statements such as 'It's been a miserable June' are not intended as information about the weather, but as a polite ice-breaker with strangers. This convention is restricted to the UK, and perhaps to older people; other social groups use different strategies to strike up a friendly conversation. This is **phatic** function, referring to the social, rather than the message, aspect of communication.

Activity 18

1   Look at the following situations where you might use private i.e *addressed to a single person* – language (spoken, written and electronic).

   • Homepage for MySpace/Facebook/Bebo, etc.
   • Introducing yourself to an attractive person at a party
   • Personal statement on a job application form
   • Note to a family member asking to borrow money

2   Add some more examples from your own experience and describe the main and the various underlying functions of each example.

3   What strategies might you use to achieve these functions?

A personal statement on a job application form has the main function of persuading the reader to give you a job or an interview. In order to achieve this, you need to show you have the necessary skills by providing information about your qualifications and experience. You also need to reveal your personality by writing about your hobbies and interests. The presentation is vital, so you need to make sure the handwriting, spelling and punctuation are all effective.

Human communication often involves the need to present oneself in a positive light. For some people, this involves a degree of boasting; others play a more downbeat or humorous role.

The subtle art of persuasion

Although declarative sentence structures make up the major part of language use, human communication is not principally concerned with passing on information. It is always interesting to consider whether there is an underlying persuasive purpose. The following text, for example, was seen on the back of a bus underneath a close-up photo of a young child's face.

>   You'll never sleep.
>   She'll never wake.

The small print 'Don't drink and drive'. Advertisers need to use subtle means to attract our attention, as we have become so familiar with the direct approach.

Independent research

Look at the campaigns on websites for various charities such as the NSPCC or Amnesty International. What tactics do they use to attract interest and donations? The visuals are often the most noticeable part, but look at the way they use language to reinforce the message.

1 Look at this extract from *The Guardian*.

Stilettos.
£129 from Selfridges.
What would you do to get your hands on a pair?
Save up?
Max out the credit card?
Kill for them?
In Liberia, the promise of fashionable shoes is used to recruit teenage girls to fight in the country's bloody civil war. **So they really are to die for. Explore the world.**

theguardian**weekly**.co.uk

The new-look Guardian Weekly
Claim your free copy
Call +44 (0) 845 000
Quote reference WIFN008

Writing about language

When you discuss the function of texts, you can use terms from:

- GCSE study (eg to entertain, persuade, inform, describe)
- everyday language (eg to present yourself in a positive light, to satisfy legal requirements)
- the linguistic toolkit you are building (eg message-oriented, phatic function).

The terms to describe the actual **structure** of sentences are: declarative, interrogative, imperative. But remember that the function of a sentence might be different from its structure, for example, the interrogative structure 'What time do you call this?' functions as a reprimand.

a At first, what do you think the function is?

b When you read to the end of the text, what do you think the function is?

c Do you think it is effective? How would it achieve its purpose and for whom?

2 Read the example response, which shows a simple application of the concepts of purpose and audience. Can you make more thoughtful comments about the functions of this text and the readership? Note how the only language comments are at the levels of graphology and lexis. Can you go beyond this to analyse semantics (meanings), grammar (sentence structure) or discourse (the overall structure)?

> The purpose of this text is to persuade. The use of different shades makes the text more eye-catching. The audience is readers of a broadsheet newspaper, so they are educated, middle-class people. You can tell that they have money, as it mentions a credit card and expensive shoes from a high-class shop. It uses some slang (Max out) to make the text lively, but tabloid newspaper readers would not be interested in global events.

What works for one group of people does not work for another. Advertisements are carefully targeted at a specific audience. The next part looks at the question of audience: who is the text aimed at and how?

What you have learned

✓ You should develop your awareness of purpose to see that language often performs a number of overlapping functions.

✓ You can add to the concepts of persuasion, entertainment and information, and consider the distinction between language as a means of passing on information and language as a means of forming social bonds.

✓ You can use these pairs of terms: message-oriented and socially-oriented; ideational and interpersonal; transactional and phatic.

Tenor

The word 'tenor' has various meanings, depending on the subject you are talking about. Pavarotti was a tenor, for example, but the tenor of a document is its general sense. This is one reason why technical jargon can become confusing. In language study, tenor is related to the concept of **audience**. It is a broader idea, though, and includes all the people in a situation. Here is a working definition from *A Dictionary of Stylistics*.

> [Tenor involves] the relationships between participants in the situation, their roles and status

This will affect the kind of language chosen, particularly in respect of the degree of formality.

Although it is not a precise, technical term, the word 'tone' is often used to describe the degree of formality or 'the kind of language chosen'. The relationship between the speaker or writer and the listener(s) or reader(s) has a shorthand term: the **addresser–addressee relationship**. When you describe this, it is useful to consider the formality scales introduced on Page 14.

Activity 20

1 Think about these situations of language use again and add some ideas of your own.

- A man writes a note of apology to the unknown woman whose room he went into in the middle of the night.
- A teacher emails the organiser of a training course at a local university to ask for confirmation of booking.
- The prime minister welcomes delegates to a conference on education.
- A music festival leaflet provides information about health and safety for everyone attending the weekend.

2 For each one, describe the participants – their relationship, roles and status.

3 How might this affect the tone or degree of formality used?

Take it further

Read *New Labour, New Language* by N. Fairclough, pages 97–118. Do you agree that Blair managed to present himself as a 'normal person', as well as a public leader?

You can see that the other three aspects of context have an influence on the tenor.

- Mode – If you are speaking to someone, you can usually become more friendly than in writing.
- Field – If you are talking about a serious subject, you might keep your language focused on the topic and not stray into social pleasantries.
- Function – If you need to apologise to someone, your role will be more humble than if they need to provide you with a service.

Language and power in social interaction

The study of language and power is now an important area of linguistics. For example, people have analysed the way Tony Blair, as prime minister, used language, and have compared it to Margaret Thatcher's style. It is interesting that Thatcher, a woman, adopted a more obviously powerful role in her interactions with the media. Tony Blair, on the other hand, often played a less assertive role, speaking tentatively and allowing people to interrupt him.

Independent research

You can find interesting ideas about the way language reveals relationships and status in disciplines such as psychology or less academic areas like assertiveness training, counselling and even sales techniques. Concentrate on a small area, such as the use of questions or negative statements. What do they suggest is the effect of such language use?

Activity 21

Use a pack of playing cards, with number 2 representing the lowest status and Ace, King, Queen the highest status.

1   In turn, each person picks a card from the pack and goes outside the room. Assume the status shown on your card and the role of someone arriving late for class.

2   Enter the room and take your place, saying whatever you think appropriate for your role and status.

3   The group should guess your status and explain their reasons. Although body language is significant, it is outside the scope of English language study. You may comment on tone and volume (see pages 39–40) of voice, as well as the words used.

Hitting the right tone

It is generally easier to find the right words in familiar (from the word 'family') situations, which we can specify in the following ways.

- **Mode**   speaking, rather than writing, because there is the chance for feedback and you can change tack, if things seem to be going badly
- **Private–public**   one person or a small group, rather than a large group
- **Relationship**   people you know, rather than strangers
- **Field**   on subjects both parties/you feel comfortable with
- **Function**   for a non-serious purpose.

Let's look at language use in more tricky situations – where the person is writing to a large group of people, who are not known on a personal level, to persuade them to change their behaviour. (Ignore the underlining in Text 1 for now; it will be referred to in Activity 23.)

Activity 22

Read these two texts and for each, assess:

a   the relative status of writer to readers on a scale of 1 to 10

b   how effective it is in achieving its purpose.

Text A letter sent by a junior school headteacher to parents

> Dear Parents
>
> We are encountering a lot of problems with the <u>payment</u> and <u>collection</u> of dinner money and need your help in resolving them.
>
> Therefore may we remind you that the cost of school meals is XXp.
>
> 5 The correct amount of dinner money <u>should be paid</u> on Monday morning in a labelled packet or envelope, regardless of the number of dinners your child will require during the week and the days that he/she will be having them. Late and incorrect <u>payment</u> of money, and an increasing amount of unidentified loose dinner money <u>being sent</u> into school, is creating a great deal of extra administration and taking up an excessive amount of the clerk's time. This means that other essential work <u>cannot be done</u> and affects the whole school.
>
> 10 Please note that if dinner money <u>is not received</u> on Monday or on the first day of the week that a child is in school and having a school meal, a dinner <u>will not be ordered</u> on following days.
>
> Your <u>cooperation</u> regarding this matter <u>will be much appreciated</u>.
>
> Yours sincerely,

Text B notice pinned above the sink in a B&B bathroom

> ## Save water!
>
> Please be so kind as to ensure that the taps are turned off completely.
>
> It is very easy to leave these taps slightly open, and they sometimes 'bounce' back a bit when you close them.
>
> Thank you very much for your help.

Identifying formal grammar

There are several accepted ways of being more formal. Often this simply means being less personal and direct. These three features of grammar are highly significant in the analysis of language and power:

- avoiding the **first** and **second person pronouns** (I/me, you) and referring in general terms to 'people' or even 'one'
- avoiding the **active voice** and choosing **passive** forms
- avoiding verbs, wherever possible, and using nouns instead (called **nominalisation**).

Activity 23

Look at the examples of nominalisation and the passive voice that are underlined in the headteacher's letter on page 28.

1   Transform these into the more direct forms, for example:

nominalisation	**verb**
<u>collection</u> of dinner money	<u>we can't collect</u> the dinner money

passive voice	**active voice**
dinner money <u>should be paid</u>	<u>you should pay</u> your child's dinner money

2   What do you notice about the use of personal pronouns in the original and the transformed text?

3   How has the tenor changed in your transformed text?

Most people feel that the B&B notice (on page 28) is written as if writer and reader share a relatively equal status. The writer shows respect to the guests and makes the request very politely, appealing to their better nature. The headteacher's letter, on the other hand, is written as if from a superior status, talking down to some badly behaved parents. The threatening tone of voice might alienate the readers, so the more personal rewritten version would be more effective.

Shifting the footing

The sociologist, Goffman uses the term '**footing**' to refer to participants' stance towards each other. In everyday language, we use this metaphor when we talk about getting off on the wrong foot or being caught off-guard, etc. Goffman points out that the footing can shift during an interaction. When we meet a person for the first time, we might start off on a formal footing, with some conventional politeness. If we find some common ground, it can change to a more relaxed footing. These changes in relationship are linked to shifts in the language used. It might be slight changes in the tone of voice, sudden introduction of taboo language or less direct ways of making requests.

Activity 24

Read this exchange of text messages with a forensic approach (ie as a language detective). It began with B phoning A, but not leaving a voice message.

A: The phones broke u wil have 2 send text that's al i can get x
B: Is that ian? I only recognise names not numbers. Alison
A: No u just tried 2 phone
B: But who are you? I an asap at texting
5 B: Just worked it out you are the bastard who nicked my stuff watch this space

(No reply)

A: sorry love but am a girl and this sim was 2nd hand I got it from stole of the market it nothing 2 do with me
B: get rid of it before you get done for it
A: Ok love thanx 4 lettin me no x

10

1   What can you tell about the participants – their relationship, status and roles? Do you think A *is* a girl? Why do you think this?

2   Does the footing change over the interaction?

3   Identify features of language use – lexis (words), grammar (sentence structures) or terms of address (names for people) – to support your points about the tenor of this text.

4   Read the two responses below. Which do you find more convincing? Why?

Theory A

The two people texting each other are not sure of the other person's identity, but they write in an informal style as if communicating with a friend. Person B seems older and better educated, as she uses more conventional spelling and punctuation, but doesn't understand predictive text. She signs off with her full name (more like a letter than a text) but never uses friendly signs like 'x'. She is in control of the exchange, asking all the questions (who are you?) at the beginning and then giving commands (watch this space) towards the end. She changes from polite language use to using slang (nicked) and taboo words in order to frighten Person A. I think Person A is a young girl, as she uses a lot of typical abbreviations (2, u) and affectionate signs, such as the 'x' for a kiss and the term 'love' to address Person B. She sounds worried about the messages, and is very polite to Person B, apologising, explaining her situation and thanking her at the end. Her polite, friendly language is in contrast to the aggression of Person B.

Theory B

The two participants begin with an awkward exchange. Person B simply wants to be clear about who she is addressing. Person A does not respond in a natural way when he or she gets the first text message. The fact that he or she withholds their name suggests a guilty conscience, even though Person B has not mentioned anything about a stolen phone yet. The footing changes dramatically after the silence. Person B changes from polite friendliness to accusations, insults and threats. Her language use becomes less standard, using slang lexis and grammar (get done for it) and no longer punctuating sentences. Under the tough exterior there is probably a bit of fear, otherwise why would she offer the helpful advice to 'get rid of it'? I think Person A is a young male; even though 'x' might be more common for females, the way he uses the term of address 'love' sounds more like a male pattern of speech. He is not well-educated (eg non-standard verb form 'broke') and seems to have a Northern accent: the misspelling of 'stole' for 'market stall'.

Writing about language

In Section A of the exam, there will often be something unknown about the context. When you are asked to give your theory, you gain more marks for providing convincing evidence, than for the right answer.

What you have learned

✓ The context is the situation, which affects and explains the way language is used.

✓ There are four important aspects to context:

- **Mode** –
  - ○ first the channel: whether speech, writing or electronic communication
  - ○ then other sub-types/genres, such as interviews, letters, emails
- **Field** – the use of vocabulary related to subject areas, such as sport or warfare
- **Function** – the reasons or aims of the language use, including overt and underlying purposes
- **Tenor** – the relationship established between addresser and addressee.

✓ The register or formality is the variety or style of language used, appropriate to the context.

✓ You should use the idea of scales, ranging from the most formal to the least formal.

✓ You can use the formality scales to analyse the connections between context and text more precisely.

3 Key constituents

Key term

key constituent

One important aspect of your approach to analysis of texts is to consider all the relevant contextual factors. Part 2, 'Looking at context', explored four important aspects: mode, field, function and tenor, including some analysis of the text. This forms part of your 'linguistic method' and is assessed in AO3. The other essential ingredient is the ability to focus on the language of the text. Text and context are two sides of the same coin (both are assessed in AO3), so it was impossible to discuss context without looking at some language features. You have already used the terms in the margin boxes in text analysis. Now this part of the book provides you with a more complete toolkit for analysing the key constituents of language.

'**Key constituents**' is quite a daunting piece of jargon, but this is what all the A-level awarding bodies have decided to call 'the important bits' of language. If you unpick the phrase, you can see that it makes sense.

What *constitutes* (makes up or forms) language? Is it just a matter of individual words or do we have to take into account the grammatical structures? Surely the sounds can have an influence if language is spoken, or the appearance if it is written down? The dictionary definition of 'constituent' is 'composing or helping to make up a whole'. 'Key' means the 'essential; vitally important parts.'

The diagram on page 11 represents the various levels of language, building up towards grammar (sentences) and discourse (texts). Let's begin at the base, with the smallest elements: graphology and phonology.

Graphology

You will know the words 'photograph', 'graphics' and even 'graphology' (in the popular sense of the study of handwriting). In language study, a 'grapheme' is the smallest distinctive unit in the writing system of a language (which most people call a letter or symbol). Graphology is the study of the visual aspects of written language, such as spelling, punctuation marks, fonts, layout and logos.

Activity 25

Note all the language texts around you in the classroom, or that you encounter in a typical day.

1   In which genres is graphology a 'vitally important part'? Think of examples where the artist's or designer's role is as important as the writer's.

2   Which examples of language use do not rely so much on their visual presentation?

3   Can you make a general statement about the types (audiences, functions, etc) of language use in which the visual aspect is a key constituent?

Most people would agree that visual impact is a key constituent for young readers. But it is more widely used than that. Visuals are used to attract attention to vital information and also for the purposes of selling. Or do you feel that *all* contemporary readers need attractive visual presentation in order to read anything? If you look at texts written at least 50 years ago, you will immediately notice a difference in the appearance of the language: the font size is generally smaller, the pages more dense with print. Some people suggest one reason is that modern texts have more competition: there is far more printed material around us, as well as competition for our attention from other media, such as radio, television, cinema and the internet.

---

lexis and semantics

semantic field, field-specific lexis, jargon, slang, colloquial, terms of address

grammar

sentence structures: declarative, interrogative, imperative, tag question, ellipsis, minor sentence, active voice, passive voice

word classes and functions: pronouns, deixis, nominalisation, intensifier

discourse

backchannel behaviour, marker of sympathetic circularity, filler, filled pause, modal expression, discourse marker, addresser–addressee relationship, footing

Writing about language

For English Language A Level, you only need to have a basic understanding of the visual choices and effects. Do not spend too much time describing the visual appearance of texts in the exam. You will gain marks for understanding the significant points, then moving on to other aspects, such as lexis or grammar.

Remember that you may not always see what the *original* version of the text looks like (in this book or the exam); sometimes you may only see a typewritten representation. You can only comment on graphology if you can see the original.

You will notice that most advertisements gain their impact from both visuals and verbal language. Advertising companies often recruit English language graduates to create the written text: a highly successful campaign for Toyota cars, for example, was written by graduates from Nottingham University. A slightly different area of persuasive language is in campaigns for various causes.

Activity 26

Look at these examples from the Government's THINK! campaign.

You're four times
it's hard to
more likely to
concentrate on
have a crash
two things
when you're on
at the same time.
a mobile phone.

Switch off! Lose control Write off car Kill girlfriend OK

1   What does each plain text version lose?

2   Comment on the effective use of visuals in each advertisement.

Are abbreviations contagious?

The controversy around mobile phones is not just about the dangers of driving while using the phone. There is a lot of media comment about the effects of text message style on students' writing skills. The consensus seems to be that other writing skills (in particular, essays) are damaged by the use of SMS, because the use of abbreviations carries over from one mode to the other. There is similar concern about the language used in chatrooms and on instant messaging services. Is this concern justified or are the facts exaggerated to make a better story? The following activities explore the use of abbreviations.

Activity 27

1   See if you can understand this text easily.

```
WERV U BIN? PPL R starting to use SMS abbreviations all the time, OTOH not everyone
understands what BCNU means. 2 SIT W/ SOM1 by MOB or email, SMS abbreviations R
GR8. IOW, JIC SOM1 sends U a MSG like this, U need a COD 2 decipher it. HTH :-)
```

The text above comes from the website of the *Concise Oxford Dictionary*. Judy Pearsall, Publishing Manager for English Dictionaries, said 'In Oxford Dictionaries we have been monitoring the phenomenal growth of text messaging with great attention: its influence is now such that we felt it was time to treat it as an integral part of English.'

2   Look at your outbox to see the way you spell words in text messages. Conduct a survey in your class and among other people you know.

3   What abbreviations do you use? Why? For each abbreviation:

   a   do you always spell the word like this? Why?

   b   do you spell the word like this in other types of written language?

Text translation

Where have you been? People are starting to use SMS abbreviations all the time. On the other hand not everyone understands what 'be seeing you' means. To stay in touch with someone by mobile or email SMS abbreviations are great. In other words, just in case someone sends you a message like this, you need a *Concise Oxford Dictionary* to decipher it. Hope this helps.

It is true that abbreviations allow the sender to be brief – this is useful for time, space and money. But is it true that people are using the number of new abbreviated words claimed in the media? Surveys among young people often come up with surprising results: many say they have never used or seen abbreviations like OTOH or even know what they mean.

Activity 28

Research the use of text-messaging abbreviations in your social group.

1   List the abbreviations you use in text messages and those used by your friends and family.

2   Look at a list of abbreviations, for example on http://www.macmillandictionaries.com/ glossaries/text.htm. Which do you recognise? Which do you regularly use?

3   Suggest reasons why some people use a lot of abbreviations and others very few.

4   Think of other writing situations where you would avoid abbreviations.

Independent research

- You can access research and debates about the effects of text message language on writing skills on many websites, eg www.literacytrust.org.uk. Do you think that new forms of electronic communication are harming young people's writing skills in more formal situations? You could use this research as the basis for the coursework writing for an oral presentation (see Unit 2, pages 128–141).
- BBC Radio 4 broadcasts regular programmes about language, often available as podcasts, for example 'Word of Mouth' presented by Michael Rosen (the Children's Laureate). He also writes an article in each edition of *emagazine* (www.emagazine.org.uk), available in print and online.

Many of the 'shock-horror' stories about language come from a lack of understanding about language variation according to context and over time. The media rarely invite language experts to discuss these issues, but there are notable exceptions. (See the Independent research box.)

Activity 29

Take it further

Read Chapter 1 in *The Language Web* by Jean Aitchison for a linguist's accessible discussion of language change and variety. Do you agree with her claim that 'the web of worries surrounding change turns out to be … somewhat like the worries each new generation of parents has about its offspring'?

Why would an effective language user change their style of language when

a sending a text message to a friend?

b writing an essay for an exam?

Use the formality scales (page 14) to demonstrate the contextual differences. Place each genre (SMS or ESS) on the line.

The first has been done as an example. Text messages are saved for a short time in the mobile phone memory. Exam papers are kept in an archive for several years.

ephemeral ———————— SMS ———————— ESS ———————— permanent

private ———————————————————————— public

interactive ———————————————————————— monologue

socially-oriented ———————————————————————— message-oriented

spontaneous ———————————————————————— planned

Writing about language

Although visual design is a significant aspect of many language texts, your AS English Language course does not emphasise this level of language. You might not be given the original text to analyse, but a plain written version. This is a clear signal to concentrate on the other levels of language (morphology, lexis, grammar, discourse). So just make brief comments on any significant aspects of layout and visual presentation.

What you have learned

✓ Graphology is the study of the visual elements of language.

✓ No technical terms and concepts were introduced. Why?

Phonology

Phonology is the study of the sounds of a language. The way language sounds is highly significant. It is much easier to disguise your identity in writing than in speaking.

> It is impossible for an Englishman to open his mouth without making some other Englishman despise him.
>
> From *Pygmalion*, George Bernard Shaw

Many people feel self-conscious about the way they sound. According to some research, people's greatest fear is of public speaking (death comes second!) Hence the metaphor used by live performers: 'I died out there.'

Although the examination gives you written versions of texts to analyse, you need to understand some aspects of the sounds of spoken language. The first is the relationship between the basic elements of speech and writing: **phonemes** and **graphemes** (letters).

George Bernard Shaw

Phonemes, sounds and letters

What is a phoneme? Is it just the technical jargon for a sound? And does each sound correspond to a letter of the alphabet? First the technical definition:

> A **phoneme** is a distinctive sound with a function in a particular language.

Activity 30

Answer the questions in the next activity to see how phonemes relate to sounds and letters.

1   How many letters are there in the English alphabet?

2   How many different sounds can you make? More than this, many more?

3   How many phonemes do you think there are in the English language? The same number as letters, fewer, more?

4   What point does the following verse (and many more like it) make?

> **'Our Strange Lingo'**
>
> When the English tongue we speak.
> Why is break not rhymed with freak?
> Will you tell me why it's true
> We say sew but likewise few?
> And the maker of the verse,
> Cannot rhyme his horse with worse?
> Beard is not the same as heard
> Cord is different from word.
> Cow is cow but low is low
> Shoe is never rhymed with foe.
> Think of hose, dose, and lose
> And think of goose and yet with choose
> Think of comb, tomb and bomb,
> Doll and roll or home and some.
> Since pay is rhymed with say
> Why not paid with said I pray?
> Think of blood, food and good.
> Mould is not pronounced like could.
> Wherefore done, but gone and lone –
> Is there any reason known?
> To sum up all, it seems to me
> Sound and letters don't agree.

In many languages, 'sounds and letters do agree', certainly much more than in English. When you study the history of English language at A2, you will understand some of the causes of this inconsistency. For now, here is an introduction to some important concepts in phonology.

Key terms

grapheme   phoneme

There are 44 phonemes in the English language (only 43, if you speak with a northern accent. See Activity 31 for more explanation.) Of these, 24 are **consonant** sounds and 20 are **vowel** sounds. You can see immediately that there are not enough letters to represent each sound. This is a particular problem with vowels, where five letters have to stretch to 20 sounds. Some doubling up is one solution, for example, using combinations of the letter 'e' to represent three phonemes:

> *pet   pert   peat*

and combinations of the letter 'o' to represent another three phonemes:

> *cop   cope   coop.*

But there are no consistent rules to explain this. 'Pert' rhymes with 'curt' and 'coop' with 'group', 'threw' and 'through'. You probably know at least five different pronunciations of the letter combination 'ough'. Hence all the time and effort spent teaching spelling and various campaigns to introduce a simplified spelling system for English.

Activity 31

Group words from the list below according to vowel sound, not spelling. In 'Received pronunciation', the first 11 words in the list (the first column) each have a different vowel sound. However, if you speak with a northern accent, you may pronounce 'luck' and 'look' the same way, so you will have 10 groups, rather than 11.

dinner	took	care	late
hell	winner	fell	wine
cat	matter	duck	that
look	cook	like	mucky
luck	mare	hatter	tart
hall	groom	smart	pat
car	baked	hare	fall
room	duke	doom	far
fare	gin	Nell	puking
mate	made	gate	
nine	hat	twins	

Variation in pronunciation

One reason for not making any change to spelling is all the different accents of English. Across the regions of the UK, and around the English-speaking world, there are variations in pronunciation. Which accent do you associate with the official spelling of a word?

For example, is 'grass' to be spelt with a long /aaah/ sound to rhyme with 'farther' or with a short /a/ sound to rhyme with 'grab'? If you choose the first, it suggests that people using the other pronunciation are 'wrong', and it does not help them spell the word. (See Part 1, page 65 for more discussion on Received Pronunciation (RP) and regional varieties of English.) What happens if everyone gradually changes to the other way of pronouncing the word (because changes in pronunciation do happen over time)?

As well as regional accents, there are other variations in pronunciation. Think of words like 'yes' or 'really'. You pronounce each one in different ways, if you are speaking quickly or slowly emphasising it. Writers can use the alphabet to represent unusual pronunciations:

> yeah, yeh, yep, yup
> reeli, rahli, rilli.

Non-standard spelling is used in representations of the speaking voice in literature, for example, and also in magazines, emails, chatrooms and text messages. The aim is not to represent the sounds accurately, but to give a flavour of a particular accent. Here are some examples from a teenage magazine.

> I just lurve   Ker-azy!   she's gonna be brilliant   squeeze 'em   bustin' for a wee

The term **'elision'** refers to the omission of sounds. This often happens in connected speech: 'she is' becomes 'she's', 'going to' becomes 'gonna', 'squeeze them' becomes 'squeeze 'em'. You can see that the apostrophe indicates a missing sound. Words ending in '-ing' are often pronounced '-in'. Strictly speaking, no sound has been omitted here; it is a change in sound. If you say such words aloud (eg 'sing' and 'sin'), there is no hard 'g' pronounced at the end of the first word. You should feel, as well as hear, the different quality of sound. The first is nasal – try saying both with your nose pinched.

Activity 32

Read aloud these examples of non-standard spelling to hear the pronunciation suggested. Comment on any similarities between the two examples.

Example A extract from the poem 'Caribbean Woman' by Jean Binta Breeze

> oh, man,
> oh, man,
> de caribbean woman
>
> oh, man, oh, man, de caribbean woman
>
> 5   she doan afraid a de marchin beat
> she doan care ho he timin sweet
> she doan care if she kill a man
> jus doan mash up she plan
>
> caribbean woman does
> 10   cry
> like rain sprinkle
> early Friday mawnin
> does
> bawl like tundastorm
> 15   late satday night

Example B text messages sent to a teen magazine

```
JST LYK 2 TELL EVRY1 DAT U'R ALL SPECIAL NO MATTA WOT ANY1ELSE SAYS! GO READAZ!
FIONA XOX

I LOVE READIN UR MAG & WANT 2 THANK EVRY1 HU MAKES IT GREAT! ALSO, ALLY ZIEGLER,
U R A COOL CUZIN! LUV U X LOTTIE T X
```

It is interesting that some distinctive features of African-Caribbean accents are being used by teenagers in general: 'DAT … MATTA … READAZ … CUZIN'.

Using IPA symbols

A vital tool for students of phonology is the IPA (International Phonetic Alphabet). If you look in most dictionaries, you will see it used immediately after the word, within slashes, like this:

> **fuse** /fjuːz/ *noun* **1** a devise for igniting a bomb. *verb* **2** to fit a fuse to.

You do not need to learn this alphabet by heart, but it helps to become familiar enough with the symbols to read words and understand the pronunciation represented.

p/eɪ/n	[pain]
ɔ:/l	[all]
eə	[air]
k/ɔ:/s	[course]
t/əu	[toe]
m/e/d/l	[medal]
p/eə	[pear]
k/ɔ:/s/t	[cast]
r/aɪ/t	[right]
p/l/eɪ/s	[place]
g/æ/m/b/ə/l	[gamble]
ɔ:	[awe]
k/æ/r/ə/t	[carrot]
ɜ:/n	[earn]
k/j/u:	[queue]
f/r/æ/n/k	[frank]
k/ɔ:/d	[chord]
s/e/n/t	[scent]
f/eə	[fair]
t/ɪə/z	[tears]
k/æ/n/v/ə/s	[canvas]
s/ɪ/m/b/ə/l	[symbol]
p/ɪə	[peer]
w/eɪ/v	[wave]
g/eɪ/t	[gate]
h/j/u:	[hue]
k/ɔ:	[core]

Activity 33

The term 'homophone' refers to words that sound the same, but have two or more different representations in writing, each with a separate meaning. For example 'bear' and 'bare'.

1 Read aloud each of the IPA transcriptions below.

2 Write down at least two words with each pronunciation. The first one has been done as an example.

Social attitudes to pronunciation

Some differences in pronunciation pass without comment. Others mark out the speaker as part of a particular social group. The concept of **prestige** refers to pronunciation considered to be superior. The opposite concept is that of **stigmatised** pronunciation.

Try substituting an /e/ sound (as in 'get') for the /a/ in the words 'happy' and 'marry'. If you use this pronunciation for 'Oh, Harry/Harriet, I'm so happy. Will you marry me?' it will sound like an upper-class character from a 1950s film. This used to be a prestige accent, but now it sounds ridiculous.

Now try dropping the /h/ in the words 'Harry and 'happy' and you will sound more like a character from *East Enders*. Other characteristics of a Cockney accent are:

• substituting a **glottal stop** for /t/ so 'better' and 'brittle' become 'be'er' and 'bri'le'

• substituting a /w/ for /l/ so 'Phil Mitchell' becomes 'Phiw Mitchew'.

These variations in pronunciation used to be stigmatised. But attitudes are changing as a wider range of regional accents are heard on radio and television. Now there is a sort of '**covert prestige**' in using previously stigmatised forms. (See the comments on Estuary English in Section B, page 80).

Activity 34

Work in groups. Say the following words out loud.

a How many different ways can each word be pronounced?

b Do some pronunciations suggest a particular region or social status?

hanging	apathetic	garage	either	scone	jewellery

Key terms
prestige
stigmatised
glottal stop
covert prestige

Stress, pitch and intonation

These aspects of spoken language are sometimes called 'supra-segmental' – quite apart from the individual phonemes. **Stress** refers to the amount of emphasis put on a syllable. Think of stress as a drum beat or rhythm, rather than extra volume. If each person in your group claps out the rhythm of their full name, you should be able to hear some different stress patterns.

Every polysyllabic word has a pattern. Can you hear that the main stress falls on a different syllable in each pair of place names?

'Manchester	Ib'iza	Liver'pool	'Birmingham	Ma'jorca	Horning'sea

Note: It is difficult to find three-syllable words with the main stress on the final syllable.

In connected speech, normally only the content words are stressed. This is shown with a mark like this ' in front of the word, for example:

I'll 'find a 'piece of 'cake.

Activity 35

1 Mark the words you stress when you say the following sentence in a natural speaking voice. You could try clapping to the beat of the sentence.

Mary is staying in Prague.

2 Now repeat the sentence, putting the main stress on the word in italics.

Mary *is* staying in Prague.

Mary is staying *in* Prague.

What is the change to meaning? If you think of the sentence as part of a conversation, imagine what the other speaker has just said.

If you put stress on one of the grammatical words, it is called emphatic or contrastive stress, because of the way the meaning changes – to emphasise or contradict something. In written English, contrastive stress is often represented by capital or bold letters. An apostrophe indicates elision on unstressed words or syllables:

Mary's staying.
Me 'n my friend.

The schwa sound

The most common phoneme in spoken English has its own name: the **schwa**. The symbol is an inverted letter 'ə'. The schwa sound occurs in nearly every polysyllabic word and is sometimes called a 'weak' vowel because it is used for most unstressed syllables, eg 'ə yə waitin tə see cəmillə' (Are you waiting to see Camilla.) The other 'weak' vowel sound is the /ɪ/ in words like 'pin', 'still', 'fit'.

Activity 36

1 Say these words out loud. They all look like four-syllable words in written form.

comfortable	vegetable	jewellery

2 How many syllables do you pronounce if speaking naturally? Where does the main stress fall?

3 Now look up the words in a dictionary. Note which syllable is marked for stress (with ') and where the schwa or /ɪ/ sound occurs.

Writing about language

Although you will only be examined on written versions (transcripts) of spoken language, you should prepare for the exam by listening to English, as well as reading it.

Pitch and intonation

Pitch and intonation are tricky to write about – and to test in exams – but are an essential aspect of meaning in spoken language. Here is a quick definition of each and a brief indication of effects. You may wish to develop your understanding of pitch and intonation for either the dramatic monologue or the spoken presentation in your coursework (see Unit 2, pages 128–155).

Pitch refers to level – whether high or low. It is hard to represent pitch in written language, except in added descriptions, for example:

> she muttered softly …
> her voice rising to a shriek …

It can be very , however, in conveying underlying meanings. (See pages 86–90 on pragmatics – the study of what the speaker, rather than the sentence, means.)

Derren Brown (of Channel 4 fame) has this to say about what pitch can reveal:

> Voices tend to be higher and louder than normal when we want to draw attention to what we are saying, and lower and quieter when we want to show withdrawal or distance from the issue. A person saying that he is not bothered by an issue may be lying if his voice pitch has risen.

Pitch also forms one physical difference between female and male voices: the latter being generally lower after the voice 'breaks' in adolescence. When you study language and gender, it is interesting to consider the attitudes towards the pitch of an individual's speech. Margaret Thatcher was advised to deepen her voice to convey more authority, for example.

Intonation refers to the tones, or tunes, over a whole utterance – whether rising or falling. This is also hard to represent in written language. A general principle is that a falling intonation signals a statement or command; a rising intonation signals a question. You may have noticed a recent phenomenon in spoken English, where people end statements on a rising tone, so that it sounds like a question. The term HRT, High Rising Intonation, has been invented to describe this. Try saying these – or any statements – ending on a rising intonation.

> I really enjoyed that film.
> I don't think that's a good idea.

Attitudes to this habit are mainly hostile, seeing it as something imported from abroad and taken up without thought by young people. Others suggest that it is a way of expressing yourself in a tentative manner, allowing others to contribute their opinion. Still others say that it is a mark of the unassertive language that keeps females from positions of power.

Take it further

Use a search engine to look for discussion about 'Uptalk' or read an interesting overview of theories and research in an article by Matt Seaton in *The Guardian* on http://books.guardian.co.uk/departments/referenceandlanguages/story/0,,555817,00.html. Do you agree that rising intonation on statements is mainly used by young females and signals a lack of status?

What you have learned

✓ Phonology is the study of the sounds of language.

✓ You should understand some key concepts in phonology: the distinction between phoneme and letter, consonant and vowel.

✓ If you are familiar with the IPA (International Phonetic Alphabet), you will be able to read written representations of pronunciation: in dictionaries and textbooks. You should, at least, understand what the terms 'schwa' and 'glottal stop' refer to. This will help you understand some variations in pronunciation, such as regional dialects. This includes aspects such as stress, pitch and intonation.

✓ You should also be aware of social attitudes towards accents.

Morphology

Morphology is the study of word structure, some of which is familiar from GCSE study. At AS level, you need to understand:

- the principles of word formation – the way words are put together
- the impact on formality – the effect on style of using particular types of words.

We barely notice word structure with familiar words, but it becomes clear with newly invented words. The website www.wordspy.com is a good place to start exploring new words as it gives a concise explanation of a word's formation plus examples of its use. Here are some examples from October 2007:

- glamping   glamour + camping
- ninja loan   a loan to someone with No Income No Job or Assets
- Potterhead   someone who is a big fan of the Harry Potter books.

From an early age, children intuitively understand the ways words are formed and create their own, for example 'killness' is a concise term for a terminal illness. You should know the terminology for this principle of word formation: a **blend**. It seems to be one of the most common ways of creating new words in the twenty-first century. More 'traditional' principles follow.

Derivation and borrowing

Let's begin with the words 'morphology' and 'morpheme'. They are each formed by the principle of **derivation**: taking a basic unit and adding extra parts.

Key terms

blend   borrowed

derivation   etymology

morpheme   prefix

neologism   suffix

root

Independent research

Use a search engine to find more examples of Shakespeare's new words, eg www.nosweatshakespeare.com. How many are still in common use today?

Activity 37

1. List other words including 'morph' or 'ology' or 'eme', for example 'metamorphosis'.

2. Does this give you enough information to work out the meaning?

3. Use a dictionary to find out the origin of each word. (It usually comes after the definition.)

4. Look up the meaning of '-eme' and 'meta-' in any 'Concise' dictionary.

Word structure is straightforward. The smallest meaningful unit of language is a **morpheme**. Every word must have at least one morpheme – the **root** of the word. Many root words in English are **borrowed** from other languages. Many are from Latin and Greek, but, for example, 'score' is a loan word from Old Norse and 'zombie' is from Kongo, a language spoken in the Congo. (**Etymology** is the study of word origins.) If you go to the webpage http://www.childrensuniversity.manchester.ac.uk/interactives/literacy/wordclasses/borrowing.asp you can test out your awareness of the origins of many English words. The optional extras are **prefixes** or **suffixes** (added to the beginning or end of words). Shakespeare invented these words from the existing root words 'heart' and 'meditate':

- dishearten   dis + heart + en
- premeditated   pre + meditate + (e)d.

Neologisms

From these three basic types of morphemes (root, prefix and suffix), the potential combinations are infinite. In fact, **neologisms** (new words) are created all the time. It is not necessary to provide definitions of new words. Their meaning can be worked out from the structure of the word and its use in context.

Take it further

Find out more about the origins of English, eg on www.ruf.rice.edu/~kemmer/Words/loanwords. Why do you think there are so many words from Latin and French, compared with borrowings from African or Asian countries?

Activity 38

1 List the existing words that have 'chew' as the root, for example 'chewable', 'rechew'.

2 Invent some new words with 'chew' as the root.

3 See if another person can supply the definition for each new word. For example, 'mischew' might be when you bite the inside of your cheek by mistake and 'chewitis' a painful condition when you keep biting the inside of your cheek by mistake.

You can see from the above activity that the principles of word formation are intuitively understood. In theory, anyone can invent a new word. A language teacher made up the word 'linkylove', for example, and started using it on her blog http://languagelegend.blogspot.com. You probably have some examples of your own.

But there are other processes before the word becomes an accepted part of the language. Some new words disappear as quickly as they appear. A word needs to be used consistently for a while by a variety of people, in writing as well as speaking. A final mark of approval is an entry in the *Oxford English Dictionary* (OED).

The status of new words

Who decides which words go in a dictionary? It is rather like a decision by a committee. A number of people must report evidence of its use to the editors of the dictionary. There is an attempt to get members of the public involved in this process on http://www.petitiononline.com/SoccerAM/petition.html:

This petition is to the OED to get the word 'bouncebackability' put in the book!

Activity 39

1 Analyse the formation of the word 'bouncebackability'.

2 Provide a definition for it.

3 Find examples of its use, using a search engine.

4 Comment on its level of formality – who uses it, where, about what.

5 Follow the same process for the word 'linkylove'.

Although 'bouncebackability' was not in the OED in July 2007, other dictionaries have accepted it as a word. *Macmillan English Dictionary* website www.macmillandictionary.com provides a definition and two examples of its use in *The Guardian* and *The Scotsman* newspapers in 2004. It has been used, not only on sports pages, but also in political comment, for example, about Michael Howard when he was leader of the Conservative Party.

Like many new words in their 'youth', 'bouncebackability' is considered to be **colloquial**, if not **slang**. These terms indicate that the word conveys an informal tone. Most dictionaries indicate their judgement about the level of formality. Remember, this is not a fixed decision. It is important to notice the date of your dictionary and try to use an up-to-date one.

Compounding

Another common principle of word formation is **compounding**. The two examples in Activity 39 joined two root words together, before adding some suffixes: 'bounce' + 'back' and 'link' + 'love'. Many compound words are so familiar that you may not notice their structure, for example, 'railway', 'homework', 'grandmother', etc.

Activity 40

1   List all the compound words in the text below.

2   Note the ones that also include some derivation.

3   Comment on the levels of formality.

Key terms

abbreviation
Standard English

> No, Dubai doesn't do it for me. If its 8-lane-mega-highways, multi-storey buildings and state-of-the-art shopping malls weren't enough, the city exists in a state of construction-frenzy to replace the natural world with its artificial mirror-image. There's the world's largest indoor ski-slope, a chill-out bar entirely formed from ice, a giant wave-cum-hotel, beside its superior 7-star rival in the shape of a sailing-boat.
> 5   Dubai's look-at-me-I'm-so-tall building remains in limbo, as more and more floors have to be added to top the latest competitor.

Abbreviations

Abbreviation is common in many areas of language use (people's names, for example), perhaps because we are always looking for shortcuts. Again, you need to consider the influence of time on attitudes to these shortened forms. When it first happens, the effect is informal, but this can wear off as people forget there was ever a full version. Consider the words 'fridge', 'vet', 'bus', 'pram'. All are abbreviations of the original word, but are now perfectly acceptable as **Standard English**.

Some abbreviations, such as 'sis', 'hubby', 'pic', however, are *only* used in informal situations or speaking, or writing for a non-serious purpose, between friends. Others like 'pop', 'mic' (for microphone), 'fan' (from fanatic) fall somewhere between the two extremes. Creating new abbreviations creates the most informal tone. For example, 'Soz, I apologe' was used as a deliberately humorous, non-sincere apology between friends.

Activity 41

Look at the following list of words taken from the first few pages of a teen magazine.

1   Note the formation of each word (borrowing, compound, derivation, abbreviation).

2   Rate the level of formality of each word on a scale of 1 to 10. Look in a recent dictionary to see if each word is listed and note any comments about its formation and level of formality or use the spellcheck tool to see if each word is accepted by the dictionary on your computer.

3   Do abbreviations tend to be more informal than other word structures?

1 fab	10 biopic	19 boy-obsessed	28 hassle	38 earth-friendly
2 shortlisted	11 micro-miniskirts	20 full-on	29 hippies	39 cutting-edge
3 gorge (boys)	12 celeb	21 hottie	30 fair-trade	40 anti-sickness
4 pint-sized	13 bra	22 wakeboarding	31 planet-friendly	(medication)
5 goalie	14 bimbos	23 showbiz	32 eco-friendly	41 stepdad
6 'mare	15 mag	24 sleepover	33 sweatshops	
7 bandmate	16 fitties	25 diva	34 recycling	
8 big bro	17 hols	26 down-to-earth	35 must-haves	
9 playlist	18 jetting off	27 fave	36 big-brand	

4   Words 29–38 came from an article about fashion that does not harm the environment. Words 39 and 40 were the only examples of neologisms in a real-life story about leukaemia. Do you think the field (subject matter of the articles) affects the level of formality in the choice of words?

Onomatopoeia and the rest

Some theories about the origins of language suggest that the very first words were based on **onomatopoeia**. Perhaps the words 'push' and 'pull' imitated the action they referred to and came about because sign language was no longer possible, when hands were occupied. Most words have no relationship to their meaning, but a few are imitative. These examples also come from a teen magazine. Can you add more?

splurge   smooch   yummy

Blends combine two existing words, for example, 'motel' from 'motor' + 'hotel' and 'skurfing' from 'ski' + 'surfing'. This is a particularly common trend in word formation nowadays. Because of this – and the element of playfulness – the stylistic effect is modern and humorous.

Acronyms are also becoming a popular method of word formation, often to name new inventions, groups or organisations, such as BASIC (Beginners All-purpose Symbolic Instruction Code) and WASP (white Anglo-Saxon protestant). If it is simply a sequence of initial letters like MRSA (methicillin-resistant Staphylococcus aureus, a notorious cause of infections in hospitals), it is called an abbreviation, or alphabetism.

Sometimes new words are created without making any changes to the form of an existing word. Instead, the word is used for a different function. The most common change of **word-class** is from noun to verb. This is commonly regarded as an 'Americanism', although it has been done for centuries without comment. (The verbs 'to mine' and 'to waltz' almost certainly began life as nouns.) However, recent examples tend to be regarded as pretentious 'management-speak'. For example, the use of 'passport' and 'ring-fence' as verbs in this statement by David Blunkett:

> If authorities passport on the additional resources and you then ring-fence, the additional £2000 uplift will be available on a ring-fenced basis.

You might also have noticed the opposite trend – using a verb as a noun in 'uplift' – and also turning a noun into an adjective in 'ring-fenced'.

Writing about language

The short answer questions in Section A of the exam may focus on lexis and morphology. You will gain marks for the use of precise terminology. For example, notice how the comments on the sentence 'I couldn't be in it appazza' in the editor's letter in Sugar Lad Mag become more focused.

- The writer does not use a proper word.
- The writer uses a made-up word.
- The writer uses a slang word.
- The writer uses a neologism.

- The word is formed by abbreviation from 'apparently'.
- The abbreviation adds the contemporary suffix 'azza', often used to shorten people's names as in Gazza.

In longer questions, always add a comment explaining the effect of the feature you have identified, eg:

This word is non-standard and does not occur in any mainstream language use. This type of ultra-modern slang creates a youthful style appropriate for the publication and its intended audience.

What you have learned

✓ Morphology is the study of word formation. You have learned the technical terms for the units that make up words: morpheme, prefix, root, suffix.

✓ You have learned some concepts for discussing the origins and forms of words: etymology, neologism, borrowing, compounding, abbreviation, onomatopoeia, blend, acronym.

✓ You have used some concepts for discussing the status of (and attitudes to) words: Standard English, colloquial, slang.

Lexis and semantics

Lexis comes from the Greek, meaning 'word', and is a more technical term for vocabulary. In the part on morphology, you explored the origins of words, their formation and the impact on formality. The next part on grammar looks at the functions of different word classes in sentence structures. This leaves the most significant thing about the vocabulary of a language:

> Lexis is the most important means we have of expressing our ideas and experience.
>
> (*A Dictionary of Stylistics*, K. Wales)

So – not before time, perhaps – this part of the book focuses on meaning. It will use three key concepts to organise useful terms for the analysis of words and meanings: **literal**, **associative** and **figurative**.

Literal meanings

Semantics is the study of the relationship between words and meaning. In some cases, this relationship is straightforward: x word = y thing. The easiest way of explaining what the word 'cup' means is to point to a cup. It is obviously more difficult with abstract nouns such as 'love'; adjectives like 'beautiful', which are relative or evaluative; and verbs used in an abstract sense, for example, 'drive me crazy'.

A dictionary definition provides (or attempts to provide) the **denotation** of a word – the thing it refer to. It may include **synonyms** (meaning the same) or **antonyms** (meaning the opposite). For example, the dictionary explains the meaning of 'baby' as a very young child, or infant, especially one not able to walk. You could add an antonym: not an adult, not a grown-up. Dictionaries often provide several definitions, showing the ways the literal meaning is extended: 'baby' also means excessively childish, someone regarded with affection, a special achievement, or concern (eg 'that project is my baby').

Activity 42

1   Explain the meaning of these words: home, lady, clever, win.

2   What methods did you use?

3   Were some harder to explain than others? Why?

You probably found it was difficult to find exact synonyms. The related words (clever, intelligent, brainy, etc) do not have exactly the same meaning. A 'lady' is not exactly the same as a 'woman' or a 'female'. If you thought of using an antonym, 'gentleman' is not always used as the exact opposite of 'lady'. In tennis, there is a ladies' championship and a corresponding men's, not gentlemen's, championship.

Associative meanings

The saying 'a house is not a home' refers to the emotional meanings associated with the word 'home'. The term '**connotation**' is familiar from GCSE study and refers to associative shades of meanings. Let's look at some ways that words acquire these shades of meaning.

For example, in recent years, politicians have talked about 'winning the war on asylum'. Is there anything odd about this combination of words? In *A Dictionary of Stylistics* by K. Wales, the term '**collocation**' (literally meaning 'located together') refers to 'the habitual or expected co-occurrence of words'. A computer corpus can provide the words that often occur before and after each individual word or you can use your memory. For example, the words collocated with the word 'war' are:

wage	<u>war</u>	against	(name of country)
win	<u>war</u>	on	drugs/crime/want/famine
lose	<u>war</u>	with	(name of country)

Now let's look at the collocation of the word 'war' with 'asylum'. The entry in the *Concise Oxford Dictionary* (1995) for 'asylum' gives its origin as:

So, the two words together mean:

> Middle English via Latin from Greek *asulon* 'refuge' (as in A-, *sulon* 'right of seizure')

<u>war</u>	on	<u>asylum</u>
attack	on	a place of safety from attack

Key terms

literal meaning

associative meaning

figurative meaning

denotation

synonym

antonym

connotation

collocation

Writing about language

When you refer to the connotations of lexis be more precise than 'it is positive/negative' and explore the collocations of the word, for example:

The word 'asylum' has begun to acquire connotations of threat, rather than its literal meaning of a refuge, where a person can be safe. This is because of its association first with ideas of madness (a mental asylum) and more recently with fears about the number of people escaping to Britain from foreign countries. The phrase 'asylum seeker' is often collocated with words signifying danger or large numbers, eg 'hordes of/the threat of asylum seekers'.

Activity 43

1   List other collocations of the word 'asylum' (from memory or using a search engine).

2   Does the connotation of 'asylum' change as the collocation changes?

Sometimes the emotive meanings of words have a stronger impact than the literal sense. The term 'asylum seekers' has gained dangerous undertones.

Figurative meanings

As well as having associative meanings, words can also be used in a **figurative** way. This term refers to the extension of meaning from a literal to a metaphorical sense. Our five physical senses are often used in abstract, figurative ways, for example:

> I <u>see</u> your point.
> She <u>sounded</u> a bit off to me.
> That left a sour <u>taste</u> in my mouth.
> It <u>touched</u> a nerve.
> I <u>smell</u> a rat.

Metaphors for love include ideas of fire, a journey, madness, etc. These few examples only scratch the surface. Once you are on the lookout for metaphors, they will pop up all over the place. The metaphors a writer or speaker uses can reveal underlying attitudes or assumptions. In the 1950s, for example, language about homosexuality used metaphors of sickness and disease, suggesting it could be 'caught' and 'cured'. More positively, banks often use gardening metaphors to encourage people to believe that money really can 'grow'. You can see that the concepts of figurative and associative language are linked.

Independent research

* Look at the website cogsci.berkeley.edu/lakoff/metaphors/ for examples of common metaphors. What types of ideas and images are associated with the abstract noun 'love'?

* Read the origin of these ideas about the influence of metaphors in *Metaphors We Live By* by G Lakoff and M Johnson (University of Chicago Press, 1980).

"He was a square peg in a round hole"

Activity 44

1. Identify figurative and associative uses of language in the extracts from *Raising Children who Think for Themselves* by E Medhus below.

2. What does the choice of lexis reveal about the writer's attitudes?

Dedication

With much fondness I dedicate this book to my greatest teachers: my husband, Rune, and my five beautiful children: Kristina, Michelle, Erik, Lukas, and Annika. Filled with eternal optimism, I also dedicate this book to my fellow parents, who, shoulder to shoulder in the foxholes of life,
5 are so willing to struggle and sacrifice for their children to defend the sacred priorities they hold dear. Their dedication, vision, and perseverance give humanity a gift of hope for the future that history has yet to behold.

Introduction

How many of us liken parenthood to a perilous journey? As parents, we are constantly teaching our children to fend off outer evils like drugs, alcohol, gangs, violence, and suicide, as well as helping them sidestep inner pitfalls like cynicism, eating disorders, irresponsibility, and poor
5 impulse control. These dilemmas can sometimes make our children's future appear downright bleak!

…

Then one day I read a story I couldn't dismiss. A young mother had killed her two-year-old son for some trivial annoyance, cut him into little pieces, fried him in a skillet, and served him to her
10 dogs. Then and there, I felt I had to do something to help stop this madness, for the world that had given me so much and for the world in which my children would have to live their lives.

…

This social reconnaissance mission inspired me to search for the most proximal cause of society's current predicament. In my earlier research, I had found that humankind usually tackles social
15 problems at the very tips of their branches rather than deep down at their roots, so that, at best, the disease is slowed but not cured. For instance, we pour money and other resources into anti-gang efforts, welfare reform, and drug and alcohol awareness programs. We do all this without ever asking ourselves one important question – *Why do we have these problems in the first place?*

Word origins

The part on morphology (pages 41–44) touched on the fact that English words are derived from a variety of language sources. You will find information about the source of a word at the end of its dictionary definition, often in square brackets. You will study the history of the language in more detail at A2. For AS, you need awareness of some significant aspects of word origins.

Anglo-Saxon formed the basis of Old English and those words still used in Modern English tend to be for basic concepts like food, family, shelter, the natural world, etc. Latin is also an important source of many English words, some coming into the English language via Old French. Other significant sources are Old Norse and Greek. In this way, English differs from Romance languages (such as French, Spanish, Italian), which are predominantly derived from a single source – Latin. Because of the variety of influences, English has a particularly large vocabulary, often including synonyms from different language sources, although such words each have slightly different collocations, connotations and levels of formality.

Activity 45

1. Use a dictionary to look up the language origin of the following words.

   kingly   royal   regal   ill   murder   homicide   smell   scent   perfume   odour

2. Compare the usual collocations of each word.

3. Comment on the connotations and level of formality.

Activity 46

Read the following extract from an open letter to *The Guardian*.

> Myra and I once loved each other. We were a unified force, not two conflicting entities. The relationship was not based on the delusional concept of folie à deux, but on a conscious/subconscious emotional and psychological affinity. She regarded periodic homicide as rituals of reciprocal innervation, marriage ceremonies theoretically binding us ever closer.
>
> 5 As the records show, before we met my criminal activities had been primarily mercenary. Afterwards, a duality of motivation developed. Existential philosophy melded with the spirituality of death and became predominant. We experimented with the concept of total possibility. Instead of the requisite Lady Macbeth, I got Messalina. Apart, our futures would have taken radically divergent courses

1 Use a dictionary to find out the meaning of the words the writer uses. Also notice their etymology (originally from Old English, or Middle English from French, Latin or Greek).

2 Try to express the writer's point in Plain English.

3 What different effect does the writer's choice of lexis convey?

Activity 47

Read the two responses below to the following question about the letter in Activity 46:
Comment on the style of this text. What are the writer's purposes and how does he try to achieve this? Which is the more revealing analysis?
Perhaps you noticed that the letter writer uses relatively simple sentence structures in contrast to the complex lexis.

Response A

The use of Latinate lexis (reciprocal innervation) creates a high register. Although the writer uses the word 'homicide', it is not clear that he
5 is referring to his own crimes. His style is highly educated, using jargon from the field of psychology and literature, perhaps because he has a university degree. He uses the
10 style of a very intelligent lawyer (as the records show), as he is trying to defend himself (before we met my criminal activities had been primarily mercenary).

Response B

The writer uses language as a smokescreen to disguise the terrible reality of his actions. Instead of saying 'I was a petty thief' he chooses Latinate lexis: 'my criminal activities had been primarily
5 mercenary'. He effectively 'blinds the reader with science' by choosing lexis from a number of academic fields. The phrase 'periodic homicide' has a bland, abstract effect compared with the plain alternative: 'we often killed children'. He creates a distant tenor between himself and the reader, suggesting that he is more intelligent. The only simple sentence is the first one: 'Myra and I
10 once loved each other.' He seems to suggest a connection between love and killing, as there is a strong semantic field of emotions (relationship, marriage) throughout. He also suggests positive connotations for killing in the collocation between 'spirituality of death'.

What you have learned

✓ Semantics is the study of meanings.
✓ You should remember the concept of semantic field (introduced in the part on Field, pages 22–23).
✓ You can organise the terms and concepts into three types of relationship between words and meanings:

Literal	Associative	Figurative
denotation	connotation	metaphor
synonym	collocation	
antonym		

Grammar

What is grammar – a, b or c?

a the most scary part of the course

b essential for good manners

c the way we make sentences.

Although the last definition sounds too simple to be true, it is the closest to an accurate definition, with its connotation of 'building'. Sometimes called 'syntax', grammar is the study of forms and structures within sentences, while discourse (see pages 56–61) looks at structures bigger than a sentence.

A **prescriptive** approach lays down the rules for 'correct grammar'. A **descriptive** approach describes in a neutral way the grammar that is in use. Some people do associate grammar with good manners. A prescriptive approach works like a guide to etiquette: it explains the rules for language behaviour at a certain point in society. This is the attitude to language use that you will often hear in 'sound-bites' in the media, whether it is Prince Charles bemoaning the poor English skills of his workers or the Conservative politician Norman Tebbit claiming a connection between loss of grammar and increasing crime rates!

Taking a descriptive approach

Although you need to understand about the strong feelings people have about language, a descriptive approach is the one used by linguists and on the A level English Language course. Some books attempt to provide a full account of all the grammatical forms and structures of English, and they run to hundreds of pages. You do not need to *know* everything about the grammar of English, but you should be *able to work out* anything you need. You can do this if you have an intuitive understanding of the basic principles of structure and access to a good reference book. First apply your intuitive knowledge of the English language in this next activity and explore your own attitudes to grammar, making sense and good manners.

Key terms

prescriptive

descriptive

Activity 48

1 Read the sentences below.

   a Which do you think are completely ungrammatical?

   b Which ones are you unsure about?

2 Explain your reasons. Which ones are to do with 'manners' and which are about making 'sense'?

- Flatpacks: hate you just don't them.
- You've gotta come 'ere quick.
- That's the sort of person I can never get on with.
- Softly flows the river Don.
- Pupils will now take less exams at A Level.
- Fat people eats accumulates.
- No worst there is none.
- If anyone is interested in this job, they should apply in writing.
- And our task is to boldly go where no man has been before.

Take it further

Find out about the basis for some of the rules of 'grammar etiquette', such as:

- You must never split an infinitive.
- Do not end a sentence with a preposition.
- Never use the plural pronoun, 'they', to refer to a singular antecedent.

Either use a search engine or read the short book *Who Cares about English Usage?* by David Crystal (Penguin, 1984).

A grammar survival kit

There is not space in this part to teach you everything you ever wanted to know about grammar. Instead, it will demonstrate some useful ways of organising and using your knowledge. It is like the joke definition of 'good taste': a person who knows how to play the accordion, but chooses not to. You cannot use every grammatical term and concept when you analyse a text. There may not be any examples of that feature. Or, if they are present, there may not be anything interesting to say about them. You must use your judgement and make choices for each particular example of language use. However, you can do some initial planning and decide on a shortlist of the most useful terms and concepts. To some extent, this will be a matter of personal choice, but some aspects of grammar stand out as particularly significant for style.

Activity 49

Here is one example of a grammar survival kit, listing some key terms.

Short of time and space in your brain? Never travel without these essentials.

Word level

pronoun:	personal versus impersonal	See Page 15
verb:	modal auxiliary	See Page 51
noun/verb:	nominalisation	See Page 29
determiner etc:	deixis	See Page 15
adverb:	intensifier	See Page 18
	discourse marker	See Page 19
	hedging	See Page 54

Phrase level

verb phrase:	passive voice (versus active)	See Page 29
noun phrase:	pre- and post-modification	See Page 53

Clause level

adverbial:	movable, optional	See Page 54

Sentence level

subordinate clause:		See Page 54
ellipsis/minor sentence:		See Page 19
interrogative:		See Page 19
imperative:		See Page 19
negative:		See Page 45

1   Which terms are already familiar to you?

2   Cut the survival kit down even further to five essential items.

3   Give reasons for your choice and compare it with another person's.

Writing about language

When you analyse texts in the exam, avoid the common fault of mentioning everything you know. Only refer to the significant features. This means that you have to add a comment explaining why you picked out that particular feature. Compare, for example, the value of these two comments on my written introduction.

1   The writer uses a formal style with a mixture of compound and complex sentence structures. There are many verbs, eg 'demonstrate'.

2   The function of the introduction is to make a clear, persuasive point. The writer gives advice by using the verbs: will, may, must. It moves from the negative 'you cannot' to the positive 'you can'.

Look back at the page references to remind yourself of the grammar terms already introduced. This part will show each of the new terms in action, but first compare your streamlined survival kit with my top five grammar concepts. I would not travel without:

pronoun   modal auxiliary   adverb   ellipsis   interrogative

The only one not already introduced in this book is the modal auxiliary. The term is a bit of a mouthful, but it is easy to identify modal verbs and interesting to analyse their subtle effects.

Modal auxiliary verbs

The part on mode introduced the term 'modal expressions' (see page 19) for words and phrases used to express the speaker's attitude to what they is saying, for example 'Honestly, I really don't believe that.' There are about 10 **modal auxiliary verbs** that have a similar function – they add meaning to, or modify, other verbs and so must be used in combination with a main verb.

Modal auxiliary verbs		+ Main verbs
Present	**Past**	+ stay/go, etc
can	could	
may	might	
shall	should	
will	would	
ought to		
must		
have to		

So, it is easy to learn the list, but what do modal verbs *do*? They perform three or four slightly different, but overlapping functions.

The pairings above indicate **present** and **past tense** forms, for example:

'I could stand on my head when I was young. I can't do it now.'

The example above shows one of the meanings modal verbs express: the degree of ability and possibility. Another person might join in with their opinion:

'You could do it; you should try.'

And then the original speaker might say:

'Mm, I might … No, I will, I must do it.'

As you see from these examples, modal verbs can also indicate degrees of obligation or necessity. The shades of meaning are not absolutely clear: is it a stronger obligation to say 'you should go' or 'you ought to go'?

Modal verbs allow us to talk about hypothetical situations. Sometimes people use the term 'conditional' to describe the function. Consider the possible replies to the question: 'What will you do, if there is a bus strike tomorrow?' You could use modal verbs to express degrees of probability and certainty: I might …, I could …, I will …

Yet another role of modal verbs is to express degrees of politeness and formality. You may (or might?) remember a teacher telling you, 'Don't say "can I", say "may I leave the room".'

Take it further

Read *New Labour, New Language*, Fairclough (Routledge, 2000), pages 6–8. Notice that this highly sophisticated analysis of political language does not use any concepts outside the survival kit. Which terms does the writer use?

Key terms

modal auxiliary verb

present tense

past tense

Activity 50

1 Read this extract from Martin Luther King's speech. (You can watch a video recording and read the full transcript on various websites, such as http://www.holidays.net/mlk/speech.htm)

Dr. Martin Luther King, Jr., 28 August 1963

But there is something that I must say to my people who stand on the warm threshold which leads into the palace of justice. In the process of gaining our rightful place we must not be guilty of wrongful deeds.

Let us not seek to satisfy our thirst for freedom by drinking from the cup of bitterness and hatred. We must forever conduct our struggle on the high plane of dignity and discipline. We must not allow our
5 creative protest to degenerate into physical violence. Again and again we must rise to the majestic heights of meeting physical force with soul force.

The marvelous new militancy which has engulfed the Negro community must not lead us to a distrust of all white people, for many of our white brothers, as evidenced by their presence here today, have come to realize that their destiny is tied up with our destiny and they have come to realize that their freedom is
10 inextricably bound to our freedom.

We cannot walk alone.

And as we walk, we must make the pledge that we shall always march ahead. We cannot turn back. There are those who are asking the devotees of civil rights, 'When will you be satisfied?' We can never be satisfied as long as the Negro is the victim of the unspeakable horrors of police brutality. We can
15 never be satisfied as long as our bodies, heavy with the fatigue of travel, cannot gain lodging in the motels of the highways and the hotels of the cities. We cannot be satisfied as long as the Negro's basic mobility is from a smaller ghetto to a larger one. We can never be satisfied as long as our children are stripped of their selfhood and robbed of their dignity by signs stating 'for white only'. We cannot be satisfied as long as a Negro in Mississippi cannot vote and a Negro in New York believes he has nothing
20 for which to vote. No, no we are not satisfied and we will not be satisfied until justice rolls down like waters and righteousness like a mighty stream.

2 Think about the full context of his speech – the historical situation in the USA, his purposes, his audience – before analysing the language.

3 Note the range of modal auxiliary verbs he uses. What is the effect?

4 What pronouns does he use – to address his audience, to refer to himself and other people? What is the effect?

5 Note his use of negatives. Does this create a negative effect?

On page 50, you saw the grammar survival kit set out on different levels, building up from single words to whole sentences. It is generally easier to notice words and sentences. Now let's look at the stages in between – phrases and clauses – taking just one example from each.

On page 50,

Now let's look at the stages in between

Key terms

phrase

premodification

post-modification

Noun phrases

The first words a young child learns are usually nouns: Mummy, Daddy, teddy, juice, and so on. The next step involves some grammar – building structures by combining single words into meaningful groups. Some grammar books use the terms 'noun groups' or 'verb groups' instead of the more traditional term used here – **phrase**.

In English, the usual pattern for noun phrases involves **premodification** – putting words before the noun. You can see the types of words used in this way from these examples of a child's language use:

> my daddy   orange juice   big teddy.

Post-modification, as the name suggests, builds onto the end of the structure, rather than the beginning. In languages like French, you can simply add the same sort of single words as are used before the noun (eg teddy big) but this does not sound 'grammatical' in English. This next example shows the way a 4-year-old child intuitively knows how to construct a complex noun phrase from the single word, 'lion' (even if it is not elegant):

> Do you mean the lion what is on the seat what goes on the toilet what you are not big enough to sit on your own?

A useful technique for spotting where a noun phrase begins and ends is 'substitution'. Try using a pronoun, such as 'it' or 'that', instead. What did it replace? That is your noun phrase.

> Do you mean <u>that</u> [the lion what is on the seat what goes on the toilet what you are not big enough to sit on your own]?

You will see from that example that post-modification of noun phrases often results in a complex style. That is because the speaker/writer needs to express something in precise detail. Complex noun phrases are a common feature of formal styles of writing, such as technical reports and academic essays. It needs to be handled well, however, as the style can easily become unwieldy.

Activity 51

1   The Campaign for Plain English selected one of the texts below for a Gobbledygook award. Which one do you think it was?

2   Find one noun phrase from each text and identify the main noun inside it.

The GENIUS project (based at the University of Reading)

The project is structured around multifaceted incremental work plan combining novel content design based on new pedagogical paradigms blended with the e-learning environments to facilitate hybrid mode of delivery. This is combined with series of educational experiments on the target learner groups with possibilities to adjust the approach and disseminate the interim and final results.

Introduction to *The Feminist Critique of Language*, edited by Deborah Cameron (1998)

I have structured this volume around three main themes: the theme of silence and exclusion, which also raises the question of women finding an authentic voice in which to speak and write; the theme of representation, in which the cultural meaning of gender is constructed and contested, and the theme of how and to what end we become gendered through our linguistic behaviour.

Clauses and adverbials

Building up from phrases, you come to the next level of **clause** structure. You may be familiar with the terms 'subject', 'verb' and 'object'. Every clause must have at least a subject and a verb, for example: Pigs / may fly. Many clauses add on an object: The children / are flying / brightly coloured <u>kites</u>.

Adverbials are worth looking at closely because they are optional extras. The other interesting way that adverbials function is that they are movable. These two factors provide you with tests for identifying the adverbial part of structures. If you think something might be an adverbial, try deleting it (Does the structure remain intact?) or try moving it to another part of the structure (Is that possible?).

Now for the reason adverbials are so fascinating. The familiar chant is 'adverbs describe how, when and where the verb happened'. This is only their 'daytime' job. To continue with that metaphor, adverbs (and adverbial phrases and adverbial clauses) have all sorts of 'undercover' functions. One is to reveal the attitude of the writer/speaker to what they are saying:

> The driver had <u>supposedly</u> been drinking.
> <u>According to the barman</u>, the driver had been drinking.

You saw on page 20 that some adverbs function as **hedges** to soften the force of a statement. Other can intensify the force of a statement:

> I <u>only</u> wanted to find out how much it cost.
> I <u>really</u> wanted to find out how much it cost.

You saw on page 19 that some adverbials (including single adverbs, adverb phrases and adverbial clauses) function as discourse markers, indicating changes of topic:

> <u>Now</u>, I want to move on to discourse.
> <u>For the final level of language analysis</u>, let's look at discourse.
> <u>Moving on to the final point then</u>, I want to look at discourse.

Activity 52

1 Read the following article from *The Guardian*.

2 Identify words, phrases or clauses that reveal the attitudes of the writer.

3 Use the two tests suggested above to see if these are adverbials.

Word of the week: innit

What word embodies Englishness? Jonathan Miller was ruminating about this, interviewed by Sue MacGregor in '50 Years On' on Radio 4 this week. Miller was discussing the influx of immigrants to this country over the last half-century and how they have become 'English'. Nationality, he said, was marked by your knowledge of ITMA, the Goon Show and Monty Python. Half-realising he was sounding like an old codger, he quickly added something for the younger generation. The children of immigrants, he observed, became 'English' when they started saying 'innit'.

The funny thing, of course, is that Miller himself could speak for days without once saying 'innit'. So was he using his ear for the demotic swirling around him in Camden Town? Or did his observation owe something to his fellow ex-Cambridge comedian, Sacha Baron-Cohen, who, as Ali G, has recently eternalised this word in the title of his compilation CD 'Ali G, Innit?'

There is some debate about the origins of the word. The OED sniffily records it merely as a 'vulgar' version of 'isn't it' (first use 1959), without noting its true versatility – replacing 'doesn't he', 'aren't they', 'wouldn't you', etc. It probably began as black British slang in the 1980s, though it has been pointed out that Indian and Pakistani English has long featured 'isn't it?' used in this way. It should be a conveniently universal tag serving exactly the same role as 'n'est-ce pas?' in French. In fact, it has remained the property of working-class adolescents.

20 Guardian readers might not know that there is an information bank for the study of teenage London English, the Corpus of London Teenage Language (COLT), based, somewhat bizarrely, at the University of Bergen, Norway. Assiduous linguists have recorded and, more painfully, transcribed 'half-a-million words of spontaneous conversations between 13- to 17-year-old boys and girls from socially different school districts'. Go to the COLT website and you'll find that two 'extra-sentential pragmatic particles' especially intrigue the Norwegian academics: 'like' (a previous word of the week) and 'innit'.

25 Such words 'reflect the highly emotive and expressive nature of teenage speech'. Papers are written and seminars given pondering the significance of sentences like 'I've told you the one about vampires, innit?' and 'I goes, you hang it up in your shower, innit?'

Yet there is a problem for both the Bergen scholars and Jonathan Miller. The linguists may not reach as far back in time as the sage of Camden Town, but they gathered their data in 1993. Are the kids still saying 'innit'? (The new habit is to say 'Isn't it' before a sentence begins.) Was Ali G, in characteristically amusing fashion, getting his slang a bit wrong?

Professor John Mullan

4 Now read this example response to the article. Notice the way the writer establishes some significant aspects of the context first. There is precise terminology to identify language features at various levels and comments explaining the connection between language choice and situation (mode, function, field, tenor).

This article is written by a professor of linguistics for a broadsheet newspaper about language use. This might suggest a formal use of language to provide academic information. Although the writer uses some subject-specific lexis to explain important facts, the lexis and grammar are often informal. The article
5 begins with an interrogative to suggest a dialogue with the reader. After some Latinate vocabulary (ruminating, discussing the influx) the writer includes slang (old codger) to lighten the tenor of the article, actually making a critical comment about the effect of more formal lexis. This mixture of the formal and informal is a pattern all through the article. References to serious institutions (University
10 of Bergen) are followed by mention of popular culture (Ali G). The sentences providing information need to be complex to give precise information. The writer adds a more conversational tone with phrases such as 'The funny thing, of course' and a direct personal address in the imperative: 'Go to the COLT website.' These language choices achieve the function of entertaining an educated readership who
15 are interested in language, but not experts in the subject.

Take it further

Use a search engine to find an archive of lively articles on language by Professor John Mullan or join in *The Guardian* blog 'Comment is Free'. You could develop one of the language topics for your spoken presentation in Unit 2 coursework.

There is <u>obviously</u> (adverb to reassure) a lot more you can learn about grammar. Remember that you can produce a revealing analysis using a limited 'palette' of terms. As with all aspects of English study, 'It's not about how much you have, but what you do with what you've got' (song lyrics by Si Kahn).

What you have learned

✓ Grammar is the study of structures within sentences.
✓ You can think of the structure as a hierarchy of levels, building up from individual words:
  ● one or more words combine to make a phrase
  ● one or more phrases combine to make a clause
  ● one or more clauses combine to make a sentence.
✓ There are so many grammatical terms and concepts, you need to be selective. Gradually build up a toolkit of useful terms for each level of structure. The grammar survival kit on page 50 provides you with a starting point.

Discourse

Discourse is, perhaps, the most fascinating area of language study. It is worth beginning with a few fundamental concepts at AS and exploring discourse further over your A2 course. The only disadvantage is that people use the term in slightly different ways. *The Dictionary of Stylistics*, Wales actually provides 10 definitions, but these can be simplified into three main aspects.

> Discourse is the study of the:
>
> 1 whole text in context, which includes aspects such as mode, function and addresser–addressee relationship
>
> 2 overall structure of written texts and spoken conversations
>
> 3 way that texts transmit an underlying ideology.

Definition 1 summarises the overall approach of A-level English Language study. This guide to Unit 1 follows the important principle of considering any text in its full context. Part 2, 'Looking a context' introduced the concepts of mode, field, function and tenor. If you prefer to avoid confusion and to use a different term, this aspect of discourse is the same as register or formality. It is not always possible to include the *whole* text – for reasons of space – but you should always consider where an extract came from.

Now let's look in more detail at Definition 2. To avoid confusion, you could refer to this aspect of discourse as **text structure** or **genre conventions**.

Overall structure of written texts

The best way to begin analysing overall structure is to look at the way texts begin and end. Many genres follow recognisable conventions. Traditional stories begin 'Once upon a time …' and end '… they lived happily ever after.' Newspapers put the most important news on the front page and sports reports on the back page.

The purpose and audience of the text can also affect the overall structure. Note the variety of **terms of address**, **greetings** (at the beginning) and **salutations** (at the end) used in interactive texts, such as letters, emails, text messages, etc.

Activity 53

1 Comment on the following examples of terms of address, greetings and salutations, and add some of your own.

Example A

> Hello darling woman!
>
> …
>
> big hugs
>
> Kath x

Example B

> Dear Friend and Admirer
>
> …
>
> Hope in all other respects you are well. Love and cheers,
>
> R and H and Des

2 What do these terms of address, greetings and salutations suggest about the context?

   a What is the mode or genre?

   b What is the relationship between writer and reader?

   c Is there any clue about the field and function?

   d What factors might explain the actual context (see below)?

The mode is straightforward, but the style of the texts may mislead you about the relationship between writer and reader.

	Example A	Example B
Mode	email to one recipient	email to a group of people
Relationship	had met once on a weekend course	are good friends
Field	the credibility of Derren Brown versus NLP (Neuro-Linguistic Programming)	the life and death of pet cat
Function	Both texts have a mainly social function, although they provide factual information.	

Both texts break the usual conventions because of the personal style of the writers. Kath is a charismatic, extrovert NLP practitioner. Richard is a witty and well-read teacher/examiner, with a strong sense of irony. (See pages 68–69 for more discussion of idiolect – an individual's distinctive style of language.)

Overall structure of dialogue

The second aspect of discourse includes the analysis of spoken – as opposed to written – language, in particular the way conversations work. You may prefer to use the term '**conversation analysis**' for this aspect of discourse. The most important concept in any conversation analysis is **turntaking**. Some research investigates the ways speakers manage to exchange turns without speaking at the same time or leaving awkward pauses. It looks at different types of signal that the turn is passing to another, such as pauses, grammatical structures and intonation patterns.

We will look at the *types* of turn and what this can reveal about the tenor – the participants' relationship, roles and status. It is always interesting to notice:

- who speaks first (*initiates* the conversation)
- who speaks most (has the longest **MLU** – mean length of utterance)
- who controls the subject (**agenda-setting** or topic shifts).

Conversations are essentially a dialogue. It is often impossible to understand what is going on from hearing one side of a conversation. The term '**adjacency pair'** refers to the two-part structures that occur in the interaction. A question needs an answer; an invitation needs an acceptance or refusal; an apology should be followed by an acceptance. This last example shows where the concept of adjacency pair can be significant – if one half is missing. You can analyse the effect, if one speaker's greeting is met with silence or a question is answered by a further question.

Take it further

You can develop your understanding of written text structure by examining the 'middles' of texts, as well as the beginnings and ends. Look at various genres, eg essays, letters or short stories, and ask yourself these questions.

- Are there clear divisions into sections/parts?
- Do these follow a predictable order?
- How does the writer signal the move from one section to the next?

Writing about language

It is rarely interesting to comment that there are adjacency pairs in a conversation. This is what normally happens. Only use this term when there is something unusual to comment on. For example:

The two speakers have an uneasy relationship, shown by the way they often break the usual conventions of adjacency pairs. B does not reply to A's first question. Later, when B apologises, A does not acknowledge it.

Key terms

conversation analysis

turntaking

MLU

agenda-setting

adjacency pair

On pages 16–18 (the part on CANCODE research), you had examples of some important concepts for analysing spoken language. These terms are also useful for discourse analysis of the ways conversations work. Here is a brief summary:

- purposefully vague language and backchannel behaviour encourage the other speaker to continue;
- filled pauses show the speaker wants to hold the floor;
- elision relies on shared knowledge;
- tag questions and markers of sympathetic circularity invite the listener to cooperate;
- discourse markers indicate a change of direction (also termed **framing moves**, eg 'well', 'moving on').

In transcripts of real spoken interactions, you will notice many non-fluency features. As well as the types of filled pause (er, erm, mm), there are often self-corrections, repetition and incomplete utterances. This is because each speaker needs to respond immediately without any advance planning. Conversations often seem chaotic on the page, with **overlapping speech** and **interruptions**. When you are listening or taking part in them, however, there is little difficulty in understanding.

Writing about language

Remember to treat spoken language as a dynamic and effective use of language in its own right. Avoid using terms like 'sloppy', 'lazy', 'vague' to suggest that spoken language is a less effective mode of communication than writing – treat it as different, but equal.

Transcription conventions

Transcriptions of conversations aim to capture the words spoken without giving a particular interpretation. For this reason, the familiar punctuation symbols of writing are not used. The term '**utterance**' refers to what is said (whereas the term 'sentence' usually applies to written language where the divisions between sentences are marked by full stops). Each speaker's name is followed by the words spoken. Other notation includes:

Key terms

framing move

overlapping speech

interruption

utterance

Notation	Meaning
(.) or (3)	brief pauses or a pause for a number of seconds
/	overlapping speech
…	unfinished utterance or interruption
SOME	capital letters indicate particular stress and volume

Independent research

You can listen to the audio file of the conversation on page 59 – and other conversations with children – on www.teachit.co.uk/technonanny. The focus is often on discourse and pragmatics. There are some transcripts with suggested questions and answers.

Activity 54

Read this extract from a conversation between a 3-year-old girl and her grandmother.

1 Can you tell from the way they interact that each person has a different agenda?

Louise:	I will pick er light orange /
Techno:	/mm hmm /
Louise:	/alright
Techno:	yeah (.) can't see it at all
5 **Louise:**	I can I am magorly
Techno:	mmm hmm
Louise:	I am really magic
Techno:	really magic.
Louise:	yes 'cos I can see the light orange can you.
10 **Techno:**	just a little bit
Louise:	I can see it a lot
Techno:	right well you are really magic
Louise:	my mummy said that (.) do you want to pick some more.
Techno:	er no I want you to do it so I can have a rest
15 **Louise:**	I think you should do SOME
Techno:	I'm tired I'm asleep
Louise:	YOU'RE NOT
Techno:	I am (.) Spike's sleeping I always want to have a little sleep after lunch
Louise:	can you just have a little rest like this /
20 **Techno:**	/yeah./
Louise:	/with your eyes open
Techno:	I have got my eyes open but I can't colour as well (2) I can talk and listen
Louise:	oh *(both laugh)*
Techno:	right I'm going to take my glasses off and have a little …
25 **Louise:**	what.
Techno:	a little rub [yawns]
Louise:	I getting pretty tired now
Techno:	are you (.) do you want to come in bed as well.
Louise:	I think I should do looking and drawling
30 **Techno:**	mm hmm OK

Louise wants her grandmother to join in the colouring; 'Technonanny' wants to have a nap.

2 Identify some evidence from the turntaking patterns. Here are some suggestions:

- Who uses interrogatives? Are these questions seeking information or do they have another function?
- How does each person seek to influence the other's actions? Are there any direct imperatives?
- What modal verbs does Louise use? Are they the same as Technonanny's?
- What adverbs does each person use as intensifiers or hedges (eg really, just)?
- What sort of backchannel behaviour (fillers) is going on and what is its function?
- When and why do they echo each other's utterances?
- How often does each refer to self ('I') or to the other ('you')?
- Who compliments and who 'boasts'?

In novels and plays, the fictional dialogue conveys characters – their feelings, motives and relationships with each other. These relationships often hinge around a balance of power. Literary dialogue is more orderly than real conversations, so it is a good place to start conversation analysis.

Activity 55

Read the extract below from the novel *Hard Times* by Charles Dickens. One of the main characters, Mr Gradgrind, is visiting a school. Comment on the following points.

a Turntaking: Who initiates? Who responds? Whose turns are longer?

b Grammar: Identify interrogatives, imperatives, negatives.

c Lexis: List the terms of address used for each of the characters.

d How does this effect the characterisation of Gradgrind, Sissy and Bitzer?

'Girl number twenty,' said Mr Gradgrind, squarely pointing with his square forefinger, 'I don't know that girl. Who is that girl?'

'Sissy Jupe, sir,' explained number twenty, blushing, standing up, and curtseying.

'Sissy is not a name,' said Mr Gradgrind. 'Don't call yourself Sissy. Call yourself
5   Cecilia.'

'It's father as calls me Sissy, sir,' returned the young girl in a trembling voice, and with another curtsey.

'Then he has no business to do it,' said Mr Gradgrind. 'Tell him he mustn't. Cecilia Jupe. Let me see. What is your father?'
10   'He belongs to the horse-riding, if you please, sir.'

Mr Gradgrind frowned, and waved off the objectionable calling with his hand.

'We don't want to know anything about that, here. You mustn't tell us about that, here. Your father breaks horses, don't he?'

'If you please, sir, when they can get any to break, they do break horses in the
15   ring, sir.'

'You mustn't tell us about the ring, here. Very well, then. Describe your father as a horsebreaker. He doctors sick horses, I dare say?'

'Oh yes, sir.'

'Very well, then. He is a veterinary surgeon, a farrier, and horsebreaker. Give me
20   your definition of a horse.'

(Sissy Jupe thrown into the greatest alarm by this demand.)

'Girl number twenty unable to define a horse!' said Mr Gradgrind, for the general behoof of all the little pitchers. 'Girl number twenty possessed of no facts, in reference to one of the commonest of animals! Some boy's definition of a horse.
25   Bitzer, yours.'

Discourse and ideology

The third definition of discourse (on page 56) refers to the way texts convey ideology. If you approach texts in this way, it moves language study closer to cultural studies and literary criticism. The phrase 'ways of seeing and saying' sums up the idea that the way we use language reveals the way we see the world. Any decision to control, or monitor, the words we choose suggests their power. For example, we might prefer not to call females 'chicks' or 'girlies' because it reflects society's treatment of women in a child-like way. Alternatively, we may decide that words have no influence – 'sticks and stones may break my bones, but words can never harm me'. (See more discussion of 'political correctness' on pages 74–75.)

You can explore discourse and ideology in the next activity (suggested by Keith Green and Jill LeBehan in *Critical Theory – A Coursebook* (Routledge, 1995).

Activity 56

1   Write your autobiography in one paragraph.

2   In small groups, discuss the questions on page 61.

The literary critic Pierre Macherey was interested in the 'gaps and silences' in a text. He claimed that what has been left unmentioned is just as significant as what has been included.

News reporting is often a good indicator of the underlying ideology of a particular culture.

Activity 57

Read the following headline and opening sentence from an article in the *Sun* newspaper.

a Which details are mentioned?

b Which are omitted?

c What underlying meanings does this imply?

GIRL 7 MURDERED
WHILE MUM DRANK AT PUB

LITTLE NICOLA SPENCER was strangled in her bedsit home – while her Mum was out drinking and playing pool in local pubs.

Take it further

Read the full article from which the extract in Activity 57 was taken: 'The Linguistics of Blame, Representations of women in the *Sun*'s reporting of crimes of sexual violence', Kate Clark in M Toolan (ed.), *Language, Text and Context* (Routledge, 1992). Do you think there are similar attitudes to women shown in tabloid newspapers over 10 years later?

What you have learned

✓ Discourse is a complex concept, but you can use it to focus on some interesting aspects of texts.

✓ Written language and spoken language may draw from the same store of words and sentence structures, but there are significant differences in the overall structure.

✓ You can use different approaches to analyse the discourse of written and spoken texts. This part introduced various terms for each:
  ● written texts structure: genre conventions for openings and closings
  ● conversation analysis: turntaking patterns.

✓ Discourse study also gives you the opportunity to move from structure into fascinating areas of meaning. This part suggested one way of analysing the underlying ideology of texts – applying the concept of 'gaps and silences' to discuss the significance of details of content.

Summary of key constituents

✓ The key constituents of language include these levels, from 'smallest' to 'largest':
  ● graphology or phonology: the sounds or visual signs of language
  ● morphology: the structure of individual words
  ● lexis and semantics: words and their meanings
  ● grammar: the structures within sentences, including words, phrases and clauses
  ● discourse: the structure of whole texts in context.

✓ You can use a limited 'toolkit' of terms effectively.

✓ You should rely on an intuitive response to select the most significant aspects for analysis.

✓ You gain more credit for analysis of a range of aspects.

Questions for Activity 56 (page 60)

- Did you begin 'I was born …'?
- Did you include material on schoolwork, hobbies, friends, etc.
- What was your final point?
- Consider the number of words spent on one topic. Does this seem an accurate reflection of the importance of that topic?
- Are there important points missed out?
- Try to assess why you included certain bits of material and left others out.

4 Tackling Section A of the exam

Section A of the exam is based on a group of short texts. You have one hour to answer a series of short answer questions on them.

The texts

The texts will all be from the same mode: spoken, written or electronic language. There will be some variation in context, for example:

- spoken introductions (giving details about person) in different situations
- book titles from different genres
- text messages sent by, or to, different people
- answerphone messages recorded by different people
- initial greetings to customers in different shops, restaurants, etc
- business cards from different organisations.

The questions

There will be four questions, totalling 50 marks (50 per cent of the marks for Unit 1).

The first short answer question will ask you to use precise linguistic terminology to identify certain features of the genre, for example:

- elision, backchannel behaviour, hedges, discourse markers in spoken conversations
- abbreviations, emoticons (visual symbols representing emotions, such as :–) for a smiley face), deixis, context-dependent language in text messages.

You should also demonstrate your knowledge of the key constituents of language by providing a second example of the feature in question.

After this short question focusing on the key constituents of language, you will have a chance to comment in more detail on the particular genre of language use, including your awareness of mode, field, function and tenor.

Another short answer question will have an element of forensic linguistics (language detective work), asking you to make decisions about unknown elements of the context, for example:

- grouping the texts according to the writer/speaker or their audience
- identifying the author of a particular text
- spotting the odd one out.

In a longer response, you should explain your brief decision above. The particular question will ask you to relate textual features to context, for example by:

- analysing one extract in detail and relating language use to a particular situation
- comparing and contrasting the language use across the data.

Read this example of a Section A exam paper. Use it as a mock exam either in timed conditions in class or completed in your own time.

Assessment objectives

25 of the 50 marks available in Section A of the exam are awarded for AO3: Analyse and evaluate the influence of contextual factors on the production and reception of spoken and written language, showing knowledge of the key constituents of language.

The other half of the marks are divided between AO1 (15 marks) and AO2 (10 marks):

AO1: Select and apply a range of linguistic methods to communicate relevant knowledge using appropriate terminology and coherent, accurate written expression

AO2: Demonstrate critical understanding of a range of concepts and issues related to the construction and analysis of meanings in spoken and written language, using knowledge of linguistic approaches.

SECTION A: LANGUAGE AND CONTEXT

Read the data provided on page 64 and answer the following questions.

1. The horoscopes were taken from four different newspapers and magazines: a women's magazine, a tabloid, a Sunday broadsheet, and a daily broadsheet.

In your response you must refer to the horoscopes.

For example

Extract: Friday's new Moon [taken from horoscope no. 1]

(i) Describe **two** language features of the text in bold.

    1.   semantic field

    2.   field-related jargon of astrology

(ii) Identify **one** more example of this type of language use from the data provided on page 64.

Ruling Mars from horoscope no.5

For each of the five extracts below:

  (i)   Describe **two** language features of the text in bold.   **(2 marks)**

  (ii)   Identify **one** more example of this type of language use from the data provided on page 64.   **(1 mark)**

                                          (Total 15 marks)

    (a)   you <u>could</u> come up with a new magic formula. [taken from horoscope no. 7]

    (b)   <u>Be</u> more present. [taken from horoscope no. 6]

    (c)   <u>Been waiting</u> for a cheque? [taken from horoscope no. 2]

    (d)   the outcome of your plans <u>is likely to be</u> something [taken from horoscope no. 4]

    (e)   a <u>friendlier</u> mood at work [taken from horoscope no. 3]

2. Explain the contextual factors that influence such use of language in horoscopes. In your response you must refer to the data provided on page 64.
     (Total 10 marks)

3. The horoscopes were taken from four different publications. Three of the publications have three extracts each in the data. One of the publications has only one extract in the data.

Identify the three groups (of three horoscopes) that come from the same publication. Choose one group and explain what the language use reveals about the audience.   **(Total 10 marks)**

4. Identify the odd one out.

Explain your decision by comparing the language use.   **(Total 15 marks)**

Language Today Texts (data)

No.1

Even if you are spread-eagled on the beach, one trusts you're hatching detailed plans for a hike up the professional ladder. Friday's new Moon opens a crucial four-month phase in your career. Short term, though, it's about patient negotiation and clearing decks. Remember, you always have options. The same goes for personal affairs, where you can keep it deliciously light (Venus) or respond poorly to provocation (Mars). Your choice.

5

No.2

Expect encouraging developments moneywise. Been waiting for a cheque, or a call from the boss? Be available on the 14th! You're confident to talk yourself up. Items you ordered for your home arrive – you can now look forward to a domestic weekend.

5

No.3

Showing how much a home move matters to you, helps it to happen. Two intriguing love developments will motivate you to get fitter. But it is a friendlier mood at work that helps you to excel. Destiny leads to the building with scarlet doors.

5

No.4

You're holding a lucky hand at present, Sag, but that doesn't mean every horse you back will gallop in first, or that every agenda you talk up will fall into place. With Mercury in contrary mode, the outcome of your plans is likely to be something other than intended. Be prepared to change tack (and expect a post-race stewards' inquiry). Above all, stay canny.

5

No.5

Afraid of Friday 13th? Not you! Ruling Mars gets lots of attention as home and money come under extra-special blessings – so bad luck is a thing of the past. If you're looking for love, you may not need go any further than the office next door.

5

No.6

Your talent is to hide from danger. It is getting difficult to find you, these days. Very soon we will stop looking, so be careful. People should, you feel, miss you more. Don't ask them why they don't, they'll very likely tell you. Be more present.

5

No.7

A project that stalled a while back could become a goldmine now, so on Wednesday check what's on that back-burner. Everything has its place – and time – and with a bit of recycling you could come up with a new magic formula. Money is heading your way.

5

No.8

Travel is no answer to your problems (you have to take yourself with you). But the local dinginess you fear to confront is truly frightening. Be strict with yourself. No, much stricter than that. Only when you have made your eyes water with the pain will you escape the nagging, dismal reality of your internal world.

5

No.9

If good ol' Easy Street is proving a hard place to locate, don't stop looking. Friday's new Moon unveils the dominant pattern of the next few months, in which your idealism and team-building powers are paramount. For the moment, however, you're at liberty to indulge in your favourite vice – indecision – but not to sit idly around. You need a plan (and a plan B, too).

5

No.10

Love me, love my dog. Don't take that literally. Or actively. But you need to be more accommodating, less judgemental, less mental altogether. Your ability to inflict bruises is one that you might consider restraining this week. There are advantages in not hurting people. Maybe you'll discover what they are.

5

B Presenting self

In this section you study the ways language varies according to the user: their age, gender, geographical background, ethnicity, occupation or status. You explore some theories about attitudes to language use, as well as some ideas about ways that meanings are implied by language use in a specific context. The final part helps you prepare for Section B of the exam by giving you a sample paper and analysing the questions and their requirements.

1 Introduction

Language is closely bound up with identity in several ways. The way a person speaks or writes provides all sorts of clues about *who* they are – their age and gender – and *where* they come from – the geographical region, as well as their ethnic, social and occupational background.

Some of these aspects of language identity may be acquired unconsciously, so that the individual has very little choice or control. It is hard – but not impossible – for a person to change their regional accent, the pitch of their voice associated with gender and idiosyncratic patterns of lexis and grammar. Impressionists rely on these sorts of ingrained language habits to create recognisable impersonations.

But language use does not only tell us about fixed identity; it can also reveal something about *how* a person chooses to present themselves. Just as some people take elocution (speech training) lessons in order to get rid of their regional accent, others may make a conscious effort to maintain all the original features – even though they no longer live among fellow dialect speakers. Margaret Thatcher was coached to lower the pitch of her voice to sound more masculine. A person, whose natural habit is to use the word 'like' repeatedly when speaking, might make a conscious effort to change this. Why?

Not only does language use reveal something about a person's background, but it causes a reaction. And this reaction is often as unconscious and ingrained as the language habits themselves. Negative judgements about people on the basis of their language are so common, but are rarely more than prejudice based on stereotypes. You can probably think of many examples, along the lines of:

> I can't stand the Liverpool accent.
> I hate the way people say 'innit'.
> Text messaging is ruining pupils' ability to write proper English.

You will already have some intuitive awareness of the links between language use and identity. Novelists and dramatists, for example, rely on this awareness to create characters through their fictional dialogue. In Unit 2, you may present characters in a narrative (page 112) or dramatic monologue (page 142). The journalism interview on page 95 involves the representation of a real person's speech. You should think about whether journalists simply *reflect* the identity of the person they are interviewing or whether they manipulate the language to *create* the character they wish to present.

Read the extracts below from an interview in *The Times Magazine*. Some names are disguised so that the identity is not immediately obvious.

1   What impression does the writer present of the person they are interviewing: their gender, age, occupation, regional and social background?

2   Identify some language features that suggest these aspects of the person's identity.

Why had H---- worn the Spider-Man costume? 'I dunno,' he shrugged. 'It were in me case, 'cause someone got me it for me birthday.'

'M---- was like, "Go on, wear it …",' continued T---.' 'Then we just hatched a plan. We love owt like that, confusing people.' …

5   When you do eventually get to stick a tape recorder in front of them, xxxx clam up. Sentences begin, then peter out. T----, so literate and perceptive in his lyrics, is tongue-tied and often inarticulate when questioned directly.

Ask them, for example, what countries they've enjoyed touring and the singer rejoins: 'I still don't feel like we're sorta like … professionals. We haven't really done that much

10   really.'

… So when people compare him to Alan Bennett, it's almost an embarrassment. 'Yeah. People go, "Oh, you'd be into him." And I'm like, "Yeah, I probably would — but gies a chance!"' He agreed to the suggestion that he got his interest in language and his attention to musical detail directly from his folks. But even that admission came over as something like

15   a revelation to him.

'I only realised that not long back,' he said, 'Me mum, not only is she a linguist or whatever, but she's always fascinated by words that mean summat. She's a big one for underlining things in books. For me birthday she gave me this book with all little things that she'd written down out of books. She's good like that. I'll be like, "What does this word

20   mean?" and she can tell me.'

Would he like to go to university? 'There's a thought. Dunno. Maybe. I'd love to proper know about summat. I struggle wi' reading a bit sometimes. I've got a couple of books in my bag but I haven't looked at them for ages. At the moment it seems like there's no time to do owt. I haven't even really writ [sic] a tune for a couple of weeks. Wi' Glastonbury and all

25   that, it's just a bit …' T---- sighed. 'It seems like there's always something else.'

Standard English and Received Pronunciation

These two concepts are crucial in order to discuss language variation. Each term refers to an abstract notion. SE (Standard English) is the form of English grammar and vocabulary that is regarded as the standard, to be taught to learners of English, and used in formal situations. RP (**Received Pronunciation**) refers to the accent, which is provided as the standard pronunciation of individual words in a dictionary. This accent does not identify the speaker as coming from a particular geographical region, but it is recognised as a marker of social status and is sometimes called 'BBC' or 'Queen's' English. The speaker sounds 'classy' or 'posh' depending on your viewpoint. The reaction to classic RP tends to be hostile and nowadays there has been a gradual shift in pronunciation. If you watch newsreels or films from the 1950s, you will notice the difference between then and now. Accent researchers estimate that only a tiny percentage of people in the UK speak a full version of RP.

You will look in more detail at the representation of regional accent and dialect in this article on page 79.

Take it further

Read or print out the article on RP on the British Library website http://www.bl.uk/learning/langlit/sounds/index.html. What do the terms 'conservative', 'mainstream' and 'contemporary' RP refer to? Why is RP changing, both in pronunciation and in attitudes to it?

Attitudes to standard and non-standard varieties

The term 'prestige' refers to the higher status of some forms of lexis, grammar and pronunciation. Is this because the standard forms are better quality and the non-standard forms simply inferior versions? In your A2 studies into language change and diversity, you will explore the origins of Standard English. With Caxton's invention of the printing press, mass communication was possible for the first time, so it was necessary to choose one of the regional dialects to use as the standard form. Not surprisingly, the dialect of the south-east (including Oxford and Cambridge, as well as London) was the choice. It is important to remember that Standard English is a dialect, but it is the one with the power and status. Simi larly, RP is an accent, but one which does not reveal the speaker's regional background.

Throughout your education, you will have studied some differences between standard and non-standard forms of English. At the level of lexis, where there are synonyms, some words are considered to be colloquial or slang, i.e. not Standard English. At the level of grammar, you may remember being taught not to use certain structures in formal situations, for example a double negative structure: 'It wasn't me what done it. I <u>never</u> took <u>nothing</u>.' Structures like this are described as 'stigmatised' – a marker of lower status.

However, social attitudes are changing in interesting ways. Regional varieties and colloquial styles are not only becoming more accepted, some are acquiring positive associations. The concept of covert prestige (meaning 'hidden' or 'underground' status) refers to the way that speakers and writers can – paradoxically – gain more status by using non-prestige forms of language. Often this is a deliberate choice of style for popular broadcasters such as Jamie Oliver. Politicians often seem to adapt their style away from the prestige forms that were part of their education. This can only be because they realise the influence of the '**demotic**' (from the same root as 'democracy', meaning language of the people).

Activity 59

1   Provide as many alternative words as you can for these concepts:

> food   sleep   uninteresting   intelligent

2   Check in a dictionary to see how each is classified – colloquial, dialect or slang.

3   What do you think are the differences in use and meaning?

Writing about language

When you analyse texts, it is useful to notice whether language use departs from the standard. Remember that it is a misunderstanding of language to use terms such as 'proper' or 'incorrect'. Although you do not gain credit for simply identifying the features (eg **The verb 'writ' is non-standard**), you may be able to make a relevant point. For example:

The journalist represents the speaker as using non-standard forms such as the past participle – 'I haven't even really writ [sic] a tune' – and draws attention to it by adding the comment [sic] in brackets. This suggests that the writer thinks it is a mistake.

Idiolect

The term 'idiolect' refers to 'the speech habits of an individual … as distinct from those of a group of people (i.e. dialect)' (*A Dictionary of Stylistics* (2nd ed.), Katie Wales, Pearson, 2001). Wales also suggests that a person's speech is as individual and distinctive as their fingerprint. If you are working on a dramatic monologue (See Unit 2, pages 142–155) you will try to create the voice of a character, by using recognisable 'voice-prints'.

It is perhaps easier to recognise a person's voice – on the telephone – than their style in writing. But idiolect does apply to written language. Of course, you will adopt a different style to suit particular situations – writing an email versus writing an essay, writing to a friend versus writing to a stranger, etc). Even so, there may be little 'give-aways' – personal language habits that other people learn to associate with your particular style.

The study of idiolect is crucial in three types of linguistic detective work: literary authorship, plagiarism and forensic linguistics.

Many literary scholars apply close linguistic analysis to texts that might, or might not be, written by Shakespeare. Others suggest that the real author of the plays must have been a different writer.

Plagiarism is the legal term for 'copying' another person's work. Universities are developing sophisticated computer programs, such as CopyCatch, to identify essays that are not the work of an individual student.

Forensic linguistics is the application of linguistic science to criminal cases. Now that technology can provide a vast database of language evidence and statistics, convictions can be made, or overturned, on the basis of language.

The case of the Unabomber

The basis for forensic linguistics is the claim that idiolect is the equivalent of a fingerprint, in other words, that each of us is unique in our language habits. But is this claim true? Here is an example taken from an interview with the forensic linguist Professor Malcolm Coulthard.

> The Unabomber, Kaczynski, was finally hunted down to his hut in the woods of Montana, from where he had been conducting a campaign of bomb threats. Of course, he denied he was the author of the documents sent to various newspaper offices and government departments over the years. The prosecution case hinged on the occurrence of certain words in the 30,000 word manifesto, which were also in a 300-word document found in his hut. Coulthard showed me the list of words:
>
> > at any rate; clearly; gotten; more or less; presumably; thereabouts; in practice; moreover; on the other hand; propaganda; and the word roots: argue; propose

This may seem odd – surely these words are pretty common?

Professor Coulthard makes another strange claim – that most of our language use is unique, once you have a string of more than seven to nine words. He even says that an individual does not repeat themselves exactly, but uses a slightly different pattern each time.

Writing about language

Understanding of idiolect is important in both sections of the exam. In Section A, there is often an element of linguistic detective work: you need to identify the writer of texts and explain your reasons. In Section B, you explain the ways a person presents themselves in speech or writing. The term 'persona' captures this idea of a particular mask, or face, that each of us can put on.

Independent research

- Use a search engine to find out more about one of the three areas of linguistic detective work. Choose some interesting details and examples for a spoken presentation for your Unit 2 coursework.
- Read the full article about the Unabomber in *emagazine*, issue 15, February 2002 or use a search engine to find websites about forensic linguistics. Why was this evidence accepted as proof that the Unabomber and Kaczynski were the same writer?

Use a search engine to check out the theory that an individual's language use is unique.

1 Take any sentence from your language use. For example, the first sentence in this activity: 'Use a search engine to check out the theory that an individual's language use is unique.'

2 Begin by typing in the first two words between quotation marks ("use a"). How many 'hits' do you get?

3 Add the third word. How many hits do you get now?

4 Continue until the result is zero. Is it more than seven to nine words?

5 Compare your results with others.

Using the first seven words from the sentence in Activity 60 gave 7470 hits, reducing to seven hits with eight words and zero hits with "use a search engine to check out the theory". Even though I was using language you might expect to find on the internet, my particular style became unique after nine words.

The Derek Bentley case

You may know about this murder case, where the 18-year-old Bentley was hanged in 1952 after his 17-year-old friend shot and killed a policeman. The film 'Let Him Have It' is a semi-fictionalised account. Bentley's family campaigned for a pardon, which was finally granted in 1998.

Courtroom scene from 'Let Him Have It' (1992)

Forensic linguistic evidence formed a crucial part of the case. The appeal cast doubt on the authenticity of Bentley's statement for two reasons.

1 **Idiolect** – The style was not convincing, given that Bentley was 'functionally illiterate' with an IQ in the bottom 1 per cent.

2 **Situation** – The police maintained that the statement was generated by asking Bentley to dictate a monologue. Bentley, however, maintained that it was a mixture: some of it a record of what he said; some question and answer ('yes' or 'no') rephrased as monologue; some the police wrote themselves.

Activity 61

Read Bentley's statement below and find evidence of:

a   Idiolect: It is not the language use of a person classed as functionally illiterate.

b   Situation: It has features of a dialogue, including answers to questions formulated by police.

Look at:

- lexis – noticeably formal words
- discourse – terms of address (ways of naming and identifying people)
- grammar – position of the adverbials 'then' and 'now'
- noun phrases – noticeably precise descriptions of places, people and times
- use of negative verb phrases.

The statement is annotated in the following way to guide you to points mentioned by the forensic linguists:

italics	– use of surname to refer to the friend 'Christopher Craig'
	– use of specific descriptive detail in noun phrases
bold	– use of adverbial 'then' and 'now'
<u>underlined</u>	– negative statements
(9)	– each sentence is numbered for ease of reference.

I have known *Craig* since I went to school. (2) We were stopped by our parents going out together, but we still continued going out with each other – I mean <u>we have not gone out</u> together until tonight. (3) I was watching television tonight (2 November 1952) and between 8 pm and 9 pm *Craig* called for me. (4) My mother answered the door and I heard her say I was out. (5) I had been out earlier to the pictures and got home just after 7 pm. (6) A little later Norman Parsley and Frank Fazey called. (7) <u>I did not answer</u> the door or speak to them. (8) My mother told me that they had called and I **then** ran after them. (9) I walked up the road with them to the paper shop where I saw *Craig* standing. (10) We all talked together and **then** Norman Parsley and Frank Fazey left. (11) Chris Craig and I **then** caught a bus to Croydon. (12) We got off at West Croydon and **then** walked down the road where the toilets are – I think it is Tamworth Road. (13) When we came to the place where you found me, Chris looked in the window. (14) There was a little iron gate at the side. (15) Chris **then** jumped over and I followed. (16) Chris **then** climbed up the drainpipe to the roof and I followed. (17) Up to **then** <u>Chris had not said anything</u>. (18) We both got out onto the flat roof at the top. (19) **Then** someone in a garden on the opposite side shone a torch up towards us. (20) Chris said 'it's a copper, hide behind here'. (21) We hid behind a shelter arrangement on the roof. (22) We were there waiting for about ten minutes. (23) <u>I did not know</u> he was going to use the gun. (24) *A plain clothes man* climbed up the drainpipe and on to the roof. (25) The man said: 'I am a police officer – the place is surrounded.' (26) He caught hold of me and as we walked away Chris fired. (27) <u>There was nobody else</u> there at the time. (28) The policeman and I **then** went round a corner by a door. (29) A little later the door opened and *a policeman in uniform* came out. (30) Chris fired again **then** and this policeman fell down. (31) I could see he was hurt as a lot of blood came from his forehead just above his nose. (32) The policeman dragged him round the corner behind the *brickwork entrance* to the door. (33) I remember I shouted something but I forget what it was. (34) <u>I could not see</u> Chris when I shouted to him – he was behind a wall. (35) I heard some more policemen behind the door and the policeman with me said: '<u>I don't think</u> he has many more bullets left.' (36) Chris shouted 'Oh yes I have' and he fired again. (37) I think I heard him fire three times altogether. (38) The policeman **then** pushed me down the stairs and <u>I did not see</u> any more. (39) I knew we were going to break into the place. (40) I did not know what we were going to get – just anything that was going. (41) <u>I did not have</u> a gun and <u>I did not know</u> Chris had one until he shot. (42) I **now** know that the policeman *in uniform* is dead. (43) I should have mentioned that after the plain clothes policeman got up the drainpipe and arrested me, another *policeman in uniform* followed and I *heard someone call him 'Mac'*. (44) He was with us when the other policeman was killed.

Language and gender

Sociologists and linguists have done a lot of research into the topic of language and gender over the past 30+ years. As often happens with theories about human behaviour, one person puts forward a theory and the next group challenge it. You do not have to write an essay *about* language and gender research in Unit 1. Your task is to *apply* your knowledge of theories to your analysis of texts. So, how much do you need to know about language and gender for your AS English Language study?

Evaluating research and theories

The most important aspect of your study of language and gender is your approach. Remember that you are studying theories, or hypotheses, not absolute statements of fact. You should keep an open mind and ask questions. For example, one theory is that in mixed-gender conversations, males interrupt more than females.

First, ask some factual questions: *who* conducted the research, *when*, *where* and *how*? The answer is Zimmerman and West, in 1975, based on statistical analysis of recorded conversations in the University of Santa Barbara, USA.

Then ask an evaluative question: Is this true in my experience? Perhaps you can think of some situations where it seems true that males interrupt more. But there may be other situations where the opposite happens. Does it depend on the individual and their particular style of interacting? Or does it depend on the people they are talking to, about what, where and why?

Then consider some critical points. Maybe the theory was true in the 1970s, but male and female roles have changed. It might be true for the USA, but not necessarily for all countries. Perhaps male university professors have a particularly dominant style of speaking. Were the women less comfortable in a formal meeting? They might behave differently in other situations. Maybe the male speakers were older than the females, had more senior positions or were simply more bossy characters.

Activity 62

Consider the following theories about language and gender in the light of your experience. Give examples that support the theory. Find examples that contradict the theory. How valid do you think each proposition is?

- Females talk more than males.
- Males use talk to be more competitive; females are more cooperative.
- Females like to gossip with each other; males prefer to discuss factual events.
- Males use more **taboo** (offensive) language than females.
- Females can't tell jokes as well as males.

A survey of research

You should have an overview of the way people have approached the subject of language and gender from the 1950s. For this, you will need a few key examples of research studies and the theories suggested. There is a catchy way to remember three important approaches to language and gender: deficit, dominance and difference.

In the early part of the twentieth century, when female roles were more narrowly defined, the 'deficit' approach assumed male language as the norm and described the ways females used language as not only different, but departures from this standard form. For example, Otto Jesperson (a man) claims:

> There can be no doubt that women exercise a great and universal influence on linguistic development through their instinctive shrinking from coarse and gross expressions and their preference for refined, and (in certain spheres) veiled and indirect expressions.
>
> From 'The Woman' in *The Feminist Critique of Language*, Cameron (ed.) (Routledge, 1998)

Key term

taboo

Take it further

- Read accounts of Zimmerman and West's research in *Women, Men and Language*, Jennifer Coates (originally published 1986, 2nd edition 1993). What does their data show about the differences between single-sex and mixed-sex conversations?

- Read some recent discussion of language and gender theories in *emagazine*. For example, Angela Goddard, issue 23, February 2004; Jennifer Coates, issue 27, February 2005; Julie Blake, issue 33, August 2006. How far do these writers agree that males and females have distinct ways of using language?

Writing about language

The terms 'deficit', 'dominance' and 'difference' are not precise descriptions of theories, but are often used in an evaluative way to refer to the underlying attitudes in research studies. You can indicate this by using the terms inside quotation marks.

Robin Lakoff (a woman) also wrote about women's language from a similar perspective, although obviously concerned about social inequalities. Her theories are interesting, but you should remember that they were not based on actual research and recorded data. Notice how she only offers suggestions about the differences between male/female language use. (I have italicised the modal auxiliary verbs.)

As an experiment, one might present native speakers of standard American English with pairs of sentences, identical syntactically and in terms of referential lexical items, and differing merely in the choice of 'meaningless' particle, and ask them which was spoken by a man, which by a woman. Consider:

a Oh dear, you've put the peanut butter in the fridge again.

b Shit, you've put the peanut butter in the fridge again.

It is safe to predict that people would classify the first sentence as part of women's language', the second as 'men's language'.

From 'Language and Woman's Place: Extract' in *The Feminist Critique of Language*, Cameron (ed.) (Routledge, 1998)

By the 1970s, movements such as Women's Liberation analysed much social behaviour in terms of male oppression. 'Dominance' studies of male versus female speech showed ways in which female speakers took up more supportive, subsidiary roles. The most well-known research is that of Zimmerman and West on interruptions. Many of Robin Lakoff's theories fit into this category, seeing female language as 'powerless' and male language as 'powerful'. For example, she claims that women use more tag questions ('Sure is hot here, isn't it?') and interrogatives ('Will you close the door?'), instead of imperatives ('Close the door.'). She comments:

Independent research

Read the two articles by Jesperson and Lakoff in *The Feminist Critique of Language* (Cameron, 1998). Note one or two key claims about female language. Then read the following chapter by Pamela Fishman. What evidence does she provide to challenge Lakoff's theories?

… women's speech sounds much more 'polite' than men's. One aspect of politeness … leaving a decision open, not imposing your mind, or views, or claims on anyone else. Thus a tag question is a kind of polite statement, in that it does not force agreement or belief on the addressee. A request may be in the same sense a polite command, in that it does not overtly require obedience, but rather suggests something be done as a favour to the speaker. An overt order (as in an imperative) expresses the (often impolite) assumption of the speaker's superior position to the addressee …

From 'Language and Woman's Place' in *Language: Social Psychological Perspectives*, Giles, Robinson and Smith (eds) (Pergamon Press, 1980)

Activity 63

Take one of Lakoff's theories below and test it against data you have collected yourself.

Females use a greater range of vocabulary to describe colours than males.

You can use a colour chart from a paint manufacturer and obscure all the brand names.

1 Ask a range of people to describe or name the colours in the range.

2 Record and analyse their responses.

3 Do your results support Lakoff's theory?

The 'difference' approach shifted the emphasis to see male versus female styles of interacting as different, rather than better or worse. Often the focus was at the level of discourse, rather than lexis or grammar, identifying different communication styles, which, in turn, lead to miscommunication between the genders. This approach to language has become a thriving industry and you may have noticed popular bestsellers such as *Men are from Mars, Women are from Venus*. Even the linguist Deborah Tannen's book *You Just Don't Understand* was serialised in a column in *Woman's Own* magazine.

Let's look first at popular (non-academic) claims about differences between male and female language use. The general points are familiar and, if we think of gender as a spectrum, seem to fit the two extremes. At one end is the macho male, a man of action rather than words, reluctant to express emotion, brusque, monosyllabic, prone to aggression. At the other end, the girly girl, loves to gossip, is emotional (hysterical even), impractical, vague and unassertive, but great at forming family bonds. What are the theories? What research evidence are they based on? Are they true for all social groups, in all situations, in all times?

Deborah Tannen makes more cautious claims. She gives one example of a wife upset by her husband's apparently unsympathetic response to her health fears.

> To many men a complaint is a challenge to come up with a solution. Mark thought he was reassuring Eve by telling her there was something she could do about her scar. But often women are looking for emotional support, not solutions.
>
> From http://raysweb.net/poems/articles/tannen.html

Her claims may also seem convincing in the light of your experience, but you should bear in mind that they are only supported by scenarios based on couples she knows, not actual recordings. However, it is generally not possible to make recordings of people having private discussions. Another criticism is that her experience is restricted to a narrow social group – probably white, middle-class, middle-aged Americans in the 1990s.

Independent research

Read *You Just Don't Understand: Women and Men in Conversation* (Tannen, 1990). There are also extracts on the internet, eg at http://raysweb.net/poems/articles/tannen.html. Note one or two theories that seem valid to you and one or two that you would challenge in the light of your experience of language use in your particular social group. You could use these as a basis for a spoken presentation for your Unit 2 coursework.

Activity 64

1   Set up and challenge some theories, using experience of your social group, for example:

    Assertion: Females love to gossip more than males.

    Challenges:

    • Definition: What exactly do you mean by the word 'gossip'?
    • Counter examples: X is a female who does not gossip. Y is a male who does gossip.

2   How would you describe your social group in contrast to that of Deborah Tannen's?

Performing gender

There is now criticism of the 'deficit', 'dominance', 'difference' approaches to language and gender. Rather than disagreeing with a particular theory, it challenges the underlying assumption of gender as an *essence* – a crucial unchanging part of a person's identity. The linguist Deborah Cameron suggests 'both sexes are fully capable of using strategies associated with masculinity or femininity' and that we should 'look at gender as a performative social construct'. The concept of 'performing' gender is convincing if you consider the possibility of males presenting themselves as young females in internet chatrooms, for example.

Even if you think that males and females are fundamentally different, it is important to consider other variables, for example, cultural variables. Are males and females the same the whole world over, regardless of age or social position? Then there are also situational variables. Do males and females use language in the same way regardless of their purposes, subject or relative status?

Take it further

Read 'Lip Service on the Fantasy Lines' by Kira Hall in *The Feminist Critique of Language* (Cameron, 1998). What examples does she give of an ideal woman from a verbal point of view: using questions to encourage men to talk; showing agreement; listening?

Activity 65

Writing about language

In Section B of the exam, you should show your knowledge of some relevant linguistic research and theories. You may find an opportunity to discuss the connection between language use and the gender of the speaker/writer. If you refer to a particular theory, remember to be tentative and evaluative, as in the example response in Activity 65.

1 Remind yourself of some claims about differences between male and female language use.

2 Give some examples where you 'perform' the extremes associated with each gender, for example, interrupting other speakers and sticking to factual matters or gossiping and talking about emotions in a cooperative way.

3 Now look again at the exchange of text messages on page 29. There was some debate about the gender of Person A (the person using the stolen mobile phone).

   a What theories and research would support the claim that Person A is a female?

   b Are there equally strong reasons for saying Person A is a male?

   c Does Person B use language in a typically female way?

An example response might be:

Person A uses terms of endearment (x, love), even when communicating with a stranger, and later acknowledges and thanks the person accusing her of theft. Lakoff suggests that such politeness is a feature of women's language. However, the only participant whose gender is known (Person B is a female) does not follow this pattern. She uses taboo language and gives direct orders. Labov's research suggests that it is women who preserve the standard forms and men who spread the use of non-standard forms. Both Person A and B use slang and non-standard language, yet we know that at least one is a female. Other factors of the situation could be significant: the conventions of text messaging are more 'relaxed'; Person A could be using the language of his or her age group; Person B's language use reflects her anger, more than her gender or age.

Independent research

Read the article on non-sexist language on the Wikipedia website. Notice that there is a warning that 'the neutrality of this article is disputed'. List some examples of gender bias in language. Do you agree with the claims made? Why do you think some readers dispute the claims?

Representations of gender

The previous parts looked at theories about the ways gender influences language use. There is also a lot of research into the differences between the ways males and females are *represented* in language. Some suggests that the English language is male-centred in certain ways. Examples such as the use of the male pronoun 'he' to refer to people in general might exclude females in job advertisements, for example. The use of the suffix '-ess' to denote a female version of an actor or waiter suggests that it is not quite the authentic, original thing. There are also marked derogatory, sexual connotations to such pairs of terms, rather than a neutral male versus female equivalence.

master	mistress
courtier	courtesan

You can see this type of bias in language if you compare the number of terms that exist to describe a sexually active female as opposed to a sexually active male.

Developments in equal opportunities have produced a gradual change in language use. Some people use the cliché 'political correctness gone mad' to object to attempts to make public language use less discriminatory language, not only against females, but also against other minority, disadvantaged groups in society. (I am one of those who regularly 'goes mad' about discriminatory language use.) The next activity tests your sensitivity to gender bias in language use.

Activity 66

Read the extracts below from an article in the *Daily Mail* about conkers and council legislation.

> It is a traditional autumn pastime that has tested and amused generations of schoolboys.

> Climbing trees to pick the perfect conker – hard enough to bring glory in playground battles – is a task requiring commitment, good judgement and more than a little courage.

> But such is the nature of today's '*nanny* state' that children are now being denied this pleasure – as council workers are dispatched to pick horse chestnuts from the trees themselves. They do so in the supposed interests of health and safety.

> Martin Callanan, the north-east's Tory MEP, said: 'Words fail me. It's the nanny state gone mad. I used to collect conkers as a lad and I never injured myself and nor did any of my friends.'
>
> Chris Brooke, September 2006

1 What do you notice about the language used to refer to the people collecting conkers?

2 What does this choice of language imply?

3 Do you think it is 'political correctness gone mad' to dislike such language use?

Take it further

Read the extracts from 'Man Made Language' (Spender, 1980) reprinted in *The Feminist Critique of Language* (Cameron, 1998) or read the introduction on www.marxists.org/reference/subject/philosophy/works/ot/spender. What does she think is the effect of language use that is biased towards the male?

Although the emphasis in debates about language gender is usually at the level of lexis and morphology – in particular about naming – the next activity asks you to consider language use at the level of grammatical structures.

Activity 67

Read the extracts below from *The Sun* and *Daily Telegraph* newspapers. They are quoted in *The Feminist Critique of Language* (Cameron, 1998) to show that this type of representation is not confined to tabloid newspaper reporters.

> A man who suffered head injuries when attacked by two men in his home in Beckenham, Kent, early yesterday, was pinned down on the bed by intruders who took it in turns to rape his wife.
>
> *(Daily Telegraph)*

> A terrified 19-stone husband was forced to lie next to his wife as two men raped her yesterday.
>
> *(The Sun)*

1 How is each gender named or referred to?

2 What do you notice about the sentence structures? (Think about how else these sentences could have been written.)

Language and age

There has been little formal research into the topic of language variation according to the age of the speaker/writer. This gives you the chance for some independent exploration of the topic. It is clear that the younger generation always invents slightly new forms of language. This is particularly noticeable at the level of lexis, but can also be seen in some grammatical structures and occasionally in pronunciation. Notice the range of terms of approval used in this extract from the networking website 'bebo':

> Back come the Tokyoblu live band as well with a couple of stonking brand ... superb!! brilliant!! wicked!! groovy!! fantastic!! wonderfull! magnificent! ...

You should consider the reasons for such constant innovation in vocabulary. One suggestion is that language acts as a badge of identity and that young people need to assert their difference from the older generation and to form exclusive 'tribes'.

Activity 68

1   Collect ways of expressing these concepts:

| approval | disapproval | intoxicated | short of money |

2   Which do you associate with particular age groups?

There are fewer examples of innovation at the level of grammar. One is the use of the generic tag question form 'innit'. You may have the 'insider' knowledge to provide more examples. The next activity focuses on the changing grammatical functions of the word 'like'.

Activity 69

1   Use a search engine to research the use of the word 'like'. Collect examples:

- as an **inquit**, or **quotative** (a verb that functions like 'said' to introduce direct speech with quotation marks): 'she was like "what are you doing?"'
- as a hedge (a deliberately vague expression): 'and stuff like that', 'it was interesting like.'

2   Listen for examples in spoken language of 'like' as a filled pause: 'And then I like picked up my bag.'

Take it further

Use a search engine to read more about Giles' theory. Give examples from your own experience of convergence and divergence. Can you think of any examples that challenge this theory, such as a person shifting their language use to become similar to another's, yet expressing some hostility or dislike?

You should also be aware of the tendency for any new forms of language to be stigmatised. Attitudes towards the two examples above are overwhelmingly negative. Despite this, their use remains common, and may also have some covert prestige within a particular social group. The sociologist Giles proposed a theory of convergence, which develops these ideas of language use as a badge of identity. This summary is taken from www.essex.ac.uk.

- **Convergence** happens when an individual adjusts his speech patterns to *match* those of people belonging to another group or social identity. Convergence expresses unity, a feeling of shared identity.
- **Divergence** happens when an individual adjusts his speech patterns to be *distinct* from those of people belonging to another group or social identity. Divergence expresses a feeling of separation, withdrawal; it draws a boundary around the in-group that a speaker belongs to and does not wish to share with their interlocutor.

People can also adjust their writing patterns to match those of a different social group. In many cases, younger writers adopt the style of older people, for example, when writing formal essays. It is necessary to imitate this style in order to produce an effective piece of formal writing. Occasionally imitation moves into forgery, if the intention is to pass yourself off as a different person. Letters excusing a child from PE can quickly be spotted as the style of the child, not the parent. The example in Activity 70 is more sinister. The text is from a criminal case in 2007, where a 15-year-old Michael Hamer pleaded guilty to the murder of an 11-year-old boy, Joe Geeling. The prosecution claimed that a letter, apparently written by a teacher, was faked by Michael.

Activity 70

Read the text of the letter.

1 Is it convincing as the style of a teacher? Identify:

- features of a teacher's style of language use
- features that betray a younger person's language use.

2 Can you produce a more convincing forgery of the style of a teacher?

Joseph,

You may have heard Year 10s have started to mentor Year 7s and they have been told to take some books to understand the difficulties some people may be having.

As you may know Michael is your mentor and will start next week.

5 Unfortunetely [sic] Michael has got some of your books, but will be unable to return them to you for two months due to surgery. So I have spoken to your mum and told her the situation and I have asked her if you could go with Michael to his house and collect them with the permission of your mother.

I have given the address to your mum and she will meet you at the house at 4.30pm tonight.

Sorry for the inconvenience.

10 L. Foley

Deputy-Headteacher

Do not discuss this with anyone else as this will cause confusion.

Thanks.

What you have learned

✓ You should be able to evaluate (not simply learn and repeat) theories. Language and gender studies can be grouped under the headings: deficit, dominance, difference.

✓ Many linguists today criticise these approaches because they ignore all the other variables that influence language use: cultural background, situation, age, status, purpose. They do not accept that gender (in the sense of being feminine or masculine) is a fundamental part of a person. Instead, they suggest the concept of performing gender. You may, of course, also evaluate and criticise this theory.

3 Wider social context

Gender and age are 'visible' personal aspects of identity, but social background also affects each person's language use. This part looks at the influence of geographical region (where you were born and brought up), occupation (your job) and power (your status).

Regional variation

At A2 you will look at language diversity and explore the use of English as a world language. It is the first language in many countries of the world (USA, Australia, parts of India and Africa) and the second language taught in schools in many others (most European countries, China and Japan).

At AS, you should be able to recognise key examples of variation in world 'Englishes', such as lexical differences between US and British English. You should also be aware of the scope of regional variation within the UK:

- national varieties associated with Scotland, Ireland and Wales
- regional dialects of England, such as those in Yorkshire and Somerset
- city dialects, for example in London, Liverpool, Newcastle and Birmingham.

You should develop the necessary skills to describe regional variation at the levels of phonology, lexis and grammar. For this, you can concentrate on the types of variation that are within your experience.

You should also consider some contemporary debates about language variation and change. What are the social perceptions of particular regional dialects? Are differences in dialects fading these days? Why?

Take it further

Use the BBC Voices or the British Library website to hear examples of some different dialects of English. You can click on a map of the UK to hear variations in pronunciation, vocabulary and grammar. For example, how many different ways is the /a/ sound in 'bath' or 'mask' pronounced?

Describing features of regional variation

Standard English is used as the benchmark for describing regional variation: how does a particular dialect differ in its pronunciation, vocabulary and sentence structures? You should observe the distinctive features of the regional dialect used in your area. Try to categorise the differences under headings. The Yorkshire variety, for example, has these noticeable differences.

Activity 71 Investigate and describe the regional variety with which you are most familiar.

Investigating attitudes to varieties

In the interview at the beginning of Section B (page 66) you looked at the way the writer represented some non-standard forms in the interview with the Arctic Monkeys. Some of these were dialect features. Here are examples of representation of non-standard forms from this interview.

Phonology	**Grammar**
• the vowel sounds in 'bath/grass' • and in 'bus/cup' • elision on the definite article in 'going t' shops' **Lexis** • some vocabulary dating from Old Norse (eg leik (play or skive), nesh, mardy, ginnel) • the contractions: owt, nowt, summat	• second person pronoun forms: thee, tha • past participles: writ, etten (eaten) • preposition: 'while (until) 10 o'clock' • forms of the verb 'to be': I were, he or she were (this may be a feature of pronunciation – the final 's' sound omitted from 'was' – rather than a grammatical difference)

The writer also comments on the overall discourse that 'sentences begin, then peter out' and Alex Turner is 'tongue-tied, inarticulate'.

As well as noting the actual differences, you should be aware of the attitudes towards such variation. You may wonder why pronunciation in the interview is shown in non-standard spelling for speakers from Sheffield, but not for the journalist himself, who is perhaps from London. Most speakers would shorten the vowel sound in 'my' to something like 'mi birthday' or 'ma mother', but the spelling would not attempt to capture it. In the interview, this particular variety of English is marked out as odd in some way. The Arctic Monkeys are portrayed as typical Northern lads, which is possibly the image they also wish to present.

Media use of regional varieties (in the choice of presenters for particular programmes) and representations of them (in adverts and fictional characters) provide a good indication of general attitudes. The tendency is to stereotype the people of that region, often in negative ways. The Yorkshire accent is used to advertise beer, bread and tea – all basic food and drink products. The accent and dialect is connected strongly, but illogically, with a lifestyle that is honest, homely, old-fashioned, unpretentious and perhaps with people who are a little bit backward or stupid.

Independent research

List all the different regional varieties used on television during one evening. Comment on the associations of each accent: the product being advertised; the qualities suggested.

Activity 72

Read the extract below from a newspaper article about a survey into attitudes.

1 What personal qualities does the survey link with an urban accent?

2 Choose one other regional variety and list the qualities stereotypically associated with it.

> The South Yorkshire accent has been branded the worst for flirting in a survey which warns city girls their South Yorkshire accent is a huge turn-off.
>
> 5 South Yorkshire was pinpointed as the worst in the study by networking website www.wannaflirt.co.uk, which also branded posh chicks with 'Sloane Square' voices and women from Staffordshire, Warwickshire and Manchester low in the rankings.
>
> But today Sheffield women hit back saying not only are they sexy but they are also very friendly and extremely proud of the way they speak.
>
> From *Sheffield Star Lite*, 17 August 2007

Some broadcasters and writers are also proud of their regional dialects. The Barnsley writer Ian McMillan was once considered too 'broad' even for Radio Sheffield, but he has not compromised his Yorkshire accent and is now regularly heard on BBC TV and Radio 3 and 4 commenting on all things literary and poetic. The novelist James Kelman represents the Glasgow accent and dialect in his novels. He is aware (because people tell him) that it alienates readers. He continues to do so, because he feels there is a deeper prejudice; it is not simply the difficulty of reading a slightly strange language. In the *Saturday Guardian*, he comments about his novel *How Late it Was, How Late*:

> During the Booker Prize controversy of 1994 much of the hostility directed at *How Late It Was, How Late* derived from the astounding proposition that the life of one working-class Glaswegian male is a subject worthy of art.

This type of uncompromising pride in language as a sign of your social roots is a factor in the use of **Black Vernacular English** (BVE). The British Rastafarian poet Benjamin Zephaniah represents his language variety in writing. He comments on some of the issues in his poem 'Translate':

Benjamin Zephaniah

> **Translate**
> Sometimes I wanda
> Why I and I
> A try so hard fe get
> 5 Overstood,
> Mek we juss get
> Afrocentric,
> Dark,
> Who in space
> 10 Who on eart
> Who de hell we writing fa?

Take it further

Read (or better still, listen to) Tom Leonard's poem 'The Six O'Clock News' and discussion of its comments on the status of Standard English and regional variations. You can find it on http://www.tomleonard.co.uk/sixoclock.shtml. What hypothetical situation is he referring to?

Independent research

You can read about Zephaniah refusing the OBE (Order of the British Empire) on www.international.poetryinternationalweb.org. What are his reasons? You could use some of this material for a spoken presentation in your Unit 2 coursework.

Key term

Black Vernacular English (BVE)

There has been a gradual shift in attitudes towards previously stigmatised varieties of English. There is covert prestige among some social groups, where young white English people use versions of Black English to acquire more 'street-cred'. There is controversy about this use of language, some people feeling that it is insincere at best and an insult to black people at worst.

Many researchers feel there is a link between language, gender and non-standard varieties. The linguist William Labov (1990) suggested that females tend to use standard forms of language and help to spread their use, for example to children in their care. On the other hand, he suggested that males lead in preserving non-standard varieties or spreading vernacular forms.

Estuary English

Another variation of English language use, which is not so much regional as social, is **Estuary English**. The term refers to a distinctive type of pronunciation that is being used by more and more people. It has some features of a 'Cockney' accent merged into a more standard RP and so probably originated around the estuary of the River Thames. It is not confined to London or the south, however. Researchers have observed the use of this accent spreading out to the north. In this sense, Estuary English is not a regional accent, but, like RP, associated more with a particular social group. Although not everyone agrees that there is enough clear evidence to say that there is a new accent, the concept of Estuary English is worth studying.

First, what are the distinctive forms? It is hard to describe an accent in writing, but imagine some speakers from the TV soap *EastEnders* as you read these examples:

- a glottal stop in place of final /t/ sound in 'about'
- changing final /l/ sounds towards a /w/ sound in 'until'
- omission of /j/ sound in words such as 'assume'.

Independent research

- You can read the debate about the DJ Tim Westwood's use of language, beginning with an article on http://arts.independent.co.uk/music/features/article69002.ece. Do you think it is an affectation or an insult? Is it significant that most of the examples given of pride in non-standard language use are male? You could use this research as the basis for a spoken presentation in your Unit 2 coursework.

- There are many websites dealing with Estuary English. Use a search engine to find one that gives a full description and/or audio clips. There is a useful summary of Estuary English in an academic paper on www.universalteacher.org.uk/lang/joanna-ryfa-estuary.pdf. List other examples of the way this accent varies from the standard. Try to use the phonetic alphabet (IPA).

Take it further

Read a critical account of the existence of Estuary English, for example on www.phon.ucl.ac.uk/home/estuary/. It includes the article that introduced the term for the first time: Rosewarne, D. 'Estuary English', *Times Educational Supplement*, 19 October 1984. What are the reasons for challenging its existence as a new accent?

What are the attitudes towards this variety of English? Attitudes to language use are strongly linked to attitudes towards the users. The high status of RP and the comparatively low status of Scouse (a Liverpool accent), for example, are less about the actual sounds than the stereotypes associated with the people who use each accent. An interesting aspect of changing attitudes is in the decreasing status of RP. In 1999, the Conservative MP Boris Johnson claimed he lost his job on television because his accent was too 'plummy'.

Estuary English is associated with contemporary media broadcasters such as Jonathan Ross and Paul Merton (yet I cannot think of an example of a female presenter!) so it accrues a certain prestige. When it is used by people living in regions outside the capital, perhaps it might suggest that they too are cosmopolitan and not tied down by any regional identity.

Language and occupation

Is language use related to a person's job? In some occupations, there is certainly subject-specific lexis. The legal and information technology worlds are obvious examples, but many occupations have a distinctive vocabulary. You should ask yourself whether the field of work influences language use at other levels, such as phonology and grammar. These days, jobs in customer service emphasise language use in their training. Employees in call centres are given manuals outlining the correct way to conduct interactions. Advice on selling techniques moves on to the level of discourse, with recommendations about the use of questions to retain the upper hand in a situation. Politicians are notorious for their habit of avoiding direct answers to questions.

You might also consider whether an individual's occupation influences their use of language in general. Does a lawyer talk like a lawyer, even at home?

For the dramatic monologue in Unit 2, you will need to capture the voice of a character and this may include features suggestive of a particular occupation. The following activity presents a parody of occupational language, rather than a real example of a teacher talking.

Activity 73

1   Read the extract from a Joyce Grenfell monologue. If possible, listen to a recording or try reading it aloud to experiment with phonological features, such as pitch and intonation.

2   What features of lexis, grammar or discourse create a recognisable stereotype of a nursery teacher?

Remember you gain credit for covering a range of levels. You could begin by analysing these features:

- terms of address: how, when and why does the teacher address other people?

- echo utterances: how often does her utterance echo the previous speaker and why?

- politeness: how often and for what function does she use 'please' and 'thank you'?

- use of pronouns: how does she use the first person plural 'we'?

- imperatives: how often does she use a plain order and how does she hint or suggest that the children do something?

- negatives: how does she 'soften' some negatives?

- lexis: is there any subject-specific (nursery/children) lexis and what semantic fields do you notice?

- positive connotations: how does the teacher put a 'positive spin' on the situation?

Children, we've had our run around the classroom, and now it's time to start our day's work. We're going to have a sing-song together, and Miss Boulting is going to play for us, so come and settle down over here, please.

Kenny, why haven't you taken your coat off? [5]

No, it isn't time to go home yet, Kenny! You've only just come.

You'd rather go home? Bad luck.

No you can't go, not quite yet.

Kenny, you've only been here for about ten minutes. [10] Come and sit on the floor next to Susan. You like Susan.

No, Susan, I don't think he wants to sit on your lap.

No, Susan, I don't think he wants to sit on your lap.

No, I thought he didn't.

Kenny! We don't want to see your tongue, thank you. [15]

No, not even a little bit of it. Put it back, please.

All of it.

And give your jacket to Caroline, I'm sure she'll hang it up for you.

Thank you, Caroline. [20]

Who is that whistling?

Sidney, you know we never whistle indoors. You can whistle in the garden, but we never whistle indoors.

Yes, I know you have just whistled indoors, but don't do it any more. [25]

And don't punch Jacqueline.

I'm sure she didn't say she liked you punching her, did you Jacqueline?

Well, I don't think it's a good idea, so we won't have any more punching. [30]

He is rather a disruptive element in our midst, Miss Boulting, but he does try to belong more than he used to, so we are encouraged, bless his heart.

You may have noticed the way she avoids direct imperatives, a feature that Lakoff suggests is common in women's, rather than men's language use. The next part, on language and power, introduces the concept of a 'mitigated' imperative and shows how its use may be affected by more than the gender of the speaker.

Language and power

Studies into language and power investigate ways that language use can establish a higher status or greater control for the speaker/writer as opposed to the listeners/readers. The use of baffling terminology is one strategy a person can take – attempting to 'blind with science'.

Activity 74

Read the extract from Ian Brady's letter to *The Guardian* on page 48 again. Note that he never uses plain words such as 'kill' or 'murder'.

1   How many words and phrases are difficult to understand?

2   Why do you think he chooses this level of lexis?

Writing about language

When you notice the use of formal features such as technical jargon, passive voice and nominalisation, remember to consider the wider effects on meaning. On the topic of Brady's letter, for example:

The writer of the letter uses such complex lexis and noun phrases that it hard for any reader to understand what he is saying. Rather than showing his level of intelligence, it suggests that he needs to present himself as powerful and cannot, perhaps, acknowledge the blunt reality of what he is saying. He is using language as a mask and trying to manipulate his readers.

The part on pragmatics (page 84) will look at another possible effects of high register lexis – a display of insecurity or pretentiousness.

Apart from lexical choice, certain grammatical structures can be significant in analysis of language and power:

- passive voice: changing from an active structure
- nominalisation: forming a noun from the original verb
- intransitivity: using verbs that do not need a direct object.

It is interesting that the first two language features are also associated with formality and impersonal language.

You may often overlook nominalisation as it is a common feature of language use. It is helpful to try alternative ways of expressing a text to make its language choices clearer.

Activity 75

1   Rephrase this text in a more direct, active, personal style.

> The <u>observation</u> of the school's code of <u>conduct</u> is a <u>requirement</u> for all pupils. The <u>maintenance</u> of orderly <u>behaviour</u> and the <u>choice</u> of appropriate clothing is essential to the smooth <u>running</u> of the school day. It is our <u>hope</u> that the <u>achievement</u> of academic <u>success</u> will be of <u>benefit</u> to all members of the school community. Any <u>departure</u> from our standards will result in <u>exclusion</u>.

2   What are the different effects of the original and the rewritten version?

3   Now try these exercises to practise your grammatical knowledge.

a   The underlined words are examples of nominalisation. Can you supply the original verb for each?

b   Some of these verbs (the transitive verbs, which take a direct object) can be either active or passive. Give an example to show the contrast, for example:

Take it further

Read *New Labour, New Language*, Fairclough (Routledge, 2000), pages 25–28. What does he suggest about the different roles of nouns and verbs?

Forms of words	Terminology
Observation	Noun
You must observe the rules.	Active voice ('rules' is the direct object)
The rules must be observed.	Passive voice

4 Read these two comments on the text above. Both interpretations of the effect are well argued. Which one do you find more convincing?

Comment A

> The writer uses nominalisation (requirement, exclusion) to create a formal tone for the text. This is because of its context: it is an official notice from the school authorities addressed to pupils and parents. It has a serious function to inform people of the rules and to warn about the penalties. The formal tone is also created by the absence of personal pronouns. The only one used is 'our hope', which creates a sense of a shared community.

Comment B

> The choice of nominalisation (observation, behaviour) rather than verbs keeps the people and actions in the background. The verbs would be more direct and specific: 'you must observe' or 'all pupils should behave'. This creates a distant tone, which may carry more authority. I think it allows the writer to be vague about some details, for example the threat of exclusion. Rephrased as an active verb, the writer would have to say more exactly who, when, where and why this will happen. The active structure sounds more threatening: 'If you don't wear uniform, we will exclude you (transitive verb with direct object) from school for a week.'

Some language and gender studies took a sideways step into questions about power and powerlessness. As with the concept of gender, power is not an absolute, unchanging aspect. The powerful status of a judge in a courtroom, displayed by language use as well as robe or wig, changes in a different situation. That same 'powerful' language use becomes less effective on the football terraces, for example.

You should also be aware of language change – or rather, changing social attitudes. If it was ever the case that the most effective way of displaying authority was to give commands, interrupt and insist on holding the floor, there are certainly more subtle ways of taking control of an interaction. There is interesting research into the language of the classroom, for example, which shows that teachers prefer to use indirect ways of giving instructions. You saw a parody of this style in the Joyce Grenfell monologue on page 81. The term '**mitigated imperative**' refers to this concept in forms such as:

> I wonder if you'd all mind stopping what you're doing and listening.
> There doesn't seem to be a lot of work going on here.
> Can we have a bit of quiet?
> I'd like everyone to listen now.

See page 85 for Speech Act Theory and implied meanings.

See page 85 for Speech Act Theory and implied meanings.

Key term

mitigated imperative

Independent research

- Read Michael Rosen's article on the 'Power of the Passive' in *emagazine*, issue 15, February 2002. What does he say about the implied meanings in the use of the passive voice in a newspaper article?

- Make a note of all the different forms used to give instructions or commands in the classroom over one lesson or a week. Can you group them according to the form – interrogative, declarative, imperative, negative, modal auxiliary verb? Is there any link with contextual factors – the speaker's age or gender; the relationship with the audience; the function or topic of the lesson, and so on?

What you have learned

✓ There is a great variety of language use across the regions of the English-speaking world. There is a distinction between these terms: accent, pronunciation, dialect, lexis and grammar.

✓ Attitudes towards regional varieties of English are not so much judgements of the sounds, but of the people who speak like this.

✓ There are gradual changes in the way that people speak. This is connected to changes in society: there is much more contact between previously isolated groups of people (with improved transport and communications) and, possibly, more democratic attitudes.

✓ Some features of grammar are significant for analysis of language and power:
  - nominalisation versus verb
  - passive versus active voice
  - transitive versus intransitive verb
  - imperative versus mitigated imperative.

Take it further

Read *New Labour, New Language*, Fairclough (Routledge, 2000), pages 95–118. He compares the less overtly 'powerful' style of Tony Blair with that of Margaret Thatcher. Is the same true for influential politicians of the current time?

4 Pragmatics

Pragmatics focuses on not so much what the *sentence* means as what the *speaker* means.

In everyday language, a 'pragmatic' approach means a 'practical' approach. There is something of this meaning in its use as a linguistic term. Pragmatics signalled a shift in interest from rather abstract matters of grammar and structure to an emphasis on meaning and the full context of language use. In many ways, pragmatics is a philosophical approach to language, asking questions about how people communicate meanings through their language use. Many interesting theories originate from philosophers, as well as anthropologists (studying human behaviour) and sociologists. Sociolinguistics is now a recognised branch of language study; it includes gender studies and regional variation, as the social context is so important in these areas.

Pragmatics is not one of the 'key constituents' of language, as meanings cannot be pinned down to any one level (phonology, graphology, morphology, lexis, grammar, discourse). This quick definition captures a fundamental contrast between the study of language form and the study of meanings in use.

You will also find less technical jargon associated with pragmatics and very few fixed, right/wrong answers. Many students find pragmatics a fascinating part of their language studies – tricky to pin down, but with great potential for exploring meanings.

Before you look at some academic theories, consider how much everyday awareness there is of the way meanings are implied in language use. Phrases such as 'name-dropping' or 'buttering someone up' refer to the difference between the outward form of the language and the underlying meanings. Think about the signals that tell you that a person is not telling the truth. The entertainer Derren Brown suggests these clues in *Tricks of the Mind*;

> probably long-winded when lying … tend to be rather superficial in his descriptions of significant events. Embellishments are suddenly skipped over, and details ignored … If you ask a liar to expand upon his story, the chances are that you'll get a repeat of what you've just heard, rather than an offering of more details.
>
> 5 … whereas in normal conversation we refer to ourselves a lot. Look out for less use of 'I', 'my', 'me' and so on, as well as an increase in references to what 'everyone' or 'no one' does or thinks, what 'always' happens, and so on, which generalise away from his own particular involvement in the story and place a distance between him and the lie.

The term 'mentionitis' is used by the main character in *Bridget Jones' Diary* by Helen Fielding, referring to the way a person keeps dropping a particular name into the conversation. According to her, this implies a positive interest in that person, even if the comments are negative.

Activity 76

Think about comments such as: 'What did you mean when you said that?'

1   Collect examples of language use that conveys underlying meanings.

2   Compare your examples with other people's in the group.

3   What other informal terms do you use, apart from the examples given above?

Writing about language

When you analyse texts, it is difficult to include the actual word 'pragmatics' in a sentence. The examiner will understand that you are discussing this area, as soon as you write: 'this implies' or 'she suggests'. You could begin a paragraph with an introductory comment, such as 'Looking at this from a pragmatic point of view …'

Some key theories

There are a number of pragmatic theories and terms often mentioned in A Level textbooks. It is better to understand two or three key theories than to learn a simple summary of many. You will then be able to apply a pragmatic approach effectively in the exam. As many of the theories are philosophical, you need time for thinking about and exploring the concepts.

Speech Act Theory

The philosophers Austin and Searle proposed their Speech Act Theory in a series of lectures in the 1970s. The key concepts have been outlined and discussed in many textbooks since. The important point that they made was that the outward, grammatical form of language does not necessarily correspond to its function. They used three pairs of terms to make this distinction:

- form versus function
- sentence versus utterance
- sense versus force.

They gave the example of declarative sentence structures and pointed out that most language use is in the form of declaratives, yet people are not using language mainly to make statements or provide information. For example, comments about the weather in some social groups serve as an introductory social pleasantry (phatic function):

> It looks a bit like rain today.

Similarly, what looks like an interrogative on the surface can function in other ways:

> What time do you call this?

The interactive function of language to create and maintain social relationships is particularly important in spoken language. The conventions for managing this will differ from one culture to another, which can be the cause of misunderstandings. The degree to which people can express themselves directly is one example. The British are notorious for indirectness – wrapping up a plain request in a lot of extra words.

Activity 77

1 How many different forms (sentences) can you use to ask someone to:

  a lend you money   c hurry up

  b go out with you   d stop talking?

2 Rank the sentences for degrees of directness and indirectness.

3 How does each link to aspects of the situation (context)?

For example:

'Lend us a tenner.' (Direct, between two close friends)

'I really want to go, but I haven't got any money.' (Indirect hint, child to parent)

'Any chance of borrowing £10?' (More direct repetition to parent)

Activity 78

Read this short extract from a conversation. The three women are drinking tea during a meeting in a hotel lobby.

Shirley:	Do you want a biscuit?
Alison:	Yes please.
Charlotte:	No thanks.
Shirley:	(to Alison) Charlotte's getting married next month.

1 What do you need to know in order to understand what Shirley means by her last comment? She is not changing the subject by mentioning marriage in a conversation about biscuits.

2 In what social contexts, might the connection (between marriage and biscuits) be missed?

Austin and Searle also introduced these three terms for analysing the ways meanings can be implied in particular situations:

- presupposition: what is already known or assumed
- inference: what the listener/reader understands or guesses
- **implicature**: what the speaker/writer was implying or suggesting.

Key term

implicature

politeness

face

positive face

negative face

positive politeness

negative politeness

Politeness theories

Many pragmatic theories are grouped under the heading of '**politeness**', but they are not concerned with manners and etiquette, in the sense of recommending the 'proper' way to behave. Pragmatics explores the ways that language users negotiate a web of human needs, such as:

- presenting a persona
- trying to be accepted/liked
- being polite/friendly to others
- managing to get what we want.

The social anthropologists Brown and Levinson have developed the concept of face (originally proposed by the sociologist Erving Goffman). **Face** refers to our public self-image. There are two aspects to this concept:

- **positive face** refers to our need to be liked and accepted
- **negative face** refers to our right not to be imposed on.

Thus politeness involves the speakers showing an awareness of others' face needs. Paradoxically, this view of politeness suggests that individuals use it to achieve their own needs. Brown and Levinson suggest that speakers use **positive politeness** strategies, such as shared dialect, informal lexis, informal grammar and more direct requests, with friends to emphasise solidarity.

Negative politeness strategies, such as more formal lexis and grammar, and indirect requests, on the other hand, emphasise respect when there is a social distance between speakers.

As with Goffman's concept of 'footing' (see page 29), the rapport between people can shift in subtle ways over the course of an interaction.

Activity 79

1   Outline a situation where the face needs of the participants shift from positive to negative, or vice versa. For example, in a teacher–student interaction, the rapport could be very friendly and relaxed, until the student breaks some rule and the teacher needs to become an authority figure.

2   In groups, two people role-play the interaction, while the others observe the language use.

Writing about language

- Remember that the term 'negative politeness' does not mean a lack of politeness, but a more formal, distant rapport

- In Section B of the exam, you have to focus on the 'presentation of self'. You might think of this as the way the speaker/ writer constructs a persona through their language use. The exam question asks you to refer to relevant research and theories. The skill lies in being able to select concepts that will be useful in your analysis..

Cooperative maxims

Perhaps the most well-known pragmatic theories are those of the philosopher Grice. He proposed Cooperative Principles of Conversation with four maxims. Grice uses the terms 'flout' and 'violate' to refer to occasions when a speaker does not adhere to the ideal cooperative principles, either accidentally or deliberately. He suggests that this *manner* of speaking conveys meanings as much as the actual *content*. It is helpful to think of each maxim in terms of a question.

- **Quantity** – If someone says rather more/less than we would expect, what do we infer?
- **Quality** – If someone says something factually untrue, what did they mean to convey?
- **Manner** – If someone communicates in an obscure manner, what do we infer?
- **Relation** – If someone changes the subject, what do we infer?

The answer to all these questions will depend on the specific context – who is speaking, to whom, about what and why. For example, a person who says very little may be shy, deliberately awkward or even aggressive in intention.

The next activity develops your understanding of the underlying pragmatic principles of Grice's maxims.

Activity 80

1   Produce five more maxims for conversation. For example, if a person drops a lot of taboo words into their speech, there are various implied meanings. If they are with friends, it may be a sign of solidarity; if it is with strangers, it often communicates hostility. If this use of language is not a deliberate choice, but a habit, it suggests something about their social background.

2   Compare your maxims with another's.

Constructing a persona

Before you tackle the kinds of questions you will meet in the exam paper on pages 89–91, think about this fictional character. The BBC TV series *The Office* created a mock documentary about the manager of a small company in Slough. The character David Brent became famous for his excruciating mixture of insecurity and pomposity. You may be able to watch this scene on DVD.

Activity 81

1   Read the script of a scene from episode 1 below, where David Brent is talking to his receptionist, Dawn.

	BRENT:	Be gentle with me today Dawn.
	DAWN:	*(exasperated)* Yeah? Why's that?
	BRENT:	Oh God. Had a skinful last night. I was out with Finchy.
		(to camera crew) Chris Finch.
		(to Dawn) Had us on a pub crawl. 'El vino did flow' …
5		*(Brent mimes drinking)*
	BRENT:	I was bl … blattered … bl … bladdered … blotto'd … Oh, don't ever come out with me and Finchy.
	DAWN:	No, I won't.
	BRENT:	There's guys my age, and they look fifty … How old do you think I look?
10	DAWN:	Thirty –
	BRENT:	*(interrupting)* Thirty – yeah … About that. Oh, but I will have to slow down. Drinking a bit too much …
		(Brent pats his belly.)
	BRENT:	… If every single night of the week is too much.
15	DAWN:	*(joking)* … And every lunchtime.
		(Beat. Brent turns, suddenly a vicious look in his eyes.)
	BRENT:	How many have I had this week?
	DAWN:	What?
	BRENT:	How many pints have I had this week? If you're counting …
20	DAWN:	I'm not counting.
	BRENT:	Aren't you? Hmm, you seem to know a lot about my drinking. Does it offend you, eh? You know, getting a little bit … a little bit personal. Imagine if I started doing that with you. I could look at you and come out with something really witty and biting like 'You're a bit …'
		(He can't think of anything.)
25	BRENT:	… but I don't. Because I'm a professional and professionalism is … and that is what I want, okay? That's all. That's a shame.
		(He strides off, leaving Dawn speechless.)

2 Work in groups to apply different approaches to this text. First note your impressions of the persona of David Brent. Which of the variables below are significant? Which are less significant?

> gender   age   region   occupation   power

3 Now use one of the concepts below to comment on the way Brent presents himself.

> positive vs negative face   footing
> cooperative principles (quantity/quality/manner/relation)

Does Brent change his persona over the interaction? Where does the change happen?

4 Identify some language features (lexis, grammar or discourse) that convey the different ways he presents himself.

5 Finally, compare the analysis of each group. Did some pragmatic concepts prove to be more or less revealing?

What you have learned

✓ Pragmatics is the study of language in use.

✓ You cannot say what an isolated sentence means. The meaning also depends on the context.

✓ Pragmatic theories help to explain the ways meanings are implied.

✓ Key theories and concepts include:

- Speech Act Theory: makes a distinction between form and function and uses the terms: presupposition, inference, implicature
- Politeness theories use the terms: indirectness, face (positive versus negative), politeness strategies (positive versus negative),
- Cooperative maxims use the terms: quantity, quality, manner, relation.

5 Tackling Section B of the exam

The exam for Unit 1 lasts 2 hours 15 minutes. It has two sections, each worth 50 marks. Section B of the exam gives you two longer texts. These are taken from the two modes not tested in Section A (spoken, written or electronic) so that you have a chance to analyse examples from all three different modes of language use in the exam.

The question will ask you to analyse and compare the ways that the speakers/writers present themselves. It will also ask you to refer to relevant research and theories.

You should leave about 1 hour to answer this question. It is worth a total of 50 marks (50 per cent of the marks for Unit 1).

Assessment objectives

25 of the 50 marks available in Section B of the exam are awarded for AO3: Analyse and evaluate the influence of contextual factors on the production and reception of spoken and written language, showing knowledge of the key constituents of language.

The other half of the marks are divided between AO1 (10 marks) and AO2 (15 marks):

AO1: Select and apply a range of linguistic methods to communicate relevant knowledge using appropriate terminology and coherent, accurate written expression.

AO2: Demonstrate critical understanding of a range of concepts and issues related to the construction and analysis of meanings in spoken and written language, using knowledge of linguistic approaches.

A suggested approach

1   Read and annotate the texts, spending 10–20 minutes:

- make brief notes on the context of each: mode, field, function, tenor
- write a summary of the persona created: age, gender, region, occupation, power
- highlight significant features of language: including grammar and discourse
- choose two or three significant theories: gender, power, pragmatics.

2   Write up your response, spending about 20 minutes on each text:

- begin by explaining and comparing the context of each
- when you analyse the presentation of self in each text, remember to:
  - support each claim with evidence from the text (going beyond graphology and lexis)
  - add some reference to theories or research
  - make clear points of comparison.

Read this example of a Section B exam paper. Use it as a mock exam either in timed conditions in class or completed in your own time.

Notation	Meaning
(.) or (3)	brief pauses or a pause for a number of seconds
/	overlapping speech
…	unfinished utterance or interruption
SOME	capital letters indicate particular stress and volume

SECTION B: PRESENTING SELF

Compare the ways the writer of Text A and the two speakers in Text B present themselves. In your response, you should refer to features of language and context. Make reference to relevant research and theories about language use.

Text A is a blog (web log) taken from the Languagelegend website. The writer is a teacher of A level English Language.

Thursday 19 January 2006

E-Julie has left the building.

So, this post is going to be a bit different to the rest, cos in this one you get to watch live as E-Julie disappears into the far horizon.

5 Is that the sound of screeching brakes of shock and horror?! Well ...

The Language Legend started out as an experiment with a particular AS English Language class, to find out whether making material available in an online format would encourage wider reading and a more independent engagement with the subject. It kinda worked pretty well, so through an email discussion forum for
10 teachers of this course, other students/teachers were invited to check it out. As time went by, all kinds of bloggers joined in the fun, and additional ideas about interactivity and the creation of online communities were explored.

It's been a cool project, and this weekend E-Julie's alter-ego is presenting the research findings, involving this and another blog project, at the annual conference
15 of the National Association of Teachers of English. If E-Julie's far less brash, confident, articulate alter-ego doesn't first pass out on the floor in a pathetic display of hyperventilating nervousness, she will be exploring why the Language Legend has to die.

One of the problems with an educational blog is that for it to become widely used,
20 it needs to speak with some kind of knowledge and authority on the subject, but in so doing it becomes less the kind of mutable, interactive space for the creation of shared and contested knowledge that grassroots blogs are, and more the kind of fixed world of teacher-centred incontestable knowledge that is at the hollow heart of much educational practice. In a bizarre twist, E-Julie has ended up recreating the
25 world she sought to help her students tunnel out of.

So, while her serious and reclusive alter-ego continues to go to work everyday at the chalkface of education, E-Julie is taking a well-earned fictional Gap Year. No doubt she'll be back – she has that prodigal daughter kind of attitude – and who knows what adventures she will have in educational cyberspace in the future. But
30 in the meantime, E-Julie has left the building.

Text B: transcript of a recording made by two friends one evening

Ali: erm if there's a mirror near by or a mirror in my field of vision I will <u>always</u> look in it I'll try and stop looking/ at my reflection /

Perry: / can I just say every time you talk the red light flashes

Ali: oooh that's 'cos I'm special

5 Perry: look

Ali: I like it

Ali: um yeah every time a mirror's around I stare in it and people often catch me doing this they think I'm really vain and narcissistic probably 'cos I am

Perry: but do ye you know when you're walking down the street and like ...

10	Ali:	and you see the shiny window like on / Waitrose
	Perry:	/ Waitrose (both laugh) yeah Waitrose
	Perry:	I I can't I can't / walk past it
	Ali:	/ you've got to not look in it but then if I don't (.) if I walk past it and don't look in it I feel like I'm being really strange when I walk past it I feel like I'm ignoring it
15		
	Ali:	<u>everyone</u> looks in it everyone looks in it
	Perry:	everyone looks in it yeah totally
	Ali:	me and Cat used to have a thing we said '<u>don't look</u> in it' because that always makes you look bad looking in the mirror and and your reflection was always a little bit like unnffhh
20		
	Perry:	sometimes like if I'm in a you know sometimes if you're in in a bit of a daydream and you're walking along the road and you walk past it and sometimes I find myself stopping and (2) (both laugh)
	Perry:	re-arranging myself
25	Ali:	packing your bits away (4) (both laugh)
	Perry:	no me badly packed kebab (4) (both laugh)
	Perry:	stop it this is serious shit man (1) anyway no sometimes I find myself just looking and just going hhmm why did I wear this ensemble (laughs)
	Ali:	hhmm for what purpose does this serve
30	Perry:	Ali I think sometimes you actually <u>forget</u> to look in the mirror (speaks directly into microphone) Ali Ali came to work and she was wearing denim hotpant shorts /with knee-high black fishnet stockings /
	Ali:	/ a skirt a skirt /
	Perry:	and football boots / excuse me sorry with the studs with the studs and what happened to your mirror that day
35		
	Ali:	um
	Perry:	huh
	Ali:	um (dramatic whisper) I only dress for myself what crap is that (.) you know what I mean people go 'oh I don't care what other people think of me' like that 'oh really'
40		
	Perry:	d'you know what
	Ali:	what
	Perry:	I I I I really care what other people think I look like and you don't care what other people think you look like do you (2) I I can tell this by the way your feet are black (both laugh)
45		
	Perry:	so um yeah sometimes I feel that Ali does forget to look in the mirror but I think that she does all the time because um
	Ali:	because you catch me
	Perry:	er yeah I always catch you
50	Perry:	as you say you dress for yourself you don't dress for anyone else whereas I dress to please (.) mainly men occasionally some girls
	Ali:	yeah that old thing do you dress for me or do you dress for other women (sound effect: myes meh meh meh)
	Perry:	we're coming away from the whole mirror ensemble can you just go and get um um an icecream and I'll turn it off.
55		

Unit 2

Exploring the Writing Process

For Unit 2 of Edexcel AS English Language you will hand in a folder containing two pieces of your own writing – one for a reading audience and one for a listening audience. Both pieces of writing are to be accompanied by commentaries.

What you will do in the course

In your coursework folder

- One piece of writing from Task 1: 1000–1500 words (30 marks)
- One piece of writing from Task 2: 500–1000 words (30 marks)
- Commentary on Task 1, maximum of 500 words (10 marks)
- Commentary on Task 2, maximum 500 words (10 marks)
- Any materials referred to in the commentaries, such as style models, drafts, recordings, transcripts, multi-media aids, bibliography.

The coursework gives you:

- time to prepare your writing for assessment
- some freedom of choice
- tasks that are both challenging and realistic
- experience of working to a 'brief' with specific task requirements and deadlines.

Over the course you will develop your writing skills within a set variety of genres, purposes and audiences, producing a journalism interview or a narrative for a reading audience and a dramatic monologue or a spoken presentation for a listening audience.

In preparation for each task, you will:

- study the techniques of the genre in a range of style models
- research your own topic, purpose and audience
- prepare, record and transcribe speakers for Task 1
- use multi-media aids for Task 2
- produce early drafts
- give and respond to constructive criticism.

For your coursework assessment, you will:

- choose one piece of writing from Task 1 and one from Task 2
- edit style in response to audience feedback and/or constructive criticism
- proofread for accuracy
- check and add word counts
- write a commentary on your process of writing for each task.

What the moderators are looking for

Your coursework folder will be assessed first by your teachers. The marks and folders will be sent to Edexcel for moderation.

Moderators use three Assessment objectives (AOs) to mark your coursework.

Assessment objective		What this means in practice
AO1	Select and apply a range of linguistic methods to communicate relevant knowledge using appropriate terminology and coherent, accurate written expression.	You should use: • clear expression with accurate spelling and punctuation (in the texts) • precise terminology to explain process of writing (in the commentaries).
AO2	Demonstrate critical understanding of a range of concepts and issues related to the construction and analysis of meanings in spoken and written language, using knowledge of linguistic approaches.	You should understand: • differences between spoken and written language • ways choice of style can alter meanings • some theories about language use.
AO4	Demonstrate expertise and creativity in the use of English in a range of different contexts, informed by linguistic study.	You should show: • ability to write for two different genres and audiences • original crafting of language to achieve purposes • understanding of style and techniques used.

Task 1 Writing for a reading audience

Task 1 gives you two choices: a journalism interview or a narrative. In both tasks you need to produce a piece of writing that will be effective for people reading it in a book, newspaper or magazine. Both tasks require you to transform spoken language into written form, so you will be able to put some of the concepts and theories from Unit 1 into practice. You will also develop some practical skills: interviewing someone, recording and transcribing spoken language.

You will need to read examples of journalism interviews and narratives to study the techniques used. You have a free choice of subject, but it must be based on a real person in both cases. You can also choose your audience and purpose for each task.

In your commentary, you will explain the process of writing.

What you will learn

Journalism interview

• interviewing techniques
• five different forms of representing speech in writing
• degrees of bias in a journalist's presentation of a person.

Narrative

• differences in structure of oral versus written narratives
• ways of shaping chronology and perspective of narratives
• use of dialogue, description and narration.

Task 2 Writing for a listening audience

How this book will help you

In this book, Unit 2 is divided into four main sections, dealing with each task in turn. Each section is free standing: you can begin with the task of your choice or even work on two tasks in parallel. You may be studying for the Unit 1 exam at the same time as preparing your coursework folder. There are links to the concepts, terms and theories needed for text analysis and you will use some of these in your commentaries.

Each section takes you through the process of writing in clear stages. It begins with researching style models and analysing key techniques, before moving on to the early stages of planning and drafting the text. The later steps develop the skills of constructive criticism and redrafting. There are suggestions for your commentary throughout each section, ending with a summary of advice for writing up your final version.

Task 2 gives you two choices: a dramatic monologue or a spoken presentation. In both tasks you need to produce a piece of writing that will be effective for a group of people listening to it in a school, college or local venue. Both tasks require you to produce a written script that will be read or performed aloud. You can include visual or electronic aids, so you will be able to put into practice some of the ideas about multi-modal texts from Unit 1 (pages 20–21). You should test your script on an audience and it might be useful for your redrafting to listen to a recording.

In order to study the techniques, you will need to listen to and read examples of dramatic monologues and spoken presentations. You have a free choice of character for the dramatic monologue and you can select your audience and purpose. The spoken presentation must be on a topic studied for AS English Language.

In your commentary, you will explain the process of writing.

What you will learn

Dramatic monologue

- ways of creating character through idiolect
- dramatic techniques, eg subtext, plot development
- performance aspects, eg voice, pitch, tone.

Spoken presentation

- organisation and structure of effective presentations
- variety of ways of presenting information
- development of appropriate rapport with audience.

How you will be assessed

A maximum of 60 marks are awarded for the two tasks you choose to submit in the coursework folder. A few marks are given for the accuracy of your writing, but AO4 is the most important – your 'expertise and creativity' in different types of writing. You will show this in your use of the techniques of the particular genre and in the way you craft your style for your chosen audience and purpose. You gain some marks for your understanding of language use, so it is important to read plenty of examples and study some theories.

A maximum of 20 marks are given for the two commentaries. For this part of the coursework you need to be able to stand back from your own writing and explain how you produced the texts. It is a more theoretical task, where you gain marks for using precise terminology and showing your awareness of concepts and theories; these must be relevant to your writing, of course.

How to succeed in English Language Unit 2

- 'Learn to read as a writer; to write as a reader.'
- Be businesslike – writing is a craft and needs plenty of practice.
- Be curious – read or listen to as much as possible in your chosen genre.
- Get started – expect your first draft to need more work.
- Look for constructive advice – professional writers, fellow students and your teachers can all offer guidance.
- Dare to be creative – experiment with fresh techniques.
- Have pride in your finished product – make sure all the fine details are polished.

A Writing for a reading audience: journalism interview

In this section you will learn how to show your skills in writing something that audiences will read. You have to submit either a journalism interview or a piece of narrative writing (see pages 112–127). In each case you will experiment with different style models before writing up a final version. You will also show your knowledge of the key concepts in English language by writing a commentary explaining what choices you have made.

1 Introduction

This section gives you a chance to produce an authentic piece of writing – the sort of thing professional writers are asked to do. You will not be doing a classroom exercise, where you try to imitate a style model from journalism by writing up a pretend interview with a famous person. As with all real writing assignments, there is a lot of preparatory work before presenting your final version. This means that you can develop various language skills as well as writing. Many of these will be valuable in the world outside the A level classroom, not just in your coursework folder.

Glossy magazines rely on their readers' obsession with celebrity to 'sell' their interviews; it hardly matters who conducts the interview or writes it up. The reverse is true for your interview task. It hardly matters who you choose to interview, as long as you know how to ask revealing questions and write it up in an effective way.

This section treats writing as a craft, with practical skills to be learned as you progress through the stages of an apprenticeship. You may not have any plans to work in journalism, but you may still be asked to conduct or write up interviews. Even if you never write an interview, this task will give you insights into the ways that journalists manipulate their readers.

On the following pages, you begin by exploring the genre, reviewing style models and analysing the different ways in which they represent a live interview in writing. Then you address the practical considerations of taping an interview and writing it up in different versions. Finally, you look more closely at your commentary. This section gives you examples and activities for these stages:

- research style models
- analyse ways of representing speech
- select a person to interview and plan your questions
- conduct and record an interview
- transcribe sections word for word
- submit a final written version of the interview (here you need to shape the words to present the interviewee in a particular way)
- add a written commentary on your writing purpose (here you must specify the type of publication, your purpose and target audience, and connect this to your style).

The written interview should be in the range of 1000–1500 words. Your commentary should be no more than 500 words long.

> **Writing your commentary**
>
> Make sure you keep notes on the key concepts in a log or journal as you work towards the final draft of your interview. In your commentary, you will explain what you learned during the process, as well as the techniques you actually used in your writing. The 'Writing your commentary' boxes will remind you about this at important stages.

Assessment objectives

Your interview write-up is assessed through AO1 (5 marks), AO2 (5 marks) and AO4 (20 marks). Your commentary is assessed through AO1 (5 marks) and AO2 (5 marks).

AO1 and AO2 marks are awarded for your understanding of the key concepts of the English language and for your ability to show this knowledge by writing clearly about them in your commentary.

AO4 marks are awarded for writing interesting and effective journalism, informed by the key concepts you have learned.

2 Exploring the genre

Activity 1

Journalism interviews are written and presented in lots of different ways. Read these short extracts from three interviews and answer the questions below each one.

Extract A The famous musician Van Morrison is interviewed by Barry McIlheney in *Word Magazine*, August 2007

The new album (…) is a mix of solo stuff and collaborations (…). How did you go about making the selection?

5 It's just a cross-section of stuff from the last decade or so. I wanted to get a mixture of guests and material that people could connect with as well as the more esoteric stuff. That's it really. There's no set formula, it's just what we ended up with.

The first track on the album is with Tom Jones. Do you and he go back a long way?

I first met Tom Jones in '64 or '65, then a while back I did a duet with him…

---

1 What do you think is the purpose of this interview?

2 What is striking about the format – the way the interview is presented?

3 The interviewer begins by saying, 'What follows is the whole of that extraordinary conversation, almost unedited.' How has the importance of the interviewee influenced the format chosen?

4 The audience is people interested in music, probably aged between their 30s and 50s. Does the style of the interview suit its purpose and audience? Give your reasons.

Extract B Ian Soutar interviews a local performer in the *Sheffield Telegraph* Arts Section, 19 January 2007

Sticky, a monthly programme of five short plays presented informally in a bar, began in 2000 in Philadelphia's notorious Bar Noir before moving to New York … Now it is coming
5 to Trippet's Wine Bar in Sheffield.

'It's like a franchise,' says Kisa Charles, a stalwart of Sticky in the US before she relocated to Sheffield and decided to introduce us to this type of guerrilla theatre. …

Kisa says: 'Our goal is to bring theatre to an audience that might not normally go to the theatre …'

---

5 What do you think is the purpose of this interview?

6 Who would read this interview?

7 How are the interviewee's words presented?

8 Ian Soutar is 'invisible' in this interview, as his questions are not given. Why do you think he chose this method? How effective is it?

Extract C Interview with forensic linguist Malcolm Coulthard, written up by Alison Ross for *emagazine* (published three times a year for A level English students), 2004

So what exactly does a forensic linguist do? 'Well, it's the application of linguistics to criminal investigations. Much of my work is concerned with the authorship of documents such as letters and
5 witness statements.'

But does he really think that style of language is as individual as a fingerprint? Surely we are all able to take on different styles, to mimic and disguise our language? I was thinking of the case of internet chatrooms, where people can adopt a different identity, too often an older man trapping a gullible young teenager. 'Yes, of course, it depends which finger you use.' Ah, so we can be pinned down in any one of
10 our different persona! Coulthard believes that it is just a case of collecting enough language data. Indeed the American legal system wants forensic linguistics to become as reliable as DNA. And with resources of computers and vast databases, this day is approaching.

9 What do you think the purpose of this interview is?

10 Coulthard's words are sometimes presented as direct speech, but sometimes there is also a summary of what he said. Find one example of each. Why have both methods been used to present the interviewee's words?

11 The interviewer is more 'visible' in this example. How are the questions represented? The interviewer's thoughts and reactions are also given. Find two examples.

Independent research

- Read the full text of the interview with the forensic linguist in *emagazine*, February 2002. Professor Coulthard talks about his evidence leading to Derek Bentley's pardon, as well as the case of the Unabomber and many more.

- Collect examples of interview articles from at least five different publications. Make brief notes of the style of the interviews and say how you think factors such as audience and purpose influences the style and format chosen.

Activity 2

There are many different reasons why interviews are presented in a particular way. Some of these reasons (or influences) are given below. Discuss how each one may influence the style of an interview.

1 Purpose Is the purpose to inform, entertain, celebrate or attack? How may each of these different purposes impact on the style?

2 Writer If the writer is famous or ordinary, how may that affect the style?

3 Interviewee Is the interviewee famous, and in what field? How may that affect the style?

4 Audience Are the readers from a particular age or interest group? How may that affect the style?

5 Publication Certain publications have a 'house style' – a consistent approach of style or format that they apply across all articles or across articles in a particular series. Can you think of any examples?

Writing your commentary

In your commentary, you might refer to the style and structure of a style model that particularly influenced you. For example, of the style of an interview with Paul McCartney in *Word Magazine*, July 2007 you might say,

'Word Magazine' is aimed at people with an interest in music, books and film. The interview with Paul McCartney, July 2007 did not simply promote him and his latest project, but gave a critical view of him. The female interviewer seemed to present the slightly mocking attitude of a younger person. I would like to experiment with a critical viewpoint in one version of my interview.

See extract on page 101

Analysing ways of representing speech

When writers produce a written version of a spoken conversation, they can do it in various ways. These choices produce different effects for different purposes. Is the intention to inform the reader of what was said as clearly and fully as possible? Or does the writer want to influence the reader towards a particular view of the interviewee? The term '**authorial intervention**' refers to the degree to which the writer shapes the original spoken words.

Let's look first at the most neutral end of the scale, where there is virtually no authorial intervention – the writer simply records the words spoken. If you want the reader to see a **verbatim** account – every word spoken, in order – you would produce a transcript. This is done in official situations, such as court cases and government meetings, because the function is to provide accurate information, without any bias. Unlike transcripts for linguistic study, these records use conventional punctuation marks to show whether the speaker intended to make a statement, exclamation or ask a question.

Here is a fascinating example from the transcripts of the Salem witchcraft trials of 1692 (now available edited and with an introduction and index by Paul Boyer and Stephen Nissenbaum on many websites, eg http://etext.virginia.edu/salem/witchcraft/texts/transcripts.html)

Independent research

You can look up Hansard on the internet and in some broadsheet newspapers. For example, see www.parliament.uk/publications/hansard.com

Q: Abigail Williams! Does this woman hurt you?

A: Yes, Sir, often.

Q: Does she bring the book to you?

A: Yes.

5 Q: What would she have you do with it?

A: To write in it and I shall be well.

– Did not you, said Abigail, tell me, that your maid had written? (Procter) Dear Child, it is not so. There is another judgement, dear child.

Then Abigail and Ann had fits.

The purpose of legal transcripts like Hansard, the official reporting of the House of Commons, is unbiased information. Drama scripts represent speech in a similar form – the name of each speaker is followed by the words spoken – but the purpose is more complex.

Activity 3

Read the two newspaper accounts of interviews below and answer the questions that follow each one. The first article from the *News of the World* refers to a controversial episode of *Celebrity Big Brother* involving the Bollywood actress Shilpa Shetty and the reality TV personality Jade Goody.

Account A

At the height of the tension Shilpa told Cleo she thought you were racist. Was she the victim of racism and bullying?

She was a victim of bullying and racism, yes. I can understand why she would have said that.

Disgusted

5 **How do you justify the comments you made to Shilpa?**

I'm not going to justify my actions because they were wrong. I was shocked to see how I behaved. I was shocked and disgusted at myself.

I don't know why I said those things to her or why those words came into my head. I wasn't thinking in my head a nasty thought.

10 I'm not making excuses because I know that it's wrong. I now know that it's offensive.

Maybe I'm just really stupid and nasty at heart. But I really don't think I am.

1   Do you think this is a verbatim transcript of an interview with Jade?

2   What do you think the writer's purpose is?

3   How is the purpose achieved?

Account B: *The Guardian* Education Supplement, James Simpson, 19 June 2007

The government's communities secretary, Ruth Kelly, laid into translation services last week on the BBC's *Politics Show*. 'Having information translated,' she said, 'means people have no reason to learn English.' 'For example,' she said, 'it's quite possible for someone to come here from Pakistan ... and to find that materials are routinely translated into their mother tongue, and therefore not have the incentive to learn English.'

Kelly seems to be making two points: that translation services are pointless and redundant; and that migrants to the UK are not motivated to learn English because everything they need is translated for them. On the first point: given Kelly's concern with integration, surely there should be more, not less, translation of information for new arrivals? But the second point raises a far deeper issue.

A government minister is yet again commenting on people's lack of English and 'unwillingness' to learn. The connection between the availability of information on housing and health in people's first languages and their motivation to learn English is a very tenuous one. Where exactly is the evidence that people don't want to learn English because translation services exist? Has any migrant to the UK ever said that they are not motivated to learn English because someone has already translated everything they need into their own language? I'd guess not.

Independent research

The six categories of speech representation are suggested by the linguists, Leech and Short in *Exploring the Language of Poems, Plays and Prose* (Short, 1996) and *Style in Fiction* (Leech and Short, 1981). Read one of these accounts. List more examples of free indirect speech. What are the effects, according to Leech and Short?

4   How does the writer represent Ruth Kelly's words (underlined)?

5   What do you think the writer's purpose is?

6   How does he achieve his purpose? Does he use any 'loaded' connotations?

In the previous examples, you saw at least two different ways of representing a person's speech in writing. Perhaps you used the term 'direct speech' for the way Ruth Kelly's words were written down, but did not know how to describe the plain technique used in the *News of the World* article. The next few pages introduce and discuss the technical terms for the representation of speech in writing.

First, here is a brief summary of each way of representing speech, moving from the least to the greatest amount of authorial intervention (interpretation by the writer).

Why do you always do that?	'Why do you always do that?' she sighed.	She asked him why he repeatedly did that.	Why on earth did he always do that?	She queried his motives.	She glared at him across the room.
Free direct speech (FDS)	Direct speech (DS)	Indirect speech (IS)	Free indirect speech (FIS)	Narrative summary of speech act (NRSA)	Narrative report of action (NRA)

In the next few pages you will practise identifying these ways of representing speech and consider their different effects.

Free direct speech

The term '**free direct speech**' (FDS) is used when the text shows only the words of the speakers, without any comments from the author. Many interviews choose this plain technique, perhaps printing questions in a different font from the answers. It is common in celebrity interviews, for example, where the questions are light-hearted and the purpose is probably agreed as a publicity exercise.

This can be the least biased form of speech representation, but, as Janet Street-Porter comments in an interview in *Word Magazine*, June 2007: 'How you write the questions delivers the answers you want.'

Activity 4

Read the extract below from an interview in *The Guardian*, 28 June 2007.
Hannah Pool is interviewing Dita Von Teese, a burlesque performer.

> **What is the difference between burlesque and striptease?**
>
> I don't really like to say that burlesque and stripping are totally different. I know a lot of burlesque dancers like to make sure you know that they are not strippers, they are burlesque artists, but I don't really agree with that. I don't think the term 'stripper' is a bad word. Gypsy Rose Lee called herself a stripper, so if it was good enough for her it is good enough for me.
>
> **You have said you find it liberating. How?**
>
> I was a failed ballerina, so I found a way to satisfy my dreams and to be a performer. One of the great things about burlesque in the old days is that a lot of the major stars were like me – maybe they weren't Ginger Rogers, but they could dance and they wanted it really bad, so they found a way to adapt accordingly. The combination of my love of glamour, my love of dance, my love of theatre, my love of style and fashion – it all sort of came together.
>
> **Don't you wish you could do all those things without having to take your clothes off?**
>
> Not at all.
>
> **Don't you worry that while it might be liberating for you, there are lots of women who are not in nice clubs, who are not having a good time?**
>
> With every profession it is not always going to be great. You just can't generalise. You can't say all strippers are abused. I've worked in some of those crappy clubs. It hasn't always been champagne and flowers and rhinestones in my dressing room, and people giving me accolades. I've worked in biker bars in Wisconsin.

1 Do you think the questions deliver the answers Hannah Pool wants?

2 What are her purpose and attitudes?

Direct speech

The term '**direct speech**' (DS) refers to the most common way of representing spoken words in novels. The words spoken are enclosed by speech marks and are often introduced or followed by an 'inquit' (a reporting clause, such as 'she said') (see Unit 1, page 76). This example is from *The Guardian* report of an interview with Ruth Kelly.

> 'For example,' she said, 'it's quite possible for someone to come here from Pakistan ...'

If the writer uses only the name of the speaker and a plain, factual verb (said, asked, replied, stated, etc), this form can be as neutral as free direct speech. The Salem witchcraft trials (see page 98) for example, could be reported like this:

> The judge asked, 'Does she bring the book to you?'
> Abigail replied, 'Yes.'

However, there are many synonyms for the reporting verbs, each conveying different connotations (shades of meaning) (see Unit 1, page 45). The writer's choice of verb suggests a way of interpreting the speaker's words.

Activity 5

1   In pairs, discuss the interpretations suggested by each choice of inquit in the box below. Which ones are relatively neutral?

'He gave me his number,' she ...

gushed	mumbled	replied
sighed	screamed	choked
apologised	stated	admitted

2   List as many others as possible.

3   Now add adverbs to each verb to suggest a variety of different interpretations, for example:

'What on earth are you doing?' he asked defensively/anxiously.

4   Now add a phrase or clause, describing the speaker's tone of voice or body language, for example:

'I never touched your bag,' she said through gritted teeth/crossing her fingers.

You can see from these examples that the use of direct speech may not be a neutral representation of a person's words. As with free direct speech, the interviewer can still control the questions and the writer can choose what to include or leave out. In direct speech, there is the possibility of more authorial intervention, in the choice of inquit (the reporting verb and supporting adverbs). In addition, the dialogue is often part of a narrative account that includes description of the people and the scene. You should notice these details as they can influence the readers' interpretation of the words. For example:

She didn't look at him at all. Staring out of the window, she said very quietly, 'I never touched your bag.'

This last example includes narrative report of action (NRA) (underlined).

Activity 6

Read the two extracts from interviews below.

1   Note the choice of inquits – reporting verb, plus adverbs, adverbial phrases or clauses.

2   Does the writer add NRA or any other description?

3   What effect do these features have on the reader's interpretation of the words spoken?

Extract A Paul McCartney interview by Sylvia Patterson, *Word Magazine*, July 2007

5   'I wasn't expecting a woman,' announces a startled Paul McCartney as I'm ushered through the presidential double doors of a mahogany-plush suite in his central London office. I wasn't expecting a dad, as it happens, which McCartney most immediately resembles, in his crumpled brown chords and casual shirt in pastel blue-green check.

Extract B Jon Ronson, *The Guardian*, 21 October 2006; http://www.guardian.co.uk/weekend/story/0,,1925825,00.html

As Noel explains to me the ins and outs of cosmic ordering, I involuntarily look dubious. Immediately, Noel changes tack to insist he hasn't gone 'off with the fairies'.

'Yes, the word cosmos might sound off-putting,' he says, 'but you don't have to call it cosmos. Cosmos is just a word. You can call it anything you like. You can call it Argos, or MFI.'

You should explain in a short paragraph (about 100–150 words) the conventions of journalism interviews and the particular techniques that you plan to use in your article. What did you notice about the style and structure of written interviews you have read? Identify several different ways of representing speech in writing. Why do you think the writer chose these ways? Think about the purposes of the article and the target audience of the publication. Apart from a record of the words spoken, note any extra comments or descriptions of the person, scene, etc. What was the effect of these? Think about point of view and bias.

Indirect speech

Indirect speech (IS) is sometimes called **reported speech**. The writer transforms the actual words spoken to emphasise the point of view of the person addressed (rather than the speaker). For example, 'I was not here last week.' becomes 'She told me that she had not been there the previous week.'

You will see that this involves some grammatical changes to the original words spoken:

• the verb	'was'	becomes	'had been'	(from past to past perfect)
• the pronoun	'I'	becomes	'she'	(first to third person)
• the adverb	'here'	becomes	'there'	(changing point of view to addressee)
• time	'last week'	becomes	'the previous week'.	

This form is often used in witness statements, so it sounds fairly neutral and 'official', for example: 'She stated that she had not been there the preceding week.'

A similar form is **free indirect speech** (FIS). It is called 'free' because the writer takes more liberties with the phrasing of the original words. This can give a flavour of a colloquial speaking voice:

> I was not here last week. (original words)
> Of course she had never been there before at all. (FIS)

This is ambiguous – the reader cannot be sure what the speaker actually said, as opposed to the writer's comments on it:

> Oh, so she had never been there before at all. Right!

Activity 7

1 Read the underlined sections in the extract below and try to reconstruct the actual words spoken in the interview.

Lynn Barber interviews Graham Norton, *Observer*, 28 October 2001

That's the whole point of these made-for-television personalities – they are not putting on an act, they are wholly themselves. But Norton has an interesting theory about this – he thinks you diverge. He thinks when you start on television you are wholly yourself, but then, over the years, you – the real you – change and age, whereas the television you is fixed for ever. 'So, you start off being yourself and then that becomes the act. I mean I used to be more like I am on television, off it – I don't think now I'm quite as full-on as I am on television, am I? But it is me. I mean I don't have to 'find my character'. It's just that's how I am in front of an audience. And I suppose it is a kind of armour. But I don't feel like I'm pretending.'

But he can't always be this sunny, can he? Surely he sometimes gets grumpy? But no, apparently he doesn't. I went round to his production office in Covent Garden and asked some of his researchers, 'Quick, dish the dirt!' but, they all said he's just so nice. He never throws a wobbly: the worst that can happen is he'll go a bit quiet some days.

He had what he calls 'a psychotic episode' in his first year at Cork University, when he stayed in his room for weeks, weeping and catching flies, and then suddenly took off to San Francisco. It was his flight to freedom, his recognition that he was never going to make his future in Ireland (where homosexuality was still illegal). He'd grown up in Bandon, County Cork, population 5000, a good Protestant boy, popular at school. He always insists he had a happy childhood, but it can't have been that happy because he spent all his time watching television. And he remembers, at 11, being freaked out by Larry Grayson, 'because I knew on some level I was like him, but I didn't want to be like that'.

---

2 What do you think Lynn Barber's questions and Graham Norton's (or his team's) answers were? Write this in the form of free direct speech.

3 Compare your version with another person's. How similar are they?

Interpreting a situation

A **narrative report of a speech act** (NRSA) is rather like the choice of inquit for direct speech. The writer can suggest shades of meaning by describing the manner of a person's speech. Emphatic behaviour, such as pleading, denying, retorting, tends to have negative connotations: if you plead, you expect failure; if you deny or retort, people often assume your guilt.

The writer in this example describes the speech act with aggressive connotations.

> The government's communities secretary, Ruth Kelly, <u>laid into</u> translation services last week on the BBC's *Politics Show*.

The writer can also summarise a section of the conversation, giving a particular interpretation:

> He related the <u>whole sorry story</u> to us.

Narrative reports of action, as mentioned on Page 103, involve our assumptions about the meaning of human behaviour.

Independent research

Use a search engine to find the complete version of the interview below. How does Jon Ronson portray the contestants on *Deal or No Deal* – in a sympathetic or mocking light? Lynn Barber's interviews in *The Observer* newspaper are also online. Her portrait of Graham Norton was quite affectionate. Can you find an example where she does 'a hatchet job'?

Activity 8

1. What are the common assumptions about the meanings of the following behaviour?

   a He looked at his feet.

   b She licked her lips.

   c He raised his eyebrows.

   d She stared straight ahead.

2. Add two more examples of NRA and see how other people interpret them.

Activity 9

Read this extract from Jon Ronson's interview with Noel Edmonds about the Channel 4 TV show *Deal or No Deal*.

direct speech

indirect speech

free indirect speech

narrative report of speech act

narrative report of action

The next morning, everyone is exhausted. I visit Noel in his Winnebago. Inside, it is very luxurious, all cream leather seats. Les Dennis's far smaller and less deluxe Winnebago is parked next to it. Les Dennis is filming a Channel 5 game show called *Speculation* in another studio.

<u>'Les Dennis can have the big Winnebago when he gets the ratings we get,'</u> Noel says.

I glance stealthily around the Winnebago for little clues that might reveal dark secrets of Noel's personal life. Noel's love life has been of interest ever since he made it known earlier this year that he asked the cosmos to provide him with a woman.

<u>Noel believes that if you order wishes from the cosmos, the cosmos will oblige,</u> as long as you follow the correct ordering protocols: you must write down your wish on a piece of paper. You absolutely have to be positive. The cosmos will not accept negative wishes. You must keep your wish general. <u>The cosmos won't, for some reason, grant overspecific wishes.</u>

<u>As Noel explains to me the ins and outs of cosmic ordering,</u> I involuntarily look dubious. Immediately, Noel changes tack to insist he hasn't gone 'off with the fairies'.

'Yes, the word cosmos might sound off-putting,' he says, 'but you don't have to call it cosmos. Cosmos is just a word. You can call it anything you like. You can call it Argos, or MFI.'

It strikes me that Noel Edmonds is probably the only modern-day spiritual guru who would even consider Argos or MFI as alternative names for the cosmos. That's the odd thing about hanging around here – the mystical people are not at all new-agey. They are retired bank managers. They work in betting shops. They are Noel Edmonds. The last time I saw Noel was 10 years ago. <u>He barged past me</u> in some country house hotel, heading for his helicopter – the epitome of the no-nonsense Conservative businessman and celebrity, off to do some deal. He was nothing like the vulnerable, spiritual Noel sitting in front of me now. If anyone doubts the extent to which mysticism has permeated the hitherto secular corners of British society, they should spend a couple of days behind the scenes at *Deal Or No Deal*.

Jon Ronson, *The Guardian*, 21 October 2006

1. How would you rank the interview for neutrality–bias on a scale of 1 to 10?

2. Identify different forms of speech representation. (Some have been done as examples.)

3. You will notice that the writer often uses direct speech. Does this form provide a neutral account of the words spoken? How does Ronson convey his opinion of Noel Edmonds?

3 Conducting the interview

Key terms

closed question

open question

This part provides some guidance on who to choose as your interviewee and how to conduct and record the interview.

Choosing your interviewee

Most interviews you read will be with famous people. It is a mistake to think that the only way you can produce an interview of interest is to make one up. This happens surprisingly often in A level coursework – an interview with Eminem or Michael Jackson based entirely on imagination. Such texts should be more accurately entitled, 'What I think Eminem might have said, if I had asked him these questions – but I didn't'. At best, such writing has no audience beyond the student's teacher, because no one would be interested in reading it. At worst, it risks a charge of libel, as it attributes made-up words to a living person.

For this task, you could go along with Andy Warhol who said that, 'Everyone will be famous for five minutes'. A good investigative journalist believes that everyone has a story to tell. Lynn Barber said, 'The best interviews – like the best biographies – should sing the strangeness and variety of the human race' (*Independent on Sunday*, 1991).

First, think of all the people you already know: family members, friends, work or club colleagues, people at school or college, etc. Ask older friends and relatives for suggestions of 'a friend of a friend'. Is there someone who:

- is particularly successful in some field
- has a challenging job or hobby
- has had an unusual experience
- has overcome a problem
- has lived in an interesting place
- has been an influence on your life?

You might want to secure an interview with a local personality. For ideas, look in the local newspaper or listen to local radio programmes. Then you need to contact the person by letter, phone or email and give them a good, clear reason to give up an hour of their time. Your choice of interviewee might give you the chance to explore an area of English language, for example, a speech therapist, a translator, a bilingual speaker, etc.

Writing your commentary

In your final commentary, you will explain and evaluate your choice of interviewee and questions. For example: There were several reasons for the choice of a young American stand-up comedian. She would be naturally articulate and amusing and she could comment on the love-hate relationship that Britain and the USA seem to have.

Planning the questions

Good interviewers are skilful at asking the right questions to get their interviewee to relax and provide interesting, personal responses, rather than brief answers. So what makes a good question? To some extent, this depends on the person you are interviewing, the topic and the purpose, but there are some general principles.

Ask open, rather than closed, questions. A **closed question** requires a 'yes'/'no' answer, eg Did you feel disappointed when you got your results? A 'yes' answer leaves you with a lot of work to do! This could be transformed into an **open question**: How did you feel …? or phrased as: 'Tell me about the day you got your results.'

Although you should not take over the conversation (as some talk show hosts do), it should be an interaction, not like an interrogation. Try to respond to your interviewee's answers. Don't just plough straight on to the next question.

Before you start on the planned questions, allow time for both you and your interviewee to relax and forget about the presence of the recorder. But the most important principle is – never record secretly. Ask permission before you record and explain what you are going to do with the recording. Your interviewee may ask to see your transcript and/or your final written version.

An important practical point concerns your recording equipment. Voice recorders on mobile phones have the advantage of being portable, but the sound quality may not be good. Your school or college may be able to provide reliable recording facilities. A digital recorder is ideal, as you can upload audio files onto your computer and edit them.

Activity 10

1 Practise recording interviews with a friend or classmate, using some of the all-purpose prompts and questions below.

Choose two prompts from list A, plus two questions from the song titles in list B. Make up one or two questions of your own. Decide whether to give your interviewee the questions beforehand.

List A prompts (used in five-minute interviews in *The Independent* online)

- If I weren't talking to you right now, I'd be …
- A phrase I use far too often is …
- The most surprising thing that happened to me is …
- A common misperception of me is …
- I'm not a politician, but …
- I'm good at …
- I'm very bad at …
- The ideal night out is …
- In moments of weakness, I …

List B questions (from song titles)

- Are you happy now?(Michelle Branch)
- Can you keep a secret? (Utada Hikaru)
- Does your mother know? (ABBA)
- Isn't life strange? (The Moody Blues)
- What are you doing for the rest of your life? (Michel Legrand)
- What's the matter with kids today? (NOFX)
- Where do you go (when you need a hole to crawl in)? (The Strawbs)
- Where have all the good times gone? (The Kinks)
- Where's your head at? (Basement Jaxx)
- Who can you trust? (Joan Lett)
- Whose side are you on? (Matt Bianco)
- Why do fools fall in love? (Diana Ross, The Beach Boys)

2 After the interview, evaluate the success of the questions. If the interview was not successful, do you think it required more skill from you as an interviewer or from your interviewee?

3 Then swap roles, so that each person has a turn being the interviewer.

Choosing a subject for your interview

After this trial run, you need to find a person to interview and think of an interesting topic. Then you should plan a list of specific questions. Keep notes of all these decisions in your commentary log.

The example interview that follows is with Kisa Charles (see the *Sheffield Telegraph* article on page 96). She is a 32-year-old American who came to live in the UK (Sheffield) in 2006 with her English partner and their two young children. She works at any job she can find, but does stand-up comedy and drama in her spare time. The main topic of the interview is the US–British divide – her perceptions of England and the way that English people see her.

These are the planned questions, but the interviewer need not stick to them rigidly – it is better to respond to any interesting direction the interviewee takes.

1 As an American, what is your view of the UK?

2 Particularly yesterday's floods?

3 You visited Oxford briefly. Did that match your image of Britain?

4 What were your reasons for leaving your lifetime home?

5 Is Sheffield different from the 'typical' UK town, in your imagination?

6 What do you like about it?

7 Dislike?

8 What are the main differences from the USA? What do you miss?

9 Do you suffer from anti-American feelings?

10 How do you respond?

> ### Independent research
>
> - There are detailed instructions for digital recording posted by Julie Blake on www.educationforum.ipbhost.com.
> - Look at advice given on a range of websites, eg on www.themediainterview.com. What different types of questions could you use?

4 Writing up the interview

Once you have conducted and recorded your interview, you need to do some hard 'leg-work': listen to the whole interview, choose interesting responses and transcribe these sections. This will be a rough transcription, where you record the words spoken, but do not include non-fluency features (See Unit 1, pages 56–59 about pauses, repetitions, fillers), unless you think they are particularly significant. Here is a section of the interview with Kisa, for example.

Note: You can use any method you like to indicate the different speakers (bold, in this case) and omitted sections (by three dots (ellipses) and round brackets (parentheses) here). The repetition 'it's true it's true' is included, because it shows how emphatic she was.

Kisa Charles

Americans have a reputation for being friendly, while the British are seen [as] a bit cold.

it's true it's true it has more to do with a formality that sort of thing … tho' there are very friendly Americans … maybe I'm a bit jaded against Americans tho' there are … maybe a bit superficial they don't want to be the bad people in the neighbourhood

5 in England it may seem a bit colder, more formal and a bit more *'Hi yes how are you'*
(phone call interruption)
we were talking about British appear to be more stodgy and cold but I think their caring and sense of community is way deeper …

that's nice to think

10 … maybe it's because I'm here now I want that to be true

A transcript represents the spoken word in free direct speech and is the most neutral version. It does not involve any authorial intervention (apart from selection of material), so it does not display your writing skills. A transcript, therefore, is a working document for you to use, not a piece of writing for assessment.

Finding an angle

Part of the journalist's skill is to select interesting details and to find an 'angle' that will shape the whole article. You need to think about your chosen audience and purpose at this stage. Will it be aimed at young females, or fans of stand-up comedy? Will it give an amusing slant on Kisa's experiences, or present a more controversial argument?

Activity 11

Read through the sections of the transcript below.

1   Which parts do you think are most interesting?

2   What audience and purpose are you aiming for?

3   Compare your ideas with others in the group.

Why did you leave your lifetime home?
… Pennsylvania it's is too far away from the rest of the world … I was very unhappy – I'm not really a political activist – but I don't like the way that country's going and I think my children will be much more well-rounded, education, more art, more history, more … compassionate … I'm a complete huge

5 anglophile wouldn't even have met my partner if he wasn't English
Was that one of the things that attracted you to him?
Yes, specially considering who introduced us … they seemed hell bent on introducing me to him … I was very reluctant till they said 'He is English' and I thought I will meet him and see what happens and luckily it worked out

10 **What about Sheffield? Is it different from a typical UK town?**
I do remember when I first arrived – town or village? You guys have so many different terms for this … there are a lot of very rural areas around here even though it's very urban you wouldn't know it if you go outside the city
for the most part it fulfilled a lot of stereotypes …I love the little walks and ways and canals.

What do you like and dislike?

I dislike that everything closes really early ... I dislike that about this whole country even Sunday is part of the weekend you don't have a lot to do you don't have to work ... you can only do it between 11 and 3

I *do* like Sheffield a lot because it reminds me of home, Sheffield and Philly are very kind of ... sisters, comparable cities.

(I thought that)

community-driven, a lot of great artists, a lot of companies that care about the community ... multi-cultural ... poor and very rich ...

Philadelphia is a lot like that so I guess that's why I like it ...

that's where my daughter got her over-friendliness because we would walk ... walk down the street, say 'Hi' to everyone smile at everyone and she got into the habit of that I think that's important

Some people say Sheffield is the biggest village in England.

Yeah I have heard this especially lately with the floods

(I disagree with you about the closing hours ...)

What do you miss?

I miss Philly cheese steaks I really wish I could have a cheese steak ... you have baps and beef on a roll I honestly believe that English people don't know what good food tastes like ... for the most part I know you suffered two world wars ... I completely appreciate that eating potatoes for a long time ... blood and haggis

But to be fair a lot of places in Philadelphia go overboard ... we consume way too much. Mitch Hedberg, my favourite comedian he said he orders a sandwich he said it was 'a cow between two crackers'. The guy says 'Anything else?' he'll say 'Yeah, a loaf of bread and 12 other people.' They just pack it full of meat ... I don't mind the portion size

I was reading something in the paper today about anti-American feelings ... do you suffer from that at all?

I was convinced when I first moved here ... When I first came here I was unemployed for longer than I've ever been. I honestly believe they didn't want an American working for them and I don't blame them cos I am very anti-American myself ...

Some cab drivers warn me 'Watch out. People don't like Americans.' But no one has ever said that to my face. I do get a lot of 'I love the way you speak'... that's very nice but that's just superficial if you ask 'do you like America' ... still despise the country as a whole ... could be justified ... not most of the Americans fault it's the government and we can't control the government

I did get booed really badly at The Lescar ... when I said 'I'm an American' ...

But a lot of friendly people a lot of nice people

I swear especially now I'm doing more shows and getting more comfortable with the material I do in my shows ... really I'm convinced I tell Jonny I will get beat up or murdered one day but he says 'Beat up'. Yeah, but I say beat up real bad, so I have to learn to walk again.

On that cheerful note, we'll finish. Thank you.

Here are some phrases and possible angles from Kisa's interview.

'I'm a complete huge anglophile wouldn't even have met my partner if he wasn't English'

Romantic angle, targeting an audience of young females

'I'm convinced I will get beat up or murdered. Jonny says 'Beat up'. Yeah, but beat up real bad, so I have to learn to walk again.'

Dark, dramatic angle, but could be given a humorous twist, for an audience interested in contemporary performance

'I honestly believe that English people don't know what good food tastes like ...

The people seem stodgy and cold.'

Quite insulting, critical points of view, for readers of a newspaper food and culture supplement

'[America] is too far away from the rest of the world.'

Discussion of the role of USA, for readers interested in modern politics – and hostile to USA

Structuring the interview

Unit 1 introduced the term 'discourse' and suggested some ways of analysing the overall structure of texts (see pages 56–61). In Unit 2, you need to put this theory into practice and create an effective structure for your written interview. Begin with the phrases that interested you most and try to find an angle for the article, bearing in mind the type of publication, your purpose and readership. Then decide on an effective point to begin and end. You need not stick to the order of the conversation itself. Here is an example, based on the interview with Kisa.

Angle

Despite all the apparent differences between the UK and USA, fundamentally the people share the same values. The article's purpose is interesting entertainment, rather than in-depth social comment, so it would appeal to people studying or working in the media (performers, writers, producers).

Beginning

It needs to grab attention, so start with either the facts about stand-up comedy or romance. This would lead on to a humorous slant on various differences and similarities.

End

This can then round off the article by returning to stand-up and her partner, with the dramatic (comic over-exaggeration?) fear: beat-up or murdered.

Producing a final version

Professional writers go through many stages of drafting and editing before their work is ready for publication. Coursework allows you the time to experiment with style and structure, try out your work on readers, and make changes right up until the deadline for assessment. Remember to treat this as a real task. Although you want to impress an audience of teachers and moderators, you can only do this by keeping your own particular purpose and audience in mind. If you make it clear that your aim is to entertain media students by writing an edgy, controversial article about aggression towards American performers, then the moderator must assess the success of your article for this context.

All writers need good critics. Although praise is welcome, it is not helpful if someone tells you everything is fine when you could make some improvements. A person who criticises your writing pays you the compliment of believing you can do better.

The next activity asks you to give constructive criticism. (Note that these examples are not the full length, of about 1000 words, required for coursework.)

Activity 12

Read the two versions of the interview below and comment on each.

a   What do you think is the purpose and audience? Which do you prefer? Why?

b   What impression does the writer create of Kisa?

c   How does the writer create this impression? Which parts of the conversation are included or omitted. What form of speech representation does the writer use?

d   What improvements need to be made to achieve the top band for AO1, AO2 and AO4?

Version A

I asked Kisa, 'As an American, what is your view of the UK?'

She replied with a laugh, 'It's very wet!'

So I asked her what she thought about the floods the previous week.

She told me, 'It was frightful. I didn't realise how many rivers were around. A lot of people got swept away which is quite terrible.'

I then asked her if she thought Americans were more friendly than the British.

'Yes,' she said, 'it's true it's true, there are very friendly Americans, but maybe it's a bit superficial. In England it may seem a bit colder, but I think their caring and sense of community is way deeper.'

10　So what were her first impressions of Sheffield?

'I do remember when I first arrived, there are a lot of very rural areas around here even though it's very urban you wouldn't know it if you go outside the city. For the most part it fulfilled a lot of stereotypes. I love the little walks and ways and canals.'

15　'Why did you leave your lifetime home?'

'I don't like the way that country's going and I think my children will get a much more well-rounded education here. I'm a huge anglophile and wouldn't even have met my partner if he wasn't English.'

I left Kisa, hoping that she continues to enjoy her new life in the UK.

Version B

I arranged to meet Kisa Charles soon after one of her stand-up gigs at The Last Laugh Club in Sheffield. Newly arrived in Sheffield after a lifetime in the mean streets of Philadelphia, I was interested to find out her impressions of this country.

5　'The British seem more stodgy and cold,' she told me. 'Though I have noticed there's quite a rivalry between the North and the South.'

I wondered what differences she had noticed.

'Well Oxford was very nice and I loved London, but Sheffield has a lot of dirty urban areas.'

10　She told me she was here because her partner is English. 'I was reluctant to meet him,' she confessed.

And now you have seen the place at first hand?

'I honestly believe that English people don't know what good food tastes like,' she exclaimed. 'I know you suffered two world wars, eating potatoes for a long time
15　– I completely appreciate that, but do you have to eat blood and haggis!'

I noticed earlier that Kisa was booed by the audience, when she stood up and announced 'I'm an American.' 'Do you suffer from anti-American feelings?' I asked her.

20　'When I first came here I was unemployed for longer than I've ever been. I honestly believe they didn't want an American working for them.'

I wondered if she could understand why.

She became defensive. 'It's not our fault it's the government and we can't control the government.' Then she looked around nervously. 'Sometimes I think I
25　will get beat up or murdered one day.'

I was tempted to say, 'This is not America, you know' but she is only too well aware of that. Instead I offered her a bit of advice 'You'll have to lighten up a bit.' As they say in America!

Assessment objectives

You can earn top marks for your journalism interview by:

- writing fluently and confidently to produce a coherent, controlled text (AO1)
- producing texts that demonstrate perceptive understanding of concepts and theories relevant to the construction of meanings in spoken and written language, eg: subtle presentation of authorial viewpoint in written interviews (AO2)
- perceptive use of genre conventions, eg controlled use of a variety of forms to shape spoken interview into effective journalism (AO4)
- informed choice of style and structure to suit clearly differentiated purposes and audiences, eg perceptive choice of style and structure achieves complex purposes (including persuasion and entertainment) for stated audience (AO4)

You may have found Version B more lively and interesting, but you should also notice how biased it is as a record of the conversation. The writer has deliberately selected and emphasised negative points. (See Unit 1, page 60 for more on this aspect of discourse.) At one point, the writer commits the 'crime' that journalists are often accused of – taking things out of context. Although Kisa did say the words 'I was reluctant to meet him', it was *not* because he was English, as the written version suggests. She actually made the point that his Englishness was a plus point. This article implies that Kisa was prejudiced against the English (see Unit 1, pages 85–86 for more on the concepts of inference and implicature.)

5 Writing your commentary

Your commentary should be about 500 words long (but no more). This means that you need to be concise and to the point. Your final commentary should include explanation of these three areas, although not necessarily in this order:

- who you chose to interview, how and why
- how you crafted your final written version to achieve your purposes for the stated audience
- what you learned about this genre from studying examples of journalism interviews and theories about representation of speech.

The main focus of your commentary is on your final written version of the interview, so this section should be the longest. Explain some significant language choices that you made in order to achieve particular effects for your intended audience and purpose. Try to comment on various levels of language because the mark scheme rewards this. You do not need to use the general terms (pragmatics, discourse, grammar, lexis, phonology) as long as you are making comments on these aspects. For example:

- **Pragmatics**   Did you imply a particular attitude towards your interviewee? How did you convey this in the way you wrote up the conversation?
- **Discourse**   How did you structure the article? How did you begin and end? What did you include and leave out?
- **Grammar**   What forms of speech representation did you use? What effects did this create?
- **Lexis**   Did you choose any idiosyncratic words from your interviewee's vocabulary? Why?
- **Graphology and phonology**   Did you attempt to represent the interviewee's pronunciation in non-standard spelling? What effect were you trying to give?

Read this example commentary on Version B of Kisa's interview (page 109). The comments show what is rewarded and why.

A brief explanation of your choice of person and focus for the interview is a useful introduction to your purpose and target audience.

> I chose to interview a young American woman. The fact that her life combines being a mother of small children and an aspiring stand-up comedian might appeal to young adults, particularly females. Because she is now based in Sheffield, the article might be of particular
> 5   local interest. I decided to focus the interview questions on her experiences of life in the UK. There is quite a lot of 'USA-bashing' in the media these days, so I thought a wide audience would be interested in Kisa's comparisons between life here and in America.

A comment on the way the writer's viewpoint of the interviewee is created at the level of discourse ✓ choice and position of material ✓ and clear reference to the original transcript

> I wanted to present Kisa as an 'edgy' character, so I deliberately
> 10   selected her more provocative comments about her experiences in the UK. I encouraged these by challenging her opinions (see the highlighted sections of transcript).

Refers to the drafting process and improvements made in response to constructive criticism

> In an early draft, I included all my questions in indirect speech: 'Then I asked her why she had moved to the UK.' I agreed with the
> 15   comment that the style sounded like a police report. I decided that the responses could either stand alone, or I rephrased the question in free indirect speech: 'So why come to England anyway?' This colloquial style is more suitable for readers of an arts magazine.

I tried to use a variety of forms of speech representation when I was writing up the interview. This was partly to vary the style, but I needed to move away from the more neutral forms of direct speech in order to put my slant on her words. I used a summary of a speech act 'She became defensive.' to suggest that she was taking the side of Americans (although she wasn't!). I also included a narrative report of action 'Then she looked around nervously.' just before her comment about getting attacked.

Shows awareness of terms, concepts and theories of speech representation

This is an example of the sort of liberties journalists can take with the truth. The recording actually shows that she was laughing and joking in a relaxed manner when she mentioned this. A more accurate viewpoint would have been something like 'In typical comedy mode, Kisa exaggerated for humorous effect.'

Shows awareness of bias and authorial intervention

The very last words have a mocking tone as I use a stereotypical American phrase 'lighten up a bit'.

Aware of regional variation and the implied meanings (pragmatics)

I structured my article in classic journalistic fashion, ending on a note that echoes the beginning. I mentioned her stand-up comedy in the opening paragraph and referred to the 'mean streets' of Philadelphia. I finished with the paradox that she feels in more danger doing stand-up in Sheffield.

Refers to discourse v overall structure

I have always enjoyed reading Jon Ronson and Lynn Barber (see Appendix 2) for their strong critical opinions on celebrities. I would have to find a publication that did not mind offending people, perhaps an independent review of the local Arts scene.

You do not have to name a specific publication, but you could include a style model that has a similar approach.

B Writing for a reading audience: narrative

In this section you will learn how to show your skills in writing something that audiences will read. You have to submit either a journalism interview (see pages 95–111) or a narrative. In each case you will experiment with different style models before writing up a final version. You will also show knowledge of the key concepts in English language by writing a commentary explaining what choices you have made.

1 Introduction

Assessment objectives

Your narrative is assessed through AO1 (5 marks), AO2 (5 marks) and AO4 (20 marks). Your commentary is assessed through AO1 (5 marks) and AO2 (5 marks).

AO1 and AO2 marks are awarded for your understanding of the key concepts of the English language and for your ability to show this knowledge by writing clearly about them in your commentary.

AO4 marks are awarded for writing an interesting and effective narrative, informed by the key concepts you have learned.

Writing stories is something that all children do from their earliest days at school. Perhaps it seems like an imaginative skill that some people have a flair for – and others don't. This coursework task emphasises the craft of producing narrative – skills that you can develop during the writing process. This is the reason for setting a specific task, rather than just telling you to go away and wait for inspiration to hit you.

You must base your written narrative on a story that somebody told to you and that you recorded. These are 'real world narratives' – news stories, personal anecdotes, autobiographical memories. This basis in the real world need not restrict your imagination – you do not have to stick to all the details in the original. It should provide you, at least, with the germ of an idea from which you can elaborate and invent to produce a fictional narrative.

In your AS coursework, your practical work with spoken and written language will complement your studies for Unit 1. For the narrative task, you will follow a process that begins with your experience as a reader of stories and ends with your final written story and commentary. This section gives you examples and activities for these stages:

1 exploring the techniques of written narratives

2 studying the structure of oral (spoken) narratives

3 finding and recording a 'real world narrative'

4 transforming the spoken word into a written version

5 experimenting with narrative techniques

6 redrafting in response to constructive criticism

7 writing your commentary, explaining your choices and how they match your audience expectation.

The narrative should be in the range of 1000–1500 words.

2 Exploring the genre

Writing your commentary

Keep notes in a log or journal as you work towards the final draft of your narrative. In your commentary, you will explain what you learned during the process, as well as the techniques you actually used in your writing. The 'Writing your commentary' boxes will remind you about this at important stages.

The process of writing begins with reading. A writer needs to understand the genre (type of text) they are working towards. Some genres have very specific conventions. The Mills and Boon romances work to a set formula – in fact, the publishers will send out a handbook of instructions to any aspiring authors. This is because they have a particular audience and purpose in mind and they know exactly what their audience wants and expects. There are other types of narratives that target a specific audience, perhaps defined by age, gender or interest group – teen romances, pre-teen horror stories, tales for sports-mad boys, spy stories, fantasy adventures, science fiction – but many narratives have a wide appeal. Once you are at the stage of redrafting your work and writing a commentary, you should consider whether you are targeting a precisely defined readership or aiming at a wider audience

So, what is a narrative? Is it the same as a story? If so, what makes a story?

Perhaps the most familiar definition is that a story must have a beginning, a middle and an end. That's obviously true in that all stories begin and end somewhere. But *where* do stories begin and end? Younger children's stories often begin with waking up in the morning and end with going to sleep at night, rather cruelly called 'bed-to-bed' stories. But another person telling the story could put a different spin on the day's events. That crafting is the crucial difference between a story and a **narrative**. A narrative involves more than just a story:

- the story (a sequence of events)
- the teller or narrator
- the tellee or narratee (audience for the story).

Key term

narrative

orientation

abstract

Analysing the structure

The narrator of the story can choose where and how it begins, for example. That choice will keep the audience in mind. Here are different types of beginning:

- **orientation**   information about time, place, characters, etc
- **abstract**   a comment ('It was so embarrassing') foreshadows what is to come
- *in medias res*   plunges the reader into the middle of the action (from Latin, meaning 'into the middle of things')
- *in ultimas res*   begins at the end, then finishes at a similar point (from Latin, meaning 'into the end of things').

The narrator also chooses how the story ends:

- **closure**   a clear resolution; many modern stories lack closure
- **summary**   a type of closure, which ties up all the ends neatly
- **moral**   ends with a comment or message.

Activity 13

Below are the first and last sentences from a range of short stories.

1   Which narrative beginnings attract your interest? Which do not? Does this suggest that certain techniques are more effective for you?

2   For each, try to describe the techniques used to begin and end each story. (You may need to use more than one term, for example: **The story begins in medias res and gives some orientation about a character and a place.**)

3   Compare and discuss your ideas with another person.

Extract A

Conradin was ten years old, and the doctor had pronounced his professional opinion that the boy would not live another five years.

And while they debated the matter among themselves, Conradin made himself another piece of toast.

Extract B

My heart was pounding.

And we knew we were safe at last.

Extract C

Every child aspires to be something when she grows up.

'Git outta the car *now*!'

I did.

Extract D

Amadeo Peralta was raised in the midst of his father's gang and, <u>like all the men of his family, grew up to be a ruffian.</u>

He did not know why he was in that tomb, <u>and gradually he forgot the world of light and lost himself in his misfortune.</u>

Extract E

One night, when I was very small, I played with the little boy next door until it was dark.

For the bridge between us was built again.

Extract F

There go the bells: one, two, three, four, five, six, seven, eight; and in the silence that follows the last chime, there goes the Leaping Lad; leaping into the abyss, pale, but proud as ever.

A Leaping Lad he was always, and not afraid, I'll gamble, when the trap fell open and he made his last leap.

Extract G

It was the week on night shift that did it.

And you can reckon out for yourself who is the real hero of this Saturday Saga.

Extract H

The yowl of a cat; a dustbin lid rattling in a yard; a car door slammed.

And with that sorted out, she did at last fall asleep.

Extract I

When she opened the door and saw him standing there she was more pleased than ever before, and he, too, as he followed her into the studio, seemed very happy to have come.

At the end she wrote: 'Good night, my friend. Come again soon.'

Extract J

There are some women who seem to be born without fear, just as there are people who are born without the ability to feel pain.

Her friends call it optimism, this conviction of hers that everything will work out for her somehow.

Extract K

It was two days before the Easter holidays when Myra told me David wanted to go out with me.

I remember over and over, when I felt beaten, gritting my teeth and saying: 'I will be Julie Christie, I will go to London.'

Extract L

My father came across the field carrying the body of the boy who had been drowned.

So we went on, with the two in the back seat trusting us, because of no choice, and we ourselves trusting to be forgiven, in time, for everything that had first to be seen and condemned by those children: whatever was flippant, arbitrary, careless, callous – all our normal, and particular, mistakes.

Extract M

The summer I was fourteen, we lived in a one-room cabin, on a hundred acres of back-concession scrub farmland.

This is what I have remembered most clearly about Buddy: the ordinary-looking wreckage, the flatness of the water, the melancholy light.

Extract N

Two old men sat on a park bench one morning in the sunshine of Tampa, Florida – one trying doggedly to read a book he was plainly enjoying while the other, Harold K. Bullard, told him the story of his life in the full, round, head tones of a public address system.

He tucked the book under his arm and walked away.

Extract O

I will wait for her in the yard that Maggie and I made so clean and wavy yesterday afternoon.

And then the two of us sat there just enjoying, until it was time to go in the house and go to bed.

Taking a perspective

Between the beginning and the closing section comes the middle – a series of events, description and dialogue. Here the writer can choose to tell the story from various viewpoints. The first simple distinction is between first and third person narration, but the effects are more complex than this.

A **first person narrative**, using the pronoun 'I', relates the events from the point of view of one character in the story. Some stories are strongly autobiographical, so the identity of the author and the 'I' may be virtually identical, eg Extract M above, taken from a collection called *Transforming Moments*. Other narratives create a fictional 'I' character, eg Extract B, written by a 15-year-old girl in a teen magazine. First person narratives sometimes create a sense of an individual speaking **voice**, using colloquial language.

This perspective has **human limitation** – the reader can only know what the narrator knows.

> ### Writing your commentary
>
> In order to research the genre, try to find a range of style models. Keep a bibliography. Also record your study of narrative techniques. In your commentary, you might mention examples that particularly influenced you. For example, **I thought the technique of 'in ultimas res' in 'The Leaping Lad' by Sid Chaplin was very dramatic, as the reader can concentrate on how and why it happened. I remember this technique was also used in the musical drama "Blood Brothers" by Willie Russell.**

Activity 14

Look again at the extracts in activity 13.

1   Which ones are first person narrative?

2   What can you tell about the identity – age, gender, social background – of the 'I' narrator?

3   Look at Extract O ('And then the two of us sat there just enjoying …') Can you find other examples that sound like a natural speaking voice?

4   Look at Extract L ('So we went on … and particular, mistakes.') Can you find other examples where the style is more carefully structured?

A **third person narrative** uses 'he', 'she' and 'they' to refer to all the characters. Sometimes, it is clear that the events are seen from the perspective of one of the characters in the story, eg Extract D, where the last sentence shows the reader what Amadeo is experiencing. So, like a third person narrative, there is human limitation.

The writer may choose, instead, the perspective of an **omniscient narrator.** The events are told from the outside. The invisible 'puppeteer' sees all, understands all and steers the reader with comments on the characters and events. In Extract D (page 113), note the underlined comments.

Key terms

first person narrative

voice

human limitation

third person narrative

omniscient narrator

showing

telling

Activity 15

1   Look back at the beginnings and endings of narratives in activity 13 and find examples of third person narration.

2   Look at Extracts F and J. What words or phrases suggest that these are the viewpoints of omniscient narrators (outsiders who make knowing comments on the characters).

The terms '**showing**' and '**telling**' refer to different narrative techniques: on the one hand, describing a scene and leaving the reader to draw conclusions; on the other, making explicit judgements on characters' motives, etc. 'Showing' is the more dramatic, cinematic technique of storytelling. First person narration can naturally involve 'telling', as the main character explains and makes comments. In third person narration, it is harder to know who is making the 'telling' comments. It must be the invisible (omniscient) narrator.

A word of warning: it is safer to use a 'showing' technique when you start writing third person narratives, as your readers may find comments intrusive and irritating, particularly if they disagree with your opinions. The next example presents a mixture of 'showing' and 'telling' from Saki, a master-storyteller.

Activity 16

Read the first two paragraphs of *Sredni Vashtar*, by Saki (the pen-name of H.H. Munro) below. Sredni Vashtar is the name of the boy's pole-cat ferret.

Independent research

You can read the complete story and others by Saki on www.classicshorts.com/stories/vashtar.html

> Conradin was ten years old, and the doctor had pronounced his professional opinion that the
> 5   boy would not live another five years. The doctor was silky and effete, and counted for little,
> but his opinion was endorsed by Mrs De Ropp, who counted for nearly everything. Mrs De
> Ropp was Conradin's cousin and guardian, and in his eyes she represented those three-fifths
> of the world that are necessary and disagreeable and real; the other two-fifths, in perpetual
> antagonism to the foregoing, were summed up in himself and his imagination. One of
> 10 these days Conradin supposed he would succumb to the mastering pressure of wearisome
> necessary things – such as illnesses and coddling restrictions and drawn-out dullness.
> Without his imagination, which was rampant under the spur of loneliness, he would have
> succumbed long ago.
>
>   Mrs De Ropp would never, in her honestest moments, have confessed to herself that
> 15 she disliked Conradin, though she might have been dimly aware that thwarting him 'for
> his good' was a duty which she did not find particularly irksome. Conradin hated her
> with a desperate sincerity which he was perfectly able to mask. Such few pleasures as he
> could contrive for himself gained an added relish from the likelihood that they would be
> displeasing to his guardian, and from the realm of his imagination she was locked out – an
> unclean thing, which should find no entrance…

1   Is it a first or third-person narrative?

2   Which parts do you think *show* the boy's view of people and events?

3   Which parts do you think are comments where the narrator is *telling* us about the boy or Mrs De Ropp?

Saki (H. H. Munro)

Activity 17

Now read an extract from later in the story, below. The boy has been keeping a ferret hidden from Mrs De Ropp.

Writing your commentary

Explain decisions you made about perspective, voice and chronology in your commentary. For example, **I decided to use a first person narrative, as it gave me the chance to get inside the head of my main character and tell the story from their perspective. I also wanted to create a colloquial voice for my narrative. This meant that my written story was quite similar to the spoken version. It was important to craft some changes, so I played about with the chronology. I think it is dramatic to plunge the reader into the action so I started 'in medias res'.**

Mrs De Ropp noticed that the visits to the shed did not cease, and one day she made a further journey of inspection.

'What are you keeping in that locked hutch?' she asked. 'I believe it's guinea-pigs. I'll have them all cleared away.'

5 Conradin shut his lips tight, but the Woman ransacked his bedroom till she found the carefully hidden key, and forthwith marched down to the shed to complete her discovery. It was a cold afternoon, and Conradin had been bidden to keep to the house. From the furthest window of the dining-room the door of the shed could just be seen beyond the corner of the shrubbery, and there Conradin stationed himself. He saw the Woman enter, and then be 10 imagined her opening the door of the sacred hutch and peering down with her short-sighted eyes into the thick straw bed where his god lay hidden. Perhaps she would prod at the straw in her clumsy impatience. And Conradin fervently breathed his prayer for the last time. But he knew as he prayed that he did not believe. He knew that the Woman would come out presently with that pursed smile he loathed so well on her face, and that in an hour or 15 two the gardener would carry away his wonderful god, a god no longer, but a simple brown ferret in a hutch. And he knew that the Woman would triumph always as she triumphed now, and that he would grow ever more sickly under her pestering and domineering and superior wisdom, till one day nothing would matter much more with him, and the doctor would be proved right. And in the sting and misery of his defeat, he began to chant loudly and defiantly the hymn of his threatened idol:

20 Sredni Vashtar went forth,
His thoughts were red thoughts and his teeth were white.
His enemies called for peace, but he brought them death.
Sredni Vashtar the Beautiful.

1 Whose view of the scene does the reader have? (third person narrator)

2 What happens? (the story events)

3 At what point is the reader left 'in the dark'? (human limitation of narrator)

4 What does the narrator imagine, or wish, is happening? (thoughts of third person narrator)

5 Why do you think the writer does not provide omniscient narration at this point in the story to tell the reader what is happening? Do you agree that the technique of 'showing' is more dramatic, or cinematic?

Plotting the timeline

The **chronology** of a straightforward narrative would be told in order, beginning with the earliest events and moving forward in time. You may know the word 'anachronism' meaning out of the usual time. The term '**anachrony**' refers to the use of flashbacks and the opposite – flash forwards – when telling a story. This may happen when a narrative begins *in medias res* – right in the middle of the action; it must happen if it begins *in ultimas res* – with the final event.

Activity 18

My father came across the field carrying the body of the boy who had been drowned.

So we went on, with the two in the back seat trusting us, because of no choice, and we ourselves trusting to be forgiven, in time, for everything that had first to be seen and condemned by those children: whatever was flippant, arbitrary, careless, callous – all our normal, and particular, mistakes.

Take the opening and closing to the story *Miles City, Montana* by Alice Munro (Extract N on page 114).

1 Mark these two events on a time-line:

   a The narrator is 6 years old. An 8-year-old boy drowns.

   b About 30 years later the narrator drives home with her husband and two daughters from a swimming pool, where no one had noticed the younger child fall into the water.

2 Suggest a progression of events to move the narrative from point A to B. Could there be any flashbacks to a time before the boy drowned? Could there be any flash forwards to a time after the car journey?

3 Exploring the structure of oral narratives

It is time to move from written to oral narratives and see whether both genres follow a similar structure and use similar techniques. The term '**real world narrative**' emphasises the fact that stories need not be fictional. When people are talking to each other, they often relate short anecdotes about personal experiences, either recent events or ones from their earlier life. Researchers have recorded many examples of people telling everyday stories about their own life and examined the structure. Perhaps the most well-known framework is the sociolinguist William Labov's six-part structure of oral narratives (1972):

1 **Abstract** – What, in brief, is the story about?

2 **Orientation** – Who, when, where, what?

3 **Complicating action** – Then what happened?

4 **Evaluation** – So what? How is this interesting?

5 **Result** or **resolution** – What finally happened?

6 **Coda** – That's it, my story has ended and I'm bringing you back to 'the present situation'.

This does not mean that every person telling a story follows this pattern exactly. Some stories may not begin with an abstract or end with a coda. The evaluation comments can come at various points during the story (similar to the 'telling' comments in a written narrative). These terms provide you with a toolkit for exploring the structure of oral narratives. Here is an example of a person responding to questions about their choice of university course (*Life Stories: The Creation of Coherence*, Charlotte Linde, reprinted on www.cs.ucsd.edu/~goguen/papers/story.html). She uses the term 'narrative' in place of 'complicating action'.

Key terms

chrnology

anachrny

real world narrative

complicating action

evaluation

result/resolution

coda

Simple narrative of personal experience	
Clause	**Structural type**
And how about the particular field?	Interviewer's request serves as an abstract
That was more or less an accident.	Evaluation of abstract
Uh, I started out in Renaissance studies,	Orientation
but I didn't like any of the people I was working with,	Evaluation in orientation
and at first I thought I would just leave Y and go to another university	Narrative (main verb: 'thought')
uh, but a medievalist at Y university asked me to stay or at least reconsider whether I should leave or not,	Narrative (main verb: 'asked')
and, um, pointed out to me that I had done very well in the medieval course that I took with him and that I seemed to like it,	Narrative (main verb: 'pointed out'). Absence of subject indicates that the verb is closely tied to previous verb, and may be simultaneous with it. Also evaluation of speaker's university career.
and he was right.	Evaluation
I did.	Evaluation
And he suggested that I switch fields and stay at Y.	Narrative (main verb: 'suggested')
And that's how I got into medieval literature.	Coda: summarises the narrative and marks its end

Activity 19

The examples below are all from an oral narrative, but are not in the original order.

1   Re-arrange them into an order that makes sense to you.

2   See whether Labov's terms provide a useful way of describing each section of the story.

C
After the fashion show in Brighton, I decided to buy one of the dresses.

A
I couldn't decide whether to get the size 12 or 10, anyway I tried on the 10. I finally got the zip done up (*mimes slow squeezing*). I was so hot, sweating. Then I was desperately trying to get it down again, my arm in the air like this, sweaty armpit (*acts it out with sounds*).

B
Whenever I wear it I have to get some one else to do it up for me. It looks really good though.

D
Oh my god it was so embarrassing, right?

E
Anyway I just marched up to the assistant, 'Yeah, the 10's great, thanks! I'll keep it on.'

F
I felt sick, SICK, I thought I was stuck for ever.

G
Take the shame! (*imitates pronunciation of catch phrase*)

H
Can you imagine what I looked like? (*horrified expression*)

Performance features

As you can see from the example above, it is not just the words, but 'the way she tells it'. Nessa Wolfson (1982) identifies a number of 'performance features' in oral narratives, which she calls 'dramatised re-enactments'. (You may wish to consider these aspects for the dramatic monologue task in Unit 2.) Wolfson's terms can be related to the narrative in Activity 19:

1   Direct speech – 'Yeah, the 10's great, thanks! I'll keep it on.'

2   Asides – 'Can you imagine what I looked like?'

3   Repetition – 'I felt sick, SICK …'

4   Expressive sounds – '(*imitates pronunciation of catch phrase*)'

5   Sound effects – '(*acts it out with sounds*)'

6   Motions and gestures – '(*mimes slow squeezing*)'

7   Conversational historic present, alternating with narrative past tense.

The term '**historic present**' refers to the use of the present tense in telling something that happened in the past. It is a colloquial form and creates more of a sense of immediate drama. The storyteller above does not use this, but it would go like this:

> So I go (present) into the changing room, right, and put the dress on. And then I got (past) completely stuck. I just marched (past) up to the desk and I says (present) – cool as you like – 'I'll wear it!'

Some obvious differences between written and spoken narratives lie in the performance aspects. The writer can use direct speech and repetition to suggest an authentic speaking voice. The narration may sometimes be in historic present throughout, but this is unusual. It would also be very unusual to address the reader directly via asides. But the physical aspects are really a feature of live speech, not written language. If the writer wishes to create any of these sound and visual effects, it would have to be done by description.

If you look at Labov's framework, there are some interesting differences between the way we tell stories when speaking and in writing. When telling a story directly in speaking, we are usually more straightforward. The oral narrative often begins with a clear introduction (the abstract and orientation) and ends with a sort of summary (the coda). Written narratives can be more artful, as readers expect to be intrigued by an unusual plot. You should be wary about mirroring the structure of oral narratives too closely. Young children's written narratives, for example, sometimes start with a plain introduction of the situation (who, what, where, when, why), relate some exciting events and finish with a safe return to normality, eg 'I woke up and it was all a dream.'

Key term
historic present

4 Finding and recording a real world narrative

So why start with a real world narrative, if it is so important to craft the written version in different ways? In the introduction to his collection of stories, *The Leaping Lad*, Sid Chaplin emphasises the importance of a writer's real life experience:

> We all start by copying; but the best copyists go straight to life.

But, although some stories need hardly any changes or additions, a writer often takes a character from here, a place from there, and puts them all together in a new situation. Chaplin continues:

> In others [stories] I combined experience and fantasy, as in *Half Moon Street*. There actually is a Half Moon Street, and the name teased away in my mind until it linked up with my own experience as a baker's boy and some anecdote I was told; then suddenly the whole thing fused, and I had a story.

It is important that your narrative is not simply a written version of a story told to (or remembered by) you. You need to fictionalise accounts of real events, or as Chaplin says, fuse experience and fantasy. The next activity gives you practice in making this transformation.

Activity 20

Work in pairs and make sure one of you has a way of timing the activity.

1. Choose one of the stimulus situations below, or add further suggestions.

   - a place you remember well from your childhood
   - a time you felt completely alone
   - your best friend or worst enemy
   - something very risky you once did
   - a really embarrassing moment
   - something you regret *not* doing
   - an event you were looking forward to for ages, but …
   - a person who turned out to be quite different from first impressions

2. Person A will speak for a minute on the subject. Person B should listen attentively, but without contributing.

3. As soon as the minute is up, Person B should take over the 'story' and talk for two minutes. Again, there should be no contributions from Person A, apart from being pleasantly attentive.

4. Finally, you can talk about how closely (or not) B's account resembled A's real experience. You may find a surprising amount of empathy – emotional, as opposed to factual, truth – in B's fictional version.

Recording an oral narrative

You can control the type of oral narrative you use as a starting point. Labov, for example, collected stories for his research based on the interview question: 'Were you ever in a situation, where you were in serious danger of being killed?' This could provide you with material for a thriller, if that is the genre you would like to work in. The topics in Activity 20 gave you ideas for other possible stimulus questions. If you want to write a story based on your own experience, you can record yourself. Otherwise choose a person who tells a good story.

Once you have an idea for a general topic, you need to set up the recording. (See 'Journalism interview', pages 104–105 for advice on equipment and ethical issues.) You want the situation to be as relaxed and natural as possible, but try to let the person tell the story without too much interruption.

Make a rough transcript of the recording. You do not have to write down every single word, but make sure you have the beginning and ending verbatim (word for word) and then note the main sequence of events, so that you can refer to changes made. Activity 21 gives you an example of a transcript so that you can apply some of your knowledge about the structure of oral narratives.

Transcribing and noting structure

When you have made your recording and transcript, try to apply the toolkit of terms for analysing the structure of oral narratives. Notice how the story begins and ends. Is there an abstract, orientation and coda? Notice whether the speaker makes the story more enjoyable by including evaluation comments or performance features. What is the complicating action and the resolution?

Activity 21

1   Read the rough transcript of an oral narrative below. It is divided into sections. The first and last parts are verbatim (word for word). The rest is abbreviated. Three dots (…) indicate that words are missing.

2   Read the comments on the first sections, then answer these questions about the following sections.

   a Can you identify any of the elements of structure that Labov suggests?

   b What performance features, suggested by Wolfson, does the speaker use?

   c What do you notice about the chronology?

   d Where do you think the main story ends? How does it end – with a moral, summary, closure?

abstract

A

uh my whole <u>childhood is filled with weird things</u> (*laughs*) but um well um I think <u>one thing in particular which I thought was very eventful</u> at least for my 10 or 12 year old adolescent self was um was <u>when I was younger</u> (*laughs*) I used to um we <u>went to elementary school near right (.) next to a roller rink</u> that we spent most of our childhood at

abstract

orientation

evaluation   *expressive sound*

B

um <u>I loved roller rinks</u> and I had the best roller skates (*laughs*) on the face of the planet um gold sparkly skates with yellow wheels and yellow laces that used to be my mum's when she was a teenager in the 60s

evaluation

C

but yeah so <u>I loved it</u> and we used to go there kind of on a weekly basis I felt very at home there … <u>my parents used to drop us off and leave us there all day</u> back when a roller rink was a babysitter … <u>no supervision</u>

complicating action

evaluation that warns of ending

flashback

D

so we went there all the time and at one point well I remember one time in particular um <u>kind of the night before</u> planning to get dropped off and planning the day's events and somehow conversation turned to bullyism um how to handle a bully …

E

flash forward

and much later in life my grandfather gave me the worst advice for handling a bully 'if a gang sets on you you pick the biggest one and jump on him … and then you pick the next biggest one …' which was terrible advice …

evaluation that warns of ending

F

but yeah, so the conversation had turned to bullyisms I guess my father's whole goal in giving me this advice just kinda giving me confidence and maybe being a tall guy it worked for him he said 'nine times out of ten' pretty good percentages I should think 'if you stand up to a bully he'll back down' well I'm very mouthy … if I'm encouraged to stand up for myself I will do it with gusto

G

so the next day my aunt and I … she was a year older than me … my mum's sister … we grew up together we were at the roller rink one day separately we got approached by these girls who thought we'd somehow gotten into their locker and stolen one of their bags (purse) it was terrible they would act like they liked us: 'Yeah let's go skating' we'd get out to the middle of the rink they'd trip us and we'd fall on our backs

H

the second time I stood up to them and said 'You think you're hot shit don't you' … my way of standing up to a bully it was hilarious … she slapped me right in the face … it escalated to violence well I guess tripping someone on a roller rink is violence … so she slapped me right in the face …

I

but luckily there were skate monitors who took us to one side … the great thing about this although the bully didn't back down I guess my adult belief in karma sort of illustrated itself because she got banned from the roller rink for life and I got a bag of ice which I later ate (*laughs*)

J

to be fair and completely off the record (*laughs*) even tho it's completely on the record cos it's recorded (*laughs*) my aunt she might well have stolen the girl's purse I don't know this for sure it's all speculation I was quite young and naive and looked up to her …

K

Heidi um I don't know everybody loves Heidi Heidi is so great, but she's so a bit selfish and a bit rotten she's really good now now she's a born again Christian she's got lots of kids she might still be slightly she puts on a good face she puts on a good face for my grandmother and the lord (*laughs*) I guess (*laughs*)

L

I loved roller rink pizza back then too oh I loved that it was delicious

Writing your commentary

- Keep notes about the way you set up your recorded spoken anecdote. Who did you choose and why? What stimulus question did you ask? In your commentary, you should refer to your rough transcript, noting any significant changes. For example, **The oral narrative began with a bit of a diversion into her past history. I wanted the written version to begin in a more focused way, so that the story was all about the incident at the skating rink. The speaker finished with some gossip about what her aunt is like as an adult. I decided to change this for the same reason – to focus on the events in childhood.**

- What did you notice about the style and structure of your oral narrative? Did it correspond to theories you have studied? You should append a transcript of your recording and refer to it in your commentary. For example, **My friend's account began with an overall evaluation of the event: 'Oh my god it was so embarrassing.' She accompanied her description of events with gestures and ended with a coda (Labov): 'Whenever I wear it I have to get some one else to do it up for me. It looks really good though.' That is not the sort of comment used to conclude written narratives.**

5 Transforming oral anecdotes into written narratives

Key term

inciting moment

In the trailer for a TV show, a voice-over intones: 'This story is a true story. Only the names have been changed to protect the innocent.' Obviously, a scriptwriter's task involves far more skill in crafting an original idea. You may find terms from scriptwriting useful as you plan the writing of your narrative.

The concept of an **inciting moment** refers to an event that creates disharmony, or destroys the balance that existed before. This is similar to Labov's concept of a complicating action. In the transcript in Activity 21, what was the inciting moment for the narrative?

1   Was it the act of physical violence against the two girls?

2   Or the alleged theft of a bag?

3   Would you go further back to the parents' advice on handling bullies?

4   Or even further back still to the use of a roller rink as a 'babysitter'?

This is rather like asking yourself, 'What's the point of the story?' Deciding on the main point, or focus, will affect the way you re-tell the story in writing, and later influence the changes you make when you redraft it. The first two decisions (in response to 1 and 2 above) for the inciting moment of the story keep the focus very much on the child's experience and the drama of the events. Number 1 places the central characters as victims; number 2 introduces the possibility of their fault. Numbers 3 and 4 take a more detached adult view on the situation. You might need to think about audience here: the first option would probably appeal most to young readers, as a simple tale of right and wrong. If you were writing for older teenagers, the second option is more challenging. The last two options have a moral slant that might be of interest to adult readers. Having said that, adults and children often enjoy the same stories, as we see in the success of many 'crossover' books, such as the Harry Potter series.

From the 'point' of the story, you could make an initial decision about narrative perspective: would first or third person be more effective?

You also need to make a decision about the starting and finishing point for your narrative, and any connected issues about chronology. Or you may prefer to leave this to inspiration – just start writing the first draft and see what happens. Certainly many writers do not know how their story ends until the moment they reach the end. However, J.K. Rowling always claimed that she had planned the final ending of the last book before she started on the first. This allowed her to plant significant clues along the way.

Activity 22

1   Read the first draft openings below to a narrative based on the transcript in Activity 21. Which do you think has most potential?

2   Comment on the differences. For each:

   a   what inciting moment does it seem to lead up to?

   b   what narrative perspective is used?

   c   what is the starting point?

A

Kerry's mum packed her off to school as usual with her roller skates in a bag and two quid in her purse. 'I'll be at Roxy's tonight,' she told her. 'Get yourself a pizza or something for tea.'

B

They say you should listen to your parents. Well, it didn't do me much good as a kid. My dad always hated authority – the cops most of all – and so did his dad before him. Come to think of it, that didn't do them a lot of good either. Both in and out of prison for petty crimes. But I still can't knuckle down and shut up, even now I've got kids of my own, if someone tries to put one over on me.

C

'That's her, the girl with a ponytail!' I watched my cousin Heidi as she told the policemen her story. 'She just came up with her big sister and shoved us both. Then they started kicking us, really hard, with their skates.'

Heidi's sobs started me off and I started crying as well. Heidi was on top form that day. I almost believed her myself.

D

I was so proud of my glittery yellow roller boots, I couldn't wait for school to end and get onto the rink. My mum let me go as long as my cousin was there too to look after me. We told her it was fine, that it was a special session for the under 12s, that it was all supervised. What we didn't tell her was that the Beaumont twins went too, and everyone in our street knew what trouble those girls were.

6 Respond to feedback and criticism

Every writer needs a good critic, someone who understands the craft of writing and is honest enough to give you constructive criticism. You may hope to get this from your teacher alone, but it would be more effective to form a sort of writer's workshop within your class. This will give you more regular and detailed feedback than a single teacher can provide and also develop your own skills of critical judgement. Although this type of feedback can be given in class, some people prefer to form smaller groups and exchange comments via email. It is sometimes easier to comment when you are not face to face.

When you read and comment on another person's story, try to give an honest account of the effect it had on you. Rather than making general statements, such as, 'It was good/bad/beautifully written/dull,' be personal and refer to yourself:

* it made me think of ...
* I liked the bit where...
* I didn't understand why...
* I wanted to know more about ...
* the ending was a bit too good to be true for me, etc.

Then ask the writer questions about the techniques used, for example:

* why did you choose a first person narrative?
* did you try any other ways of beginning the narrative?
* do you think it could end in a different place?
* why didn't you mention the girls' name?
* did you mean to include a flashback to the mother's childhood?

Activity 23

Read the written narrative below based on the story in the transcript in Activity 21. The writer could not decide how to end the narrative. Give constructive criticism to steer the writer towards some cuts, some changes and a decision about the ending.

a Begin with personal comments.

* What aspects work well for you? What parts are less successful?
* What does the point of the story seem to be? (Try to summarise it in a sentence or two.)

b Then comment on techniques (you can read some comments in the margin)

* What changes has the writer made to the original spoken version?
* Note the narrative techniques used: perspective, voice, chronology.

c Finally, make one or two suggestions to the writer, for example:

* try beginning the narrative at the roller rink, then use flashbacks
* you could end with the discovery that Heidi *had* stolen the bag.

> *begins with abstract, hinting at the climax, so almost* in ultimas res

> *colloquial first person voice*

As a young girl of 12, I remember trusting – perhaps a little too much – in what my parents told me. I thought it was wonderful to have such trust, until <u>the point when</u> it was slapped out of me. (Literally.)

I loved to roller skate. <u>Not this</u> 'new-fangled' in-line skating phenomenon. But real old-
5 school, four wheels, moveable ankles, corner-cutting, 'wish you were in a roller derby' skating.
I even have the most beautiful skates ever to roll over this planet. Two shiny gold and yellow works of art. My skates were handed down to me from my mother. They were hers when she was younger. I'm sure they acquired most of their mileage <u>during the 60s and 70s,</u> when there was absolutely nothing to do in the Pennsylvania suburb where she grew up except to smoke
10 cigarettes and skate. They were malleable yet supportive leather skates coloured completely with the shiniest gold glitter between the calves-skin and a transparent slathering of plastic. They were accented with yellow wheels and yellow laces. An absolute monstrosity in some folks eyes but absolute beauty in mine.

> *flashback to mother's era*

My mother was the oldest of eight children. Her youngest sister Heidi, my aunt, was only
one year older than me when I was born. This, more than any common interests or goals,
would cement our adolescent partnership.

comment from wiser perspective

We went to the same elementary school. And being a year younger I, while longing for
attention and approval, annoyed more than a few of Heidi's teachers, spoiling their academic
projects by informing the other students of what they were, before the teachers had a chance
to. Serves them right for not having a new lesson plan each year. They must have known that
scores of siblings would pass through their classrooms, having to complete the same clove
gingerbread ornament for their Christmas tree as their older sister or brother.

knowing comments in parenthesis, like asides

Though the teachers lacked originality in my 12-year-old eyes, one thing my school had
going for it was its strategic location. You see, directly behind my school – not more than
10 yards away was the neighbourhood roller rink. We used to cue up, at least once a month,
in the halls of Cornwells Elementary School and anxiously await the trek that so many of
my aunts and uncles walked. It's a journey that would continue, like clockwork, for future
cousins and uncles and brothers. Only a five-minute walk around the school playground
to the coolest and absolutely most fun place in my childhood experiences – the Cornwells
Roller Rink.

direct spoken address to audience, as if oral narrative

Of course, these class trips weren't enough for me. Heidi and I spent practically every
weekend in that rink as well. My favourite meal at the time was the abysmal (though
I'm sure I could enjoy a slice right now) roller rink pizza. The owners of this venue were
friendly and knew many of my predecessors. My father would drop us off in the morning.
After hours of action and small-town dramas we would be picked up, a little wiser from the
experience. But I never imagined that one of the most vivid lessons that I would learn at my
favourite childhood hang-out would be exactly how naive and clueless my father could be.

'telling' comment from older perspective in more formal lexis

flash forward

To be fair, maybe my father's advice would of worked as a percentage game. Six times
out of ten, in which case I was just unlucky. (Though I have always been a lucky person, in
fact recently I had my fortune told by a man and was told I had a very lucky face. I asked a
friend of mine who also had her fortune read by the same travelling 'artist' if he told her she
had a lucky face and she, flabbergasted, exclaimed 'He said I had a very unlucky face!')

aside, more like unstructured spoken narrative

It was the beginning of summer and we were still basking in the 'no-more-school-
for-three-months' freedom feeling. I remember sitting around my grandmother's house
on Friday evening, planning the next days' events. Of course, what we did was a given:
skating. Only the ornamental details needed to be discussed: who would do the honour of
transporting, would we be allowed to scarf gelatos afterward, etc.

Then the conversation turned to the annoying topic that plagued any US suburb in the
80s: bullyism. Once adolescents in our town didn't have to worry about the daily grind of
school and helping their single-parent mothers with dinner, they could focus on tormenting
as many children as possible. Something that wasn't really tolerated in our elementary
school environment but with the freedom of a suburban town – anything was possible.

rather complicated 'telling' about characters outside the main story

'We'll just steer clear of trouble' I optimistically chirped, I was more concerned with how
much mileage I'd accomplish on my skates this summer.

'Well, you know' my father began, 'if you stand up to a bully – nine times out of ten,
they'll back down.'

I was amazed and my 12-year-old mind wasn't an idiot. I knew that those odds were
something that, with my charisma and moderate confidence, I would happily play. I had
developed, in that moment, armed with my fathers 'insider intelligence' (he'd never been
wrong before), a bravado that most American 12-year-olds aren't graced with. I went to bed
that night dreaming of roller discos in a Brave New World.

irony, which signals disaster to come

The day was filled with roller pizzas and pair-skating, sometimes with Heidi: scouting
who'd we really like to skate with or kiss, other times with shy suburban boys that we would
later introduce to the world of tongue kissing and minor vandalism. Heidi and I weren't
inseparable, which gave us individual freedom.

flash forward establishes world of character

Remember to print off at least one early draft of your writing before you make revisions to it.
It may be useful to save each successive draft in a separate file. You can then look back and
comment on changes, or even return to an earlier version that you feel is the most effective.

7 Experiment with techniques in redrafting

Professional writers redraft many, many times. Although people can come up with the occasional example of a piece of literature that just sprang from nowhere in a wild outpouring of inspiration (Coleridge's poem 'Khubla Khan' is often mentioned), the aim of AS coursework is to develop the craft of writing and to use the knowledge and understanding of language gained from Unit 1. For this reason, you must submit at least one early draft of your final narrative and this should show some substantial, thoughtful editing changes.

Feedback from fellow students should give you a sense of the effects of your narrative. But readers – even your teachers – are likely to be as polite as possible and avoid saying anything directly critical. You will need to take a further step to identify areas for improvement or change.

Activity 24

1   Can you read between the lines of these comments on the story in Activity 23?

   •   'direct spoken address to audience as if oral narrative'

   •   'aside, more like unstructured spoken narrative'

   •   'rather complicated 'telling' about characters outside the story'.

2   What changes does the writer need to make?

Here are more direct evaluative comments explaining why this narrative needs some improvement in order to achieve top band marks.

Overall: This is a lively and engaging narrative.		
AO	Comment	Mark
AO1: written expression	Lively, varied and accurate, with some lapses in control	mid/low top band
AO2: perspective, chronology voice and style	The style is effective for first person narration in the voice of a young teenager. Although the style captures the voice well, it sometimes veers too far to the colloquial to be really effective in a written narrative. The more formal comments from an older perspective add some interesting ideas, but too many tend to 'dilute' the impact of the story. There are interesting flashbacks and flash forwards in chronology, but sometimes there is too much backstory given. The narrative would be stronger with more 'showing' and a less 'telling'.	Band 2
AO4: control over changes from spoken to written narrative	An effectively written narrative, which could show a little more crafting to change the structure of the oral version. The first person telling voice is engaging, but there could be more variety with inclusion of description (of places, people and key events) and dialogue. This would allow more dramatic 'showing' of the climax, rather than 'telling'. It needs a better awareness of the impact of spoken narrative techniques and more use of the range of techniques for written narratives.	borderline Band 3/4

Assessment objectives

You can earn top marks for your narrative by:

•   writing fluently and confidently to produce a coherent, controlled text (AO1)

•   producing texts that demonstrates perceptive understanding of concepts and theories relevant to the construction of meanings in spoken and written language, eg use of perspective, chronology, etc to shape written narratives (AO2)

•   perceptive use of genre conventions, eg original use of a variety of narrative techniques to transform original spoken version (AO4)

•   informed choice of style and structure to suit clearly differentiated purposes and audiences, eg thoughtful choice of style and structure to achieve ambitious purposes and audience (AO4)

8 Writing your commentary

Assessment objectives

You can earn top marks for your commentary by:

- choosing a range of appropriate terminology to discuss your own language use (including grammar, discourse and pragmatics) (AO1)
- explaining and evaluating the impact of a range of linguistic choices in the stimulus texts and your own writing (AO2).

Your commentary should be about, but not more than, 500 words long. This means that you need to be concise and to the point. Your final commentary should include explanation of these three areas, although not necessarily in this order:

- the ideas your oral narrative provided for your plot, character or themes
- how you crafted your final written narrative version, making changes that were effective for your purpose or specific audience
- what you learned about narrative techniques, from studying examples of written narratives and theories about the structure of oral narratives.

The main focus of your commentary is on your final written narrative, so this section should be the longest. Explain some significant language choices that you made in order to achieve particular effects for your intended audience and purpose. You will need to discuss changes from the oral transcript and any made in redrafting. You will gain credit for commenting on a range of language levels. Remember that any comments about the overall structure (beginnings and endings), perspective and chronology come under the heading 'discourse'. Comments on style and voice may include reference to grammar as well as to lexis. If you tried to create a sense of a spoken voice, this would come under phonology, represented by graphology. You do not need to use the general terms (pragmatics, discourse, grammar, lexis, phonology) as long as you are making comments on these aspects. For example:

- **Discourse**

  I used first person narrative to capture the perspective of a 12-year-old girl.

- **Grammar**

  Some minor sentences suggest a colloquial, spoken voice.

- **Lexis**

  I did use some more formal lexis to give an overview of the morals of the situation.

- **Graphology and phonology**

  I used brackets to indicate comments made as asides and italics to show emphatic stress. These were performance features of oral narratives that I tried to recreate in my written narrative.

Assessing the commentary

Read the example commentary below on the roller skating story. It is about 500 words long, excluding any quotes. It refers to a redrafted version that added an ending and made some changes suggested in the previous sections. The teacher/moderator's comments show what is rewarded and why. Note that it is a 'model' example, illustrating what you should aim to produce and written by the writer of this book, not the writer of the original story.

I wanted to write a story based on a childhood experience of my own, so rather than record another person, I tried to tell the story as spontaneously as possible to a friend. I think such a realistic story would be of interest to other teenagers and young adults, who could identify with the main character and the situation. I
5 enclose a copy of a style model from a collection called 'Transforming Moments'. I think readers would enjoy the combination of humour and fear in the story. Most people remember a time when they felt bullied, or afraid of older kids. I also thought that the setting – a roller rink in the USA – had plenty of colour and interest. I spent my childhood in the States, so I am familiar with the scene and
10 the way people talk.

When I made written notes on the recording, I noticed several things that influenced my final written version. Although the climax seemed to be the attack by the older girls, I realised there was an interesting moral dilemma: was the main character – and Heidi – really an innocent victim?

15 My first draft had focused on the consequences of standing up to bullies, so I included lots of comments about my grandfather and his advice. Readers said there was generally too much 'telling' about the family background and not enough dramatic showing of the inciting moment. In my final draft I changed the focus to the attack itself. [example quoted] I left out the adult characters and developed
20 Heidi more.

My first draft was written in the first person. This is essentially my own perspective, so I found it a natural colloquial voice to use. [example quoted] Some comments that there was not enough crafting of the original oral story made me try different styles. The third person perspective was very flat in style, so I
25 abandoned that and tried to re-shape my first person point of view.

I decided to plunge in 'ultimas res' as a dramatic beginning. I dropped the hint that Heidi was not honest in the opening paragraph [example quoted] to foreshadow the ending. The style of this was the more formal voice of the older person looking back on the events [quote and example of lexis and grammar].

30 The bulk of the story concerned the attack at the skating rink. Here I redrafted to include much more description of the scene as well as dialogue between the girls. I think this 'showing' rather than 'telling' is effective.

I ended the story on a note of doubt. The main character is beginning to realise that Heidi is not the wonderful person she looked up to as a child. This ending
35 actually mirrors the structure of my oral version, though, at the time I thought it was a diversion that didn't really fit in.

I think the combination of a child's view of a situation with the more cynical view makes the story more satisfying for young adults.

Reference to the stimulus oral narrative explains some decisions about the plot structure.

Explains changes made in redrafting, with reference to relevant concepts about narrative techniques.

Shows awareness of the concepts of perspective and the different effects on style.

Shows awareness of overall structure and links this to comments at the level of lexis and grammar.

Evaluates own narrative techniques.

Explains the structure of the ending, comparing spoken and written versions.

Evaluates the effectiveness for purpose and target audience.

C Writing for a listening audience: scripted presentation

In this section you will learn how to write a script for something that audiences will listen to. You have to submit *either* a spoken presentation on a language topic or a dramatic monologue (see pages 142–155). In each case you will use your experience of listening to these genres to produce an effective script of your own. You may choose to test out your script on an audience before redrafting and writing up a final version. (You may also, if you choose, submit a recorded version of your monologue or presentation to show the moderator how the text works in its spoken form.) You will also show knowledge of the key concepts in English language by writing a commentary, explaining what choices you have made.

1 Introduction

Assessment objectives

Your scripted presentation is assessed through AO1 (5 marks), AO2 (5 marks) and AO4 (20 marks). Your commentary is assessed through AO1 (5 marks) and AO2 (5 marks).

AO1 and AO2 marks are awarded for your understanding of the key concepts of the English language and for your ability to show this knowledge by writing clearly about them in your commentary.

AO4 marks are awarded for writing an effective script for the topic, audience and purpose you have selected, informed by the key concepts you have learned.

What is meant by a 'spoken presentation'? It is:

- a talk or lecture – so it is *not* interactive like a lesson
- delivered by a single speaker
- often supported by multi-media aids (OHTs, handouts, digital presentation slides)
- to inform or instruct (with elements of entertainment and possibly persuasion)
- delivered to an audience present in the room (or occasionally broadcast on radio or television).

For this coursework task, there are additional requirements. The presentation must be scripted – so not delivered impromptu or based on brief notes. It must also be on a topic introduced as part of the AS English Language course, perhaps something controversial in the media. There should be between 500–1000 words on the page and the presentation should take about five to ten minutes to deliver.

You have to specify the audience you aim to address. It will help if you choose a local setting, for example, your classmates, prospective AS language students. You will be able to test the material on your audience and make revisions in the light of feedback comments. Ideally, you should deliver your own script, but you may use another person to read it for you. You can choose whether to record the presentation. The presence of cameras or recording equipment can be daunting, however.

Of all the coursework tasks, this is the writing and speaking skill you are most likely to use once A level studies are behind you. Spoken presentations are now a common requirement of most university courses, providing an alternative mode of assessment to essays and reports. Job interviews will often ask for a short presentation before the question and answer session. In the workplace, you may find that you are asked to deliver an oral presentation to colleagues or clients. This surge in popularity of spoken presentations has led to a small industry of advice on effective public speaking, generating manuals, DVDs, courses and even hypnotherapy to overcome fears!

As with all the coursework tasks, this section will take you through a recommended process of writing, beginning with your experience as a listener in this case, through choosing your topic to preparing your script. It will finish with advice on pulling together all the ideas gained into a final commentary for your folder. This section gives you examples and activities for these stages:

- researching the genre and analysing techniques of spoken presentations
- choosing your topic
- preparing a script, including any visual and audio aids
- testing and redrafting your script
- writing a commentary on your writing process, explaining the techniques you used to achieve your purposes for the stated audience.

2 Exploring the genre

In one sense, this is the genre you are most familiar with: over your 11 or more years of education, you have been on the receiving end of countless spoken presentations. The downside is that there is very little evidence of this genre in 'concrete' form – written scripts or spoken recordings. For the most part, you will need to explore your memory and begin to take notice of any future presentations. Here are two areas to begin with.

Although most lessons are interactive, there is often a period of 'chalk and talk', where the teacher spends uninterrupted time explaining or introducing the topic. If your school/college has assemblies, these might include a talk from a member of staff. There may be visiting speakers for some of your A level subjects or visits to conferences with a series of speakers.

You should also explore documentary programmes on television. Many of these use the full range of audio-visual techniques, but some rely on a single narrator for much of the information.

The next activity introduces an ongoing activity, which you will work on during your AS year as you attend conferences, watch recorded programmes or listen to talks on any of your AS subjects.

Activity 25

Compile a list of examples from your experience of one person speaking in a planned manner to inform an audience. For each example, note the topic, purpose and audience. Did they hold your interest? Was the information clear? How did they begin and end the talk? Did the speaker use any other aids such as handouts?

The next few pages focus on key areas of spoken presentations: the overall structure and the rapport with the audience.

Analysing structure and techniques

When you look at the overall structure of spoken presentations – the way they begin and end, and the organisation of material in the middle – you are analysing language use at the level of discourse. (See Unit 1, pages 56–61.)

Although you will find that there are as many different ways of organising a talk as there are different speakers, the advice given in manuals tends to follow this simple formula:

> Tell them what you are going to say; say it; tell them what you have said.

If you look again at an example you collected for Activity 25, you should find evidence of these three sections:

- **beginning**   outline aims, content
- **middle**   sequence of the main points, each explained/illustrated with examples
- **end**   summary of main points.

It may sound dull or obvious, but that is a useful general structure to follow when your main purpose is to provide clear information or instruction. You should have very good reasons for departing from it. You may think that your audience, for example, is already familiar with the topic and would feel patronised if you spelt out the details in such simple detail. Or your purpose may include an element of persuasion or entertainment, so you prefer to begin in a more unusual way to attract the audience's attention. Before you consider exceptions to the rule, it is important to understand why the standard structure of informative talks follows this pattern.

It is partly to do with the **channel** (the medium, in this case of sounds to communicate language via the sense of hearing). Speaking is transitory, with no chance to press a pause or rewind button. Research has shown that active listening (as opposed to simply hearing words) requires some preparation or prediction. A clear introduction, listing the scope of the talk, gets the listener ready by narrowing down the infinite field of possibilities.

Writing your commentary

- Make sure you keep notes on the key concepts in a log or journal as you work your way through the task. The 'Writing your commentary' boxes will remind you about this at important stages.

- Keep a record of scripted spoken presentations that you have listened to. What ideas did you get for effective techniques?

Independent research

Watch some of the programmes from *The Routes of English* by Melvyn Bragg on BBC Education. As well as the content, notice the way the information is presented for a listening audience.

Take it further

Read some chapters from *The Language Web: The Power and Problem of Words*, Jean Aitchison. These were first presented as a series of lectures (the 1996 BBC Reith Lectures), so you can consider the way the information is organised for a listening audience.

Key term

channel

Written texts do this as well with titles, headings and introductions. In fact, contemporary textbooks (with an informative or instructive purpose) borrow techniques from spoken language. Nowadays, you will often see a chapter begin with a clear summary of the aims and content. It might also end with a checklist of key terms or summary of points that have been introduced.

This basic structure is easier said than done. As a speaker, you have to be absolutely clear in your own mind what it is you want to say. Once you have worked this out, the scripting moves along quickly. Look at some examples of beginnings, middles and ends.

Tell them what you are going to say

This principle works well in various modes. If your purpose is primarily to provide clear detailed information to a group of people, it helps to orient the readers/listeners with an overview, rather than plunging straight into specific facts. Writers can use visual techniques – leaflets often begin with a contents list, for example. Speakers need to use different oral techniques to highlight and clarify points.

Activity 26

Below are three versions of 'beginnings' for informative texts on an aspect of intonation.

1   Which is the:

- script for a talk
- notes for the speaker
- textbook introduction.

2   What visual techniques does the writer use? How can the speaker achieve similar effects?

HRT

definition and examples

origins

implied meanings

Phonology

Key terms: intonation; rising; falling; high-rise intonation (HRT)

This section looks at common intonation patterns and explores the use of a rising intonation at the end of statements. It will attempt to answer these questions:

- what?
- where?
- who?
- how and why?

I am going to talk about a phenomenon known as HRT. Not the medical term, but a linguistic label – high rise intonation – used to describe the way people sometimes make statements sound like questions, by letting their voice go up at the end.

First I will define the term precisely with some examples.

Then I want to look at various theories about the origins of this way of speaking. Where did it come from? Who uses it?

Finally I will discuss its implied meanings. Why do people use HRT? What do they mean? What effect does HRT have on listeners?

Now look at an exception to the beginning–middle–end rule. In the BBC Radio 4 Reith lectures, Professor Jean Aitchison began Lecture 1 in the following way:

> Is our language sick? You might think so, judging from complaints: 'The standard of speech and pronunciation in England has declined so much … that one is almost ashamed to let foreigners hear it', moaned a writer in a daily newspaper. 'The language the world is crying out to learn is diseased in its own country', ranted another. 'We are plagued with idiots on radio and television who speak English like the dregs of humanity, to the detriment of our children,' lamented yet another.
>
> But why? At a time when English is a major world language, is it really in need of hospital treatment? A wide web of worries, a cobweb of old ideas, ensnares people as they think about language – any language – and this must be swept away.

Professor Jean Aitchison

Activity 27

1 What does Professor Aitchison tell the listener about the content of her talk?

2 What do you think her purpose is in beginning in this way?

Later, at the end of the next paragraph, she begins a clear summary:

> I shall look at some key linguistic topics which illustrate these themes: how language changes, how it began, how children learn it, and how we remember words.

Then she mentions the topic for the first talk: language change and states:

> Naturally, language changes all the time. This is a fact of life.

None of this quite follows the rule, but those lectures were so acclaimed that they have been made into a book. Remember that you must understand the conventions of a genre before you can take the risk of breaking with convention.

Say it

Let's return to the standard advice for the format of a spoken presentation. The 'middle', or main body, of your talk is the longest, most important part. You should divide it clearly into sections that match the claims in the introduction. So, in the example about HRT, the beginning promises the listener three things: definition, theories about origins and implied meanings.

A written text can use graphological features (see graphology in Unit 1, page 31) to signal discourse structure: punctuation and paragraphing, as well as font size and type. A speaker can use phonological features: pauses, volume, pitch, stress and intonation (see Unit 1, pages 39–40). But the actual pronunciation is not generally scripted: an effective speaker uses their voice to make the points clear and memorable. The writer of a presentation will use certain lexical items and grammatical structures to make the structure clear.

The term 'discourse marker' (see Unit 1, page 9) refers to words or phrases such as 'let me first say', 'moving on to my next point', which signal the structure. (An alternative term for this function is framing move; this is often used for more informal spoken language, such as the use of the words 'right' or 'OK' to signal a change of topic.) The introduction to a presentation might use the discourse markers 'first', 'then' and 'finally' to make the three-part structure clear. The main body of the talk should also use techniques to signal the structure of the argument. It is important, for example, to:

- highlight the main point
- to make it clear when you are adding some subsidiary points
- to signal that you are leaving the main track to mention a little anecdote
- to show that you are now moving on to a new point.

There are various ways of doing this in language, either at the level of graphology/phonology, lexis or grammar. For example:

- brackets, commas or dashes indicate that this part is an added explanation
- conjunctions (but, yet) indicate an opposing point
- (and, furthermore) indicate a similar point
- phrases such as 'for instance' indicate a specific example of a general point
- interrogatives can introduce a new discussion topic.

Activity 28

Read the script below for the middle of the presentation on HRT, started in Activity 27. It deals with the third main point: implied meanings. It will be easier if you either read the script aloud yourself or listen to someone reading it aloud.

1 Identify any words and phrases that function as discourse markers. What do they signal to the listeners? The first one has been done for you.

2 What graphological features (spelling, punctuation, paragraphing, etc) indicate the way this would be spoken aloud? One has been done as an example.

> *Indicates that the speaker is now moving on to the first main point.*

> *To be pronounced as a quotation, perhaps with a 'rabbit ears' sign.*

So what does HRT mean? The first thing to say is that most people claim to be irritated by it. Those people that use it must be oblivious that they do. It is described as a 'habit', a word which generally has negative connotations, suggesting something repeated mindlessly. And why are they so irritated? I suggest – and this is simply my take on the subject – that it's because this habit is a recent change, and all changes tend to cause anxiety. Not only is it new, but it is associated with 'outsiders'. It is, quite simply, 'not British'! And yet, young people, especially young females, are adopting these alien ways. You can see how these circumstances play on all the usual fears, whether it's about food, clothing, sexual behaviour … and so on.

If a certain style is associated with the young and with females, this can have two very different effects: either seen as desirable, or seen as powerless. In this case, I feel the evidence points more to the 'powerless' end of the spectrum. Indeed, if you look at the quotes on your handout, the reactions to HRT often use words like 'nervous tic' or 'afflicted'. The connotations are of a physical impediment.

That seems to be it, then. HRT is used predominantly by young females, copying traits originating in USA or Australia, signifying their slavish aping of these popular cultures and marking them out as lacking in conviction.

But surely we could take a more open-minded look at this recent phenomenon. Rather than making assertive statements, these speakers offer their point of view in a tentative manner that allows listeners the space to join the discussion. I suggest that HRT is a democratic intonation pattern!

Tell them what you said

If you are going to follow the standard recommended structure, the end of a spoken presentation is easy to write as it must be virtually the same as the beginning and follow the order of the main sections of the middle. It is a matter of personal style whether a speaker chooses to end with a flourish or to keep it plain and simple. The listeners' main needs – getting information or instruction – are met by a plain, simple recap of the main points.

You may think it is important that the audience leave feeling entertained as well. In that case, you would aim to add something a little different. Do not forget your main purpose, however. Think back to your examples of spoken presentations (in Activity 25). Were there any lively or amusing ways of ending? Here is the way Professor Aitchison rounds off the topic of her first Reith lecture, before offering a 'trailer' for the next one. The title was 'A web of worries' and she introduced the main topic as – worries about language change.

> Variation in speech is the norm. Our linguistic wardrobe contains a range of speech styles, which we suit to the occasion. Toddlers and tax-inspectors need to be addressed in different ways. Tennis-players, cricketers and taxi-drivers each have their own specialised vocabulary, some words of which are now widely used. Change often happens when one particular variant expands its usage, and spreads across a broader area. But which variants should be used where and when still causes arguments as sharp as barbed wire, especially as nowadays being 'matey' is often more important than being 'proper', resulting in increasing approval of informal styles of speech, including swearing.

Activity 29

1 Script two endings for the talk on HRT, one plain and simple, the other more entertaining.

2 Compare your ending with others. Comment on the effectiveness of each one.

Creating rapport with the audience

Getting the style right is almost as important as the structure of a talk and is part of the assessment of this task.

As a listener to presentations, you will have experienced the full range – from lively and effective, through dull and confusing, to patronising and pointless. A clear structure is the essential skeleton for any informative talk. But the human touch is also significant. There are all sorts of electronic forms of teaching materials, but – even though brilliantly researched and produced – people tend to respond better to a real person, and the presence of other students.

You should think about the profile of your audience:

- who are they – their background, interests, needs, etc
- where are they – in a familiar situation, large lecture hall, new city, etc
- what is their purpose in coming to listen?

But remember that there is more to tenor than just the audience. Also consider the addresse–addressee relationship. Who are you – an expert, a colleague? And why should they listen to you?

You will remember speakers who assumed you knew nothing and others who thought you understood far more than you did. It can be irritating to hear a speaker make assumptions about your collective lifestyle, for example, 'For all you little ladies out there, who love a bit of pampering!'

Your experience should make you an expert in addressing a teenage audience. Think about what tenor is – and is not – effective between the speaker and this type of audience.

Writing your commentary

You will be commenting on how your writing is informed by audience needs, so make sure you keep a note of your decisions about establishing an effective rapport with your target audience.

Independent research

Use a search engine to access the *How to Give a Bad Talk* website. How would you rank the ten pitfalls?

Activity 30

1 Work in groups and devise a list of things to avoid when giving a spoken presentation. You might want to consider the effectiveness of techniques such as alliteration, humour or references to youth culture.

2 Then present your points in an ironic way – advise the audience to do what you really think they should avoid. For example, 'Always start your talk with an apology, like this:

3 Feedback and come up with your class's top ten tips.

- Sorry, but …
- I know this subject isn't interesting …
- I don't really know much about it …

- I'm very nervous/not good at speaking in public …
- I've forgotten my notes/the handouts …
- You probably think 'what's this idiot droning on about?' …

The question of how to build rapport is not only a linguistic one, although language use plays a part. Areas such as psychology and social anthropology probably have as many (or as few) useful pointers to give you on this area. In a sense, you are on your own here. That need not cause dismay – you are as much an expert as your teachers and moderators. The old proverb, 'the proof of the pudding is in the eating' is relevant here. You can judge the value of any techniques by trying them out and seeing what reaction you get.

Read through this list of advice suggested by an experienced speaker at student conferences. How far do you think these are likely to be effective techniques?

- People make judgements on the basis on the first few seconds of an encounter – make sure your opening words are spot on.
- Forget the triumph of style over substance – the content and ideas are more important than any flashy tricks.
- Focus your attention on the audience – the talk is for their benefit, not yours.
- Remember the Chinese proverb 'I hear and I forget, I see and I remember, I do and I understand' – create active opportunities for the audience to do things, even if only to answer a question.
- Endings should be prompt and sweet – always finish on time and leave them with a feeling of confidence, in you, in themselves, in the subject.

---

3 Choosing a topic

One of the biggest problems at the planning stage is trying to cover too much. If you go on to study A2 English Language, this issue will come up in your choice for the coursework investigation. You might begin with a topic you are broadly interested in, for example, language and gender. But, whole books have been written on this subject; a couple of thousand words can only scratch the surface. Think small!

The following activity was used on a training course for presenters on BBC Radio Sheffield.

Activity 31

1   Assign one of these topics to each person in the group, either:
    • a colour of the rainbow – red, orange, yellow, green, blue, indigo, violet, or
    • a day of the week – Monday, Tuesday, etc.

2   Write a script on your topic that takes *exactly* two minutes to read aloud.

3   Each person should read their script. The others will listen and notice whether the timing was exact.

4   Give feedback comments on the experience. How difficult or easy was the scripting and timing? How were your nerves as a public speaker?

Narrowing the focus

If you have no particular topic in mind, use the following three headings to remind yourself of the scope of the course:

• key constituents
• contextual factors
• wider social context.

1	Let's say you are interested in the key *constituents* of language.

↓

2	From this area, you pick *grammar*.

↓

3	You could narrow this down further by picking one aspect of grammar – *adverbs*.

↓

4	Now you need to find a particular focus or an angle on the topic. It is time to start thinking in question form: what is the *function* of adverbs?

↓

5	You might narrow it down even further and pinpoint one specific function – to reveal the *attitudes* of the speaker or writer.

Independent research

If you wonder how single words could be interesting as a topic, read the article by Alison Ross in *emagazine*, issue 14, December 2001 or read Michael Rosen's lively comments on the word 'do' in *emagazine*, issue 18, December 2002.

Activity 32 Follow similar steps to narrow the focus on context or wider social context.

This process may have led you from an abstract concept to a specific topic or question that intrigues you. But it is probably better to begin with issues that are of current interest. Media debates should provide some starting points. Here are some recent (in 2007) examples from daily newspapers.

- Do women really talk more than men?
- Should the new voice for the speaking clock have a regional accent?
- Why do people use text messaging for sensitive news?
- Why do interviewers interrupt so much? (John Humphrys' interviewing style)

You can use a search engine to find newspaper articles on these or other language debates. The archives generally go back for several years.

So far, the emphasis has been on using effective techniques to make a spoken presentation clear and lively. But this task can be more straightforward or challenging depending on the topic.

Activity 33

Compare the following ideas for talks to AS students.

a What abbreviations do young people use in text messages? (based on a list from a newspaper article)

b How widespread is the use of abbreviations in text messaging? (based on data from 20 people, including both genders and different age groups)

c What are the attitudes to Estuary English? (based on handouts provided by the teacher and a survey of the class)

d Is there such a variety as Estuary English? (based on own research on the internet and recordings of speakers)

The top band of marks refers to an *ambitious* language topic and *research*. You will see that the second topic in each case introduces new ideas to the audience and involves more independent research. However, you must be careful not to choose such a difficult topic that you fail to get it across to your audience in an effective way. You can see that choice of appropriate topic is a really important factor in this task.

Independent research

For more ideas for spoken presentations, read some popular language books. Perhaps the most accessible is *Mother Tongue: The English Language*, Bill Bryson. Lynne Truss has produced a follow-up to her bestselling *Eats Shoots and Leaves* called *The Girl's Like Spaghetti: Why, you can't manage without Apostrophes!* Try to listen to recordings of Melvyn Bragg's BBC radio series or read the book version, *The Routes of English*.

Activity 34

1 Working in groups, make sure each person gets a different daily newspaper. You could use an online edition.

2 Read through to find any stories with a language comment. (You may find that the tabloids have little of interest to language students.)

Writing your commentary

Keep a record of all the reading and research you have done. You will need to present an accurate bibliography for the topic of your spoken presentation. For this, you should list all websites, books, newspapers, TV and radio programmes.

4 Preparing a script

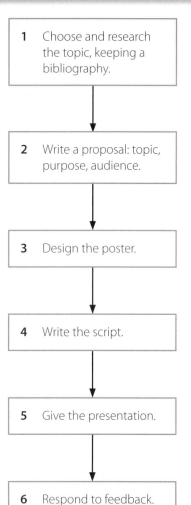

1. Choose and research the topic, keeping a bibliography.

2. Write a proposal: topic, purpose, audience.

3. Design the poster.

4. Write the script.

5. Give the presentation.

6. Respond to feedback.

As with all writing tasks, you need to practise the skills before you produce the final version of the script. This genre (spoken presentation) is probably less familiar to you than the other three tasks (journalism interview, narrative, dramatic monologue) and for this reason, a dry run would be useful.

A poster presentation is a mini version of the full task. It allows you to experiment with a potential topic and develop some of the necessary techniques. A poster presentation, as its name suggests, is based around a poster or billboard. The poster provides all your visual input: a picture, a title, diagrams, key points. Your audience gathers around the poster as you talk them through the topic.

You should follow the process in the margin in preparation for both the dry run and your final presentation.

Here is an example:

> **Topic:** The media's fascination with celebrity, and what this reveals about our society's underlying attitudes and values. (*The Practice of Critical Discourse Analysis: An Introduction*, Bloor and Bloor; en.wikipedia.org)
>
> **Proposal:** I want to provide an interesting introduction for AS students to critical discourse analysis, by focusing on the media obsession with trivial news about the royal family.
>
> **Poster design:** see below
>
> **Write script:** see Page 137

Princes are still powerful

'Prince William & Kate Middleton Head to Scotland'
(*The People*, 13 October 2007)

So?

What is discourse?

'communicative practices expressing the interests and characteristic 'ways of seeing and saying' of a particular socio-historical group or institution; these are always definable in terms of relative power or powerlessness.' (Rob Pope)

What is critical discourse analysis?

It views 'language as a form of social practice' (*Language and Power*, Fairclough) and focuses on the ways social and political domination is reproduced by text and talk.

Script

On a day when wars raged, hundreds starved and scientists made medical advances, why was the break-up of a lad and lass front-page news?

I am talking, of course, about Kate Middleton and Prince William. I know he is heir to the throne, but this isn't even a birth, marriage or death. The recurring choice of trivial news – provided it is associated with celebrity – is significant for those interested in English language. We are looking at language here, not at the level of pronunciation, vocabulary or grammar, but at language in its widest sense: the whole text in its full social context.

This definition of discourse is probably familiar to most A-level students. No longer do we analyse texts without thinking about:

- what they are – the text type or genre
- what they are trying to achieve – the purpose, or function
- who is involved – the writer and reader, and their relationship, or tenor.

We look at the overall structure: how the text begins, what features make the progression clear, how the text ends. The word 'discourse' often refers to spoken language, and the study of the way people interact.

So, how does a front-page news story about William and Kate <u>interact</u> with the reader? It <u>assumes</u> that the reader is interested in their relationship. It <u>implies</u> that it is important.

It is useful to think of another part of the definition of discourse:

'communicative practices expressing the interests and characteristic 'ways of seeing and saying' of a particular socio-historical group or institution; these are always definable in terms of relative power or powerlessness.' (Rob Pope)

Everyone knows that the 'communicative practices' of tabloid newspapers show their obsession with sex, and, more recently, with celebrity. But it is not only the tabloids that run stories about the royal family in a lead position. *The Guardian*, the *Independent*, *The Times*, the *Telegraph* have regularly placed Diana or her sons on the front page and many more inside. BBC Radio 4, considered so dull and middle-class by most students, also featured this story prominently.

As for questions of 'relative power', the monarchy may have lost its power in any real sense, but the media are only reflecting the way we, the 'masses', still look up to them, anxious for any little titbit thrown in our direction.

Giving the presentation

When it comes to the point of 'going live' with your presentation, you do have a few options. You can, if you wish, ask another person to present the script for you – you are assessed on your ability to write for a listening audience, not your performance skills. You may choose to record the presentation, so that you can assess how effective it is as spoken language.

Responding to feedback

The experience of giving a talk often provides all the feedback you need. A sensitive speaker can sense the points where the audience is losing interest, where it needs to slow down or speed up. If you also ask the audience to summarise what they learned from your presentation, this will give you some ideas about the structure – perhaps you need to signal the main points more clearly. The example above chose not to follow the standard three-part structure, as the purpose was to stimulate interest with provocative ideas. The writer might choose to add more clarity on a redraft.

Activity 35

1   Read the script for a presentation below or listen to someone reading it aloud.

2   Rate the script on a scale of 1 to 10 for:

- **topic**   Is it suitable for AS English Language? Is it well researched?
- **purpose**   Does it give clear information? Is it lively and interesting?
- **audience**   Does it have an effective rapport with the audience of AS students?
- **structure**   Is there clear signalling of the beginning, main points and end?
- **techniques** Does it use audio or visual aids (handouts, slides, etc)?

3   Then see if you agree with the moderator's comments.

Plain English

Speech

Good morning/afternoon. Many of you here will no doubt be wondering and thinking 'What exactly is Plain English?' Well, the phrase 'plain language' (meaning the same
5   thing) may be more familiar to you and is described as a communication style that focuses on considering the audience's needs when writing. It recommends avoiding unnecessary words and avoiding jargon, technical terms, and long and ambiguous sentences. Furthermore it does not only focus on the lexis used but also on the presentation and layout.

10 It means that any confusion that may occur within society as a result of complex language used by organisations such as the government will no longer. It is estimated that the cost of confusion incurred is £600m and with the use of Plain English much of this unnecessary cost would be avoided.

The Plain English Campaign was established in 1979 after founder Chrissie Maher
15 OBE publicly shredded hundreds of official documents in Parliament Square, London in protest at the unnecessary complexity of the language used in government documents. The campaign organisation has since aided the UK government so that the public information they produce is as clear as possible. The campaign is not only in the UK. In fact, the campaign has more than 11,000 members ranging across 80
20 countries. It is also very established and recognised, reassuring the public that if the campaign's distinctive 'Crystal Mark' is on a document, it is written in Plain English. This has been a big step forward for the campaign as it now means that it is recognised nationally and internationally.

Now, many of you will have heard and possibly used the term 'gobbledygook'. It
25 was a phrase used widely by the campaign and refers to unnecessary terminology that could confuse people. A nurse who emailed the campaign had received a memo that was in gobbledygook. She said that this 'makes us feel hoodwinked, inferior, definitely frustrated and angry, and it causes a divide between us and the writer.' I have here an example of what she is referring to: 'At base level, this just comes
30 down to homogenised asset innovation.' I don't know about you, but it took me a few attempts at reading this before I eventually understood it. Now imagine a whole letter written like that – very confusing! In my opinion, this phrase could be re-written as 'working more efficiently'. This way, everybody in the business world understands clearly and there will be no confusion.

35 Now we have established what we should not use, let me give you a guide on how English can be written using Plain English. First, use short sentences. By doing this, the point you are trying to make can, in most cases, be delivered in a more direct, concise way where the reader can understand clearly what is meant to be understood.

40 Second, use 'you' and 'we'. If in a business situation, this makes the business feel more united as it includes everybody together. By referring to people in the third person, for example as 'the HR department', there is no link between different areas of a business. While this might sound funny now, if introduced and used by

everybody, it could create a unity throughout the business that makes a lot of
45 difference.

Presentation is another key factor in Plain English. It is not only the language used
but also the way it is presented. Huge blocks of text are very unappealing to the
eye. By breaking it up, with gaps between paragraphs and lists, readers will be
encouraged to read on, thinking about and digesting the information they have just
50 read. Also, when you are trying to emphasise a point try not to use capital letters
as it means you are shouting. Use bold instead. This is much clearer and easier on
the eye as capital letters can be confusing. Layout is also extremely important.
Letters should be written so that they are easy to read. Do not fill space for the
sake of it, but instead try to leave clear gaps. Titles should not be overwhelmingly
55 large but should be larger than the main bulk of the text in order to differentiate
the two. You could also use lists, which are excellent for splitting information
up while also giving clear concise information. Lists are brilliant for instructions
are there is no way that they can be argued with. Lists of items to be taken on a
holiday, for example, are clear and much more user-friendly as they can be ticked
60 off.

Plain English also encourages the use of positive language and, at all costs, avoiding
negative language. A phrase written negatively, such as: 'If you don't renew your
membership, we won't allow you to use the equipment' could be threatening for the
reader and discourage them to renew their membership. By writing this phrase
65 using positive language, for example 'Please renew your membership so that you
can continue to use the equipment at your leisure', it will encourage the reader
to renew their membership as it seems that they will gain great benefits if they
do. You will always get a better response if you emphasise the positive side of a
situation.

70 Well I hope you all now have a good idea and understanding of Plain English and the
campaign. Please feel free to ask me any questions you may have and I will do my
best to answer them! Thank you.

Teacher/moderator comments

This is an appropriate topic, with some interesting research clearly explained. There is a respectful rapport established at the beginning and end.

In order to achieve top band marks, there needs to be more awareness of the genre. This text probably works better on the page, as some of the complex sentences need to be read a second or third time. The style in the first half is more suitable for a written essay. It becomes more effective as a spoken text in the latter half, where there are some lively examples to illustrate the points.

A redraft should include more interactive techniques (questions, direct address) at the beginning to capture interest immediately. The writer should include more visual aids to add variety of input and improve the clarity of information.

It is significant that the writer called the text a 'speech'. This suggests a one-way monologue, using voice only. The next part looks at possibilities for including more than just a single voice.

5 Using multi-media and visual aids

The mark scheme refers to the use of techniques such as visual aids or even the use of digital slides (eg PowerPoint), which can include audio and visual clips. Remember that it is the ideas in your presentation that carry most weight, so do not rely on flashy gimmicks to dazzle the audience. A handout or simple visual aid will meet the criteria for the top band, if it is effective.

Let's take the written script from Activity 35 and see how the use of other aids could improve its effectiveness. Possible aids might include:

- printed handout – A4 typewritten, with clear layout
- OHTs – transparencies with visual material to use on an overhead projector
- flipchart – usually only used to add impromptu written material for small groups
- digital slide show – using software to create, store and project material onto a screen.

Now look at the 'bare bones' of the presentation. This is a useful exercise when you have written your first draft. Make a summary of the main points in each paragraph and check that they flow from one to another in a logical order. The summary can be used as your notes for the talk.

Activity 36

What aids could you use to illustrate or support some of these sections of the talk?

What is Plain English?

- avoid unnecessary words, jargon (lexis)
- avoid long, ambiguous sentences (grammar)
- improve presentation and layout (graphology)

Benefits: £600m costs
History of campaign
Gobbledygook: examples

Style guide

- use short sentences
- use personal pronouns: you, we (not third person)

Presentation advice

- break up text – paragraphs, lists
- emphasis – bold, not capitals
- white space
- titles
- lists

6 Writing your commentary

Your commentary should be about 500 words long (but no more), so you need to be concise and to the point. Your final commentary should include an explanation of these three areas:

- the topic you chose, why and how you researched it
- how you crafted your final written version to achieve your purposes for the stated audience
- what you learned about this genre from studying examples of spoken presentations and the use of multi-media aids.

The main focus of your commentary is on your final written script for the presentation, so this section should be the longest. Explain some significant language choices that you made in order to achieve the particular effects in this genre for your intended audience and purpose. Try to comment on various levels of language as the mark scheme rewards this. You do not need to use the general terms (pragmatics, discourse, grammar, lexis, phonology) as long as you are making comments on these aspects. For example:

- **Discourse**   How did you structure the presentation: using or changing the standard format? What discourse markers did you use to signal the structure? What rapport did you establish between speaker and audience?

- **Grammar**   What sentence structures did you use in order to make it particularly effective as spoken information?

- **Lexis, morphology and semantics**

  What technical jargon did you use and why? Did you use more colloquial semantic fields? What was your purpose?

- **Graphology and phonology**

  How did you design the presentation of any visual aids for maximum clarity and interest? Did you consider any aspects of spoken delivery when making (or listening to a recording of) your presentation?

Assessment objectives

You can earn top marks for your commentary by:

- choosing a range of appropriate terminology to discuss your own language use (including grammar, discourse and pragmatics) (AO1)
- explaining and evaluating the impact of a range of linguistic choices in the stimulus texts and your own writing (AO2).

Assessing the commentary

Read the example commentary below on the Plain English presentation. It was written as a first draft, before including any multi-media aids. The teacher/moderator comments indicate that there is some awareness of style, but a tendency to make simple, general claims. There is no reference to any style models.

In order for this speech to be successful I had to take into account a number of features. The main purpose of the speech was to inform and also partially to entertain as I did not want the audience to become bored as the subject was not the most interesting and not to everybody's
5 interests.

The tone of the speech was informal as the age range within the audience was unknown and could have been quite broad. An informal tone was taken so that it would appeal to most of the audience. The informality also contributes to the entertaining element within the speech.

10 Due to the informality, the lexis was mainly monosyllabic and disyllabic. This meant that all age ranges will gain an understanding. However, there were a few exceptions where polysyllabic lexis was used. Words such as 'unnecessary' and 'complexity' are more complex but are still accessible to most of the audience.

15 Throughout the speech I was directly addressing the audience in a manner where they felt that they had to continue to listen, for example, 'Many of you here will no doubt ...' The continuous involvement meant that they could not stop listening and felt more involved and part of the speech. Furthermore the use of rhetorical questions meant that the audience
20 had to think about what I was saying in the speech and they therefore understood it much more. An example of this is: 'what exactly is Plain English?' In this example, which was towards the beginning of the speech, much of the audience would not have known what Plain English was, so would now listen to the explanation in much more detail.

25 The use of mainly declarative sentences throughout helped to fulfil the purpose of the speech, which was to inform. Declarative sentences give mainly fact and statements in a manner where they are easy for the listener to understand. If I was to use imperatives, which would also give fact; the listener would have felt on edge as imperatives are often
30 commands which are not as friendly. An example of a declarative sentence is: 'You will always get a better response if you emphasise the positive side of a situation.' I have also included a number of simple sentences to break the speech up. Although simple sentences would have more effect in written examples, it does break up the speech and allows more pauses
35 for the speaker, for example 'Presentation is another key factor in Plain English.' Simple sentences also get straight to the point and I used them mainly as the opening sentence to a new topic area in the speech. It also made it much clearer to the audience when there was a topic shift.

Premodification was used so that added detail could be given to the
40 audience and also to emphasise a point. By saying 'extremely important' it highlights that this issue cannot be overlooked. By using premodification it does mean that the audience will take more notice and will also make them continue to listen as they want to know the reasons behind it.

Overall, the speech was written in an informal manner so that it appealed
45 to as much of the audience as possible, and also so that it was more entertaining. The use of features such as rhetorical questions and also directly addressing the audience meant that they were listening all the time and remained focused.

Explains purpose and topic of talk with understanding of multi-functional texts.

General awareness of register, relating purpose and audience to style. Needs to be more specific about the audience.

Gives general examples of informal lexis being short words. Not entirely valid point or accurate, however (many polysyllabic words).

Comments on tenor and discourse: pronouns and questions, with quotations.

Uses precise terminology for grammar: declarative, imperative, simple sentence.

Precise terminology, but makes a minor, unconvincing point about effect. Other techniques would be much more effective to emphasise points and make audience take notice.

Picks out two general points as evidence of success. A more critical approach would show more understanding. This speech is not really informal overall and there could be more use of interactive features such as questions.

D Writing for a listening audience: dramatic monologue

In this section you will learn how to write a script for something that audiences will listen to. You have to submit either a spoken presentation (see pages 128–141) or a dramatic monologue. In each case you will use your experience of listening to these genres to produce an effective script of your own. You may choose to test out your script on an audience before redrafting and writing up a final version. You may, if you choose, submit a recorded version of your monologue or presentation to show the moderator how the text works in its spoken form. You will also show knowledge of the key concepts in English language by writing a commentary explaining what choices you have made.

1 Introduction

Key terms

monologue

idiolect

sub-text

Writing your commentary

- Keep notes in a log or journal as you work towards the final draft of your monologue. In your commentary, you will explain what you learned during the process, as well as the techniques you actually used in your writing.

- Make sure you keep notes on the key concepts in a log or journal as you work your way through the task. The 'Writing your commentary' boxes will remind you about this at important stages.

A **monologue** is a discourse of *one* speaker, ranging from a person alone speaking to themselves, to one person addressing a large public audience. So what is a *dramatic* monologue? For the purposes of this coursework task, the requirements are that it must be scripted for a single voice to perform to a listening or watching audience. It must also have an entertaining purpose and be 500–1000 words long. It will help you in redrafting your monologue if you can get someone to perform and record it, but this is not an essential requirement.

For Unit 1, you studied **idiolect** – the way each individual's language use can be like a fingerprint or signature (see pages 68–69). You also looked at more general characteristics, such as the distinctive features of a particular regional dialect, or of a social class, occupation, age group or gender. This coursework task will develop your understanding of these concepts. You will explore ways that dramatic monologues use the relationship between language and identity to create characters.

In Unit 1, you also studied pragmatics – the ways in which meanings are implied in language use (see pages 84–87). Effective scripts leave much unsaid, for example characters indirectly reveal hints of their motives. The playwright Harold Pinter uses the literary term '**sub-text**' to refer to underlying (or 'pragmatic') meanings:

> It is the pause which shows to the audience that the real preoccupation of the characters, the unspoken subtext, is going on beneath the surface, but that it is unable to come into the open.

Assessment objectives

Your script for a dramatic monologue is assessed through AO1 (5 marks), AO2 (5 marks) and AO4 (20 marks). Your commentary is assessed through AO1 (5 marks) and AO2 (5 marks).

AO1 and AO2 marks are awarded for your understanding of the key concepts of the English language and for your ability to show this knowledge by writing clearly about them in your commentary.

AO4 marks are awarded for writing an effective drama script for the character, audience and purpose you have selected, informed by the key concepts you have learned.

This section will take you through the process of writing, from your experience of listening to dramatic monologue, through choice of character and situation to the scripting of a final draft for your folder. This process will provide ideas for your commentary, which will be brought together in the last part. This section gives you examples and activities for these stages:

- researching and analysing the genre
- devising a character and situation
- writing and redrafting your script
- writing your commentary.

2 Exploring the genre

The most famous dramatic monologues are probably *Talking Heads*, written by Alan Bennett and performed by various actors on television. This part will introduce some shorter examples by less well-known writers. (Although all the examples are monologues, in the sense that each one is the voice of a single character, some extracts are taken from longer drama scripts or comic sketches which involve other characters.)

Exploring idiolect

The idea of a distinctive 'voice-print' is used by dramatists (and novelists) to create fictional characters. To some extent, this relies on stereotypes, rather than fully rounded, realistic characters. So, in fiction, we have stock characters, such as the smooth villain, the innocent girl. Comic sketches use parody to portray the typical schoolteacher, football manager, checkout girl, farmhand, public-school boy, IT geek, etc. For example, the comedian Peter Cook portrays an arrogant judge in the following extract. (You can watch and listen to all four characters that Peter Cook portrays on www.youtube.com; search for Clive Anderson Talks Back.)

Alan Bennett

apparently inarticulate discourse with many filled pauses

speaking slowly and hesitantly

> I hanged a boy at school for erm,
> it was really <u>er</u>, <u>dumb insolence</u>
> was the <u>er</u>, he was looking at me
> in that particular way, you know,
> irritating look and <u>er</u>, when I say
> I hung him – <u>or is it hanged</u>, I
> never know which – well I <u>strung</u>
> <u>him up</u>.

lexis indicates age and class of speaker

repeated use of filled pauses shows he is determined to hold the floor

inappropriate grammatical quibble

extreme contrast when collocated with 'irritating'

Independent research

Watch some of Alan Bennett's *Talking Heads* monologues on DVD. You could also read the scripts (BBC Books, 1988).

The annotations pinpoint revealing features of language use at various levels. Notice that there are no comments on graphology, as this version is a transcript, not a script designed by the author, so comments about the visual form are irrelevant. Overall you might move on to pragmatics and comment on the implications of his muddled manner of expression – perhaps it suggests an underlying lack of honesty.

In Unit 1, you studied the presentation of self, including such aspects as gender, age, occupation and region (see page 65–89). In addition, the section on idiolect refers to the way style can reflect an individual, including a particular personality. The next activity asks you to use your intuitive awareness, as well as any skills developed by language study.

Take it further

Read some dramatic monologues by the poet Robert Browning, eg 'My Last Duchess', 'Fra Lippo Lippi', 'Porphyria's Lover'. What do you think is dramatic about these poems? What sort of character is created by the monologue? What situation is the character in? Do you think these poems would be effective as a spoken performance?

Activity 37

Read the following first six short extracts.

1. What can you tell about the characters – gender, age, occupation, region, personality, etc?

2. Match the voice in the 'mystery' text G to one of the six characters identified from extracts A–F. Explain your decision by referring to language features. (This is like one of the questions in Section A of the Unit 1 exam – see page 63.)

A

So I put the kettle on and start setting up the shop. Delivery had come over the weekend and the Saturday girl with the pink hair had made a right pig's ear of my lovely display, god bless her, she just doesn't know any better, but I really can't abide her dungarees – dungarees? I can't see that catching on. Makes her look a bit ... funny, y' know? Anyway, what'm I on about? Oh that's right, so I walk over to the window display to sort out her dodgy handicraft – and no word of a lie, I wish I were lying, there's a bloody great puddle under the mannequin with the dodgy perm!

B

The glamour of a caped crusader's life has worn thin and I am no longer satisfied with the inequalities within our working relationship. A super side-kick can only take so much. I am 28 years old and, to be honest, the tights and cape have become a social embarrassment. The girls only talk to me to get to you. They love that mean mysterious man in black look. That's another thing. Why are you the one who gets to wear black, while I prance around in crimson and green? I might as well wear sequins and a feather boa! The humiliation of answering to the name 'Boy Wonder' at my age can damage a man's self respect.

C

Have you heard about Billy? Apparently he was so outrageous and out of it at Becky's party, that Becky's Dad had to phone his Dad and get him to come and get him out of the cellar, because he wouldn't come out on his own, because he was so out of it. It's odd 'cos Becky hasn't got a cellar. I think that Billy was fine and that Becky's Dad was so out of it that he started seeing stuff and thought they had a cellar when they don't. Becky's Mum's mad anyway.

D

It's funny you should mention that though, 'cause I was talking to my daughter last week, and it turns out she's going on holiday to Morocco! Funny place to go I thought, but then she's like that, quite adventurous really, she drinks milk made out of rice! Well, she has to get herself jabbed you see, and I says to her, I says, 'Why don't you come with me on Thursday, see Dr Barnett and we'll keep each other company', she says, 'No mum, you can't get it on the NHS', I says 'What d'ya mean', she says 'You have to go Private!'

E

You're right, in a way. You didn't do anything. They'll be able to write that on your tombstone. You don't oversleep; you don't lose or forget thing;, you don't make a mess; you don't skip meals, then gorge on crisps and chocolate; you don't fall out with your friends, drink too much, stay up all night and sleep all day.
And I guess that's my problem - I'm always doing something, and often it's the wrong thing. Because, somehow, I feel that I am not the same. I am different, an alien, who has to concentrate all the time to pass for normal.
If you really did learn by your mistakes, I'd have a PhD in life, or something.
But it doesn't work like that. Where are the happy endings in life? You see, I don't find out that it's a mistake, until it's too late.

F

Statistics show that this year's intake of sinners has fallen again. Our main competitor has been gaining ground again. We have to move with the times. The 1980s with its 'Greed is Good' philosophy has gone.
We are losing popularity with the young in particular and cannot allow this dangerous upward spiral in moral values to continue. The 'Diana' effect has seriously undermined our stock and, other than sending a few more journalists into the world, we must pull ourselves out of this rut. I am pleased to report that today's youth are reacting very well to the Alco-pops campaign and plans for Alco-sweets are already underway.
On the down-side, the big corporations, which used to be our main allies, are going for the touchy-feely mentality. Body Shop, Coca-Cola and even Sony are cleaning up their act and are actually refusing to exploit any third world countries. At least Virgin trains, with their consistently late departures, have been sending a steady stream of blasphemers in our direction.

G

You will not believe the day I had! So I came in this morning at 8:30 – no hang about it was 8:45, I got waylaid when I bumped into our Colin's ex on her way to salon to get her eyelashes permed, she's looking really lovely since she got that job at M-power, or whatever you call it. Anyways, I get in at 8:45, went into back room, put kettle on, didn't think anything of it. No – it was 8:30, I remember now! I'd got the early bus in as I woke at 7 from next door's builders banging two bricks together outside my bedroom window. Anyway, it doesn't matter …

Independent research

Go to www.youtube.com to see some of these comic monologues in action; search for Peter Cook with Clive Anderson or the Rowan Atkinson 'Hell' sketch.

Representing the spoken voice on the page

Standard spelling and punctuation represent a general, conventional pronunciation of words and sentences – a question mark indicating a rising intonation on a question, for example (see more on graphology, pages 31–34). But a scriptwriter often wants to indicate particular sound qualities of a person's speech: their accent, volume, stress, pitch and intonation.

Activity 38

Read the following extracts from *Radioactive Monologues for Women – for Radio, Stage and Screen*, M. Calderone and M. Le Conte. If possible, listen to someone reading each one aloud.

1   What does the voice convey about the character?

2   Then look at the script on the page. What non-standard spelling is used to convey a particular voice?

3   What punctuation is used to convey a particular voice?

A

All make sense in the end. You n'me. Our own little home. Do it up a bit, like. Lick o'paint. Put a throw over that thing. Frame on picture there. Love that picture. Sez somethin', dunt it? Really somert special about that. Only ever notice it when I'm … (Pause.) Be able to decorate won't we? Once we're settled. Nice blue carpet. Blue or green at any rate, long
5 as it's furry. Able to walk barefoot then. Barefoot in us dressin' gowns. Couple o' lamps. Bookshelf. Sofa. Coffee table. Spiderplant. Video. Hoover. Keep it all clean. Washin' machine. Go Kwik Save on Sunday. Economise. (Pause.)

From *Redundant* by Leo Butler

B

What? Look at what? What card? Where?

Ink blots! Oh my God, it's the ink blots! He's giving me the ink blots! I knew it!

What can I see? Well, that's a … it's a sort of … well … it looks like a kind of …

I mustn't see any blood! I mustn't see any phallic symbols, or violence, or threatening
5 *clouds, or …*

Two drunken men! It's two drunken men fighting, isn't it? No, no, no! I don't mean that!

No violence!

From 'Blots', from *Listen to This* by Michael Frayn

C

And we leaned – he leaned – I set my back against the rail and it … just … We were gone: we were over. I saw us leave the window. I looked – past him, my hands reached past him to try to hold something, there wasn't anything … just blue … And I didn't black out. I thought – very clearly … This is bad. This is real. And it's true, you see everything pass before your
5 eyes. Everything. Slowly, like a dream, and Marty was … Marty was climbing up me and screaming and we turned … over … once … and … we went through an awning … Sloan's … Which saved my life … And I broke every bone in my face. I have a completely new face. My teeth were all shattered; these are all caps.

From *Blue Window* by Craig Lucas

Exploring pragmatics

One way of thinking about pragmatics is to ask the question: What did so-and-so mean when they said that?

There are many informal terms used to talk about implied meanings. Perhaps you already know the word 'mentionitis'? If you type the word into a search engine, you will find it used in many contexts. The theory is that if a person repeats a name often – even if they claim to dislike them – it shows that there is some love interest. So, repetition can imply underlying obsession. You might think, for example, that the character in Extract C is attached to Billy. In a contradictory way, vehement denials are often taken as a sign of guilt.

There are many other beliefs in popular psychology about ways to tell if someone is being deceitful. In the TV programme *Big Brother: On the Couch* (8 July 2007), a psychologist claimed that speech disturbances such as filled pauses and repetition indicate negative emotion under the surface. Derren Brown (*Tricks of the Mind*) claims that the length of a person's explanation can indicate its truthfulness:

> … probably long-winded when lying … tend to be rather superficial in his descriptions of significant events. Embellishments are suddenly skipped over, and details ignored … If you ask a liar to expand upon his story, the chances are that you'll get a repeat of what you've just heard, rather than an offering of more details.

The amount of specific detail in both Extracts A and G would suggest an honest, if mundane and uninteresting, account.

The playwright Harold Pinter also suggests that the amount a person speaks is significant:

> There are two silences. One when no word is spoken. The other when perhaps a torrent of language is employed. This speech is speaking of a language locked beneath it. That it is continual reference. The speech we hear is an indication of that we don't hear. It is a necessary avoidance, a violent, sly, anguished or mocking smokescreen which keeps the other in its place. When true silence falls we are still left with echo but are nearer nakedness. One way of looking at speech is to say that it is a constant stratagem to cover nakedness.

You should notice that these theories from psychology and drama are similar to some pragmatic theories from linguistic philosophy. Grice's *Maxim of Quantity*, for example, also suggests that the amount a person speaks is significant.

Take it further

If you are interested in drama, look for examples to support Harold Pinter's ideas about silence – or a torrent of speech. Do you agree that speech can be a 'smokescreen' or a 'stratagem to cover nakedness'? What do you think he means by claiming that silence leaves us 'nearer nakedness'?

Independent research

You should use your understanding of pragmatic theories to inform the writing of your dramatic monologue. Apart from the philosopher Grice, you should look again at the theories about 'face' and 'positive or negative politeness' proposed by Brown and Levinson (see page 86).

Writing your commentary

You gain credit for commenting on language use at various levels. Pragmatic theories will be relevant when you discuss the way your character uses language and the meanings that are indirectly implied.

Activity 39

Read the following extract from *An Experienced Woman Gives Advice* by Iain Heggie. The experienced woman of the title is Bella, an attractive teacher who enjoys gardening and has a young lover Kenny. The character Nancy thinks that she is a more suitable girlfriend for Kenny and climbs over into Bella's garden to tell her. She is furious to hear that Bella has decided to dump Kenny and advises Nancy to do the same.

> Nancy: So thank you. Thank you for all that high-flown bull-shit. Thank you for admitting that this this *boy* has knocked you off your perch. (Him and all the dozens before him who have ditched you. I don't blame them.) Because you haven't ditched him. He's ditched you with all your pathetic rules and laying down of the law. Every last one of those guys had the
> 5   sheer spunk to *walk out on you* before it was too late for them. (And I mean that in a nice way.) Thank you. Because you might well be bitter and twisted, but at least you've shown me, you've shown me *again* who I am. How *worthwhile* as a human being I am. Don't think when you were appearing to open your heart and help me out I didn't know exactly how it was going to end. I knew it would end with you trying to get me out your garden,
> 10   out of your life and to pretend to yourself people like me don't exist. I knew *all along*. And I enjoyed every competitive bloody second of it. So I am going to ask him to see me again. I am. I am going to go up and wait for him and tell him he's going to see me again. That we're right for each other. I am. I am. I am. So thank you. Thank you. Thank you.
> (*She climbs over the fence.*)
> Thank you, you poor pathetic bitch.

1   What do you feel the character has left unsaid? For example, does she really mean the following statements?

   - 'Thank you ...'
   - 'how worthwhile as a human being I am ...'
   - I knew it would end with you trying to get me out of your garden ...'
   - 'I enjoyed every competitive bloody second of it ...'
   - I'm going to ask him to see me again ...'
   - 'we're right for each other ...'
   - 'you poor pathetic bitch'

2   How did the writer suggest that we should not take all her statements at face value?

Structuring your monologue

A comic monologue creates a parody of a recognisable 'type' of person for humorous effect. A dramatic monologue needs more than this – a situation involving more than one character, a plot with a climax and resolution and, possibly, some development for the main (speaking) character. The extract in Activity 39, for example, comes near the end of a 'love-triangle' situation, involving two characters as well as the speaker. So, what techniques does a dramatist use to develop the situation or plot? First let's compare it with the techniques of narrative fiction (see pages 112–118).

In dramatic monologues, the 'story' is all from a first person perspective, with no omniscient narrator 'telling' the audience what is happening. Another concept from narrative theory is that of a 'flawed' or 'unreliable' narrator, a person whose view of events cannot be taken at face value. In dramatic monologues, the central character is always unreliable, so the audience must work to create their own version of the story being told to them.

The plot of a narrative often develops in chronological order. In a dramatic monologue, it is likely that all the significant events have already happened by the time the speaker begins. To maintain the interest and tension, the audience needs to piece the 'story' together as the character gradually reveals the situation.

When www.teachers.tv ran a competition to write a short, school-based monologue, they provided tips on the website. The first tip uses the term 'hook' to give advice about the most effective way to begin a dramatic monologue.

Start late – 'the hook'

Grab people's attention. Don't start at the beginning of the story the character wants to tell but towards the end of it, enticing the audience to find out what happens next, as well as wondering what led to this.

One change people often make to a first draft is to plunge into the 'story' at a later point, with less explanation. You should look at the end point of the drama and then experiment with various possible beginnings.

Two useful concepts from drama and scriptwriting refer to techniques for gradually revealing the situation to the audience:

- **foreshadowing**   hints and clues about what is going to happen
- **dramatic irony**   a mismatch between what the audience realises and what the character fails to understand.

Key terms

foreshadowing

dramatic irony

Activity 40

1   Read the end of this monologue from *He Walked on Water* by Viv Ratcliffe. The speaking character is a receptionist in a doctors' surgery.

2   Then look at the opening few paragraphs, Extracts B–G. Try reading each one aloud. What does the audience learn about the main character, situation and other characters?

3   Which would make the most effective opening and why?

4   Would you keep the other paragraphs? If so, in what order?

Independent research

Read the monologue *The Caretaker* by Tony Marchant (search for 'The Caretaker', Sample monologue, on www. teachers.tv). Look out for foreshadowing and dramatic irony in the opening four sections. After each one, note what the character mentions about other characters and the situation. What does this suggest to the audience? How does the remaining part of the monologue maintain interest once the main dramatic event has happened?

Extract A Final section of the monologue

I couldn't be expected to know he'd got meningitis. I mean, I'm not trained in the art of medicine. Doctor Goodheart said we're lucky his wife had the forethought to call an ambulance otherwise I'd be up on a charge of manslaughter. Manslaughter! I've never harmed anyone in my life and now look at me. Stood outside the Labour Exchange with my P45 looking like I've got conjunctivitis I shouldn't wonder. And I didn't even get the chance to rescue my cactus. God knows what will happen to it now. Well that's what you get for being a caring person. The Apostles weren't treated like that. No. They were instructed to carry on the good fight, metaphorically speaking, and wasn't that precisely what I was doing?

Pause

My appointment's in five minutes.

Fiona dabs at her eyes

Hankie's soaked through.

She peers into her vanity mirror

I can't go in looking like this. I'll frighten any prospective employers off!

Her voice tails to a whisper.

But I'm not laughing. I just don't understand.

Extract B

I should have been a doctor; after all I must know as much as them by now what with the amount of queries I handle each day. Would have made a good one at that. Mrs Stevens said it often enough so there must be something in it; though why she was qualified to say so beats me. Still I do think she had a point: ha, ha, ha. 'Fiona,' she'd say, 'the number of times you've saved me a visit.' Well you
5 can't bother the doctor for every little minor ache and scrape, I reply, and she always sounded suitably humbled. She died three weeks ago: cancer of the pancreas the coroner said, but what with her having IBS and the symptoms being so similar, it got misdiagnosed …

Extract C

Short list today. Doctor Goodheart commented on it earlier. Used to be brimming when I first came here. Doctor hadn't a minute to call his own. Can't understand where they've all gone to: area's overcrowded as it is, ooh and what an area. Nothing but grey and black for miles around. It's the forges … the soot from those chimneys! …

Extract D

He's been a long time with Mrs Harper – name and a half that, Harper, because that's exactly what she does do: harp on. Ha, ha, ha. You need a sense of humour in a place like this; they're all so miserable. What with their coughings and splutterings. I do my best to cheer them up though. We– ell it doesn't hurt to laugh; costs nothing I tell them and anyway, I think they feel much better when I counsel them to
5 count their blessings: 'There's always someone worse off. Think of the starving in Africa' and that does the trick every time. I said that to Doctor Goodheart and he mumbled something about the area being deprived. It's deprived alright. Deprived of a sense of humour. Ha, ha.

Extract E

Only two more to see then we've done. Early dinner today, I don't doubt, that is providing he doesn't spend half an hour with each patient. It should be ten minutes but does he listen to me? Does he! He listens to them right enough, but me! What's the good of my trying to get the patients to consider him when he won't consider himself?

Extract F

Empty pews again. That should be 'chairs', I know, but honestly, it's becoming more like my local church than a doctor's surgery. Where is everybody? Perhaps the Second Coming's been and no one's bothered to inform me. That would explain the emptiness. I mean, you don't visit the doctor when you're alright, do you? And He was good at healing the sick. Our Lord, I mean; not unlike the doctor – bit of a miracle
5 worker himself judging by the absences …

Extract G

Had a phone-call earlier. 'I'm not feeling too well; could I have a home visit?' says this patient – can't rightly say I recognise the name: Marter, or something similar – anyway I said, 'I'm not feeling so good myself, but you don't catch me bothering the doctor. Can't you take an aspirin or something? He's a busy man; he can't be at everyone's beck and call, you know.' 'But I've got a stiff neck and I feel ever so hot.'
5 Oh, I do hate it when they get that 'I'm sorry for myself' air.

Writing your commentary

Try to find style models for creating a range of characters of different ages, gender, social background. At least keep a bibliography, listing title and author. Note whether they are comic monologues or present a dramatic situation. Record your study of dramatic techniques. How did the writer represent/create an individual spoken voice? What situation was the character in? What other characters were suggested in the scene? Was there a sub-text? In your commentary, you might mention examples that particularly influenced you, for example:

I wanted to use foreshadowing right from the beginning of my monologue, as Tony Marchant does in 'The Caretaker' by mentioning his hopes for his family, just before he talks about the school musical, which leads to the break-up of his marriage.

3 Devising your character and situation

It is important to choose a character that you can empathise with and who has some dramatic potential – a fatal flaw perhaps. Alan Bennett's monologues successfully create lonely, elderly, northern female characters. You should move away from this range of character types to ones that you understand. It's important to 'hear' a person's speech mannerisms if you want to recreate their idiolect on the page. Sometimes it is easier to choose a person, or type, that irritates you – you will be more aware of distinctive features of that voice and personality. Also aim for a situation that you understand. It is not at all satisfying to read a monologue about an elderly man with Alzheimer's, written by a young female with no experience of – or empathy for – the situation.

News stories can give you ideas for dramatic situations involving ordinary people, for example:

- a young person missing after an exam/argument with a boyfriend/haircut
- a botched post office robbery where the incompetent robber handed a slip of paper with their name and address written on the back
- a lottery winner who hid the news from their family
- a student excluded from school for wearing a religious symbol/tattoo.

You might be interested in a minor character in a novel, film or soap opera and wonder 'who they are'. Or perhaps you wonder about ordinary people from the many 'reality' TV shows, who are placed under the spotlight in an unnatural situation for a short time – who are they back in their real life?

You could try creating characters from a list of 'vital statistics' to see which ones might work for you. Look at the following activity for an example of this kind of random character creation.

Activity 41

1 Make cards for each of the characteristics below and place them under the headings given. Add more of your own ideas for occupation and region. Pick one card from each group to create a character type. Make a few different characters in this way

Gender	Age group	Occupation	Region
female	teenager	student	London
male	20s	DJ	USA
	30 something	call centre manager	Yorkshire
	40 going on 14	unemployed	Home Counties

2 Now suggest a dramatic situation for each character.

3 Decide which character you will use in your dramatic monologue and what situation they are in.

Writing your commentary

How did you choose your character and situation? Did you use any drama techniques to develop the character and create a situation? You should mention these in your commentary. For example: **My idea for a monologue came from a news story about a missing boy whose parents claimed everything was perfect. I thought they probably didn't understand their child at all!**

Developing characters

The technique of hot-seating is used in drama improvisation to develop understanding of a character – their background, personality, motivation, etc.

Activity 42

Work in small groups of four to six people. In turn, each will take the 'hot seat' as the fictional character chosen to be the basis of a monologue.

First, plan some questions. These should range from factual, specific details to more general, probing enquiries, for example:

- Have you any brothers or sisters?
- What do you usually have for breakfast?
- What did you want to be when you were a child?
- What frightens you?

4 Scripting for performance

You have considered the genre of dramatic monologue and the purpose – entertaining with some tension. So now you need to think about the third variable – audience.

In the case of literary genres like narratives and drama, the audience is often hard to define beyond the obvious: 'the audience for this dramatic monologue would be people who enjoy dramatic monologues'. If you suggest that only older, middle-class people enjoy literary genres, you are showing a limited awareness of notions of age and class. The immediate audience for your monologue will be your classmates, and then your teachers and the examiners. However, you should consider not just *who* will be the audience, but *how* and *where* they will experience your monologue.

If you were submitting your work in the hope of getting it performed, your immediate audience may be an editor assessing your written script. However, most people cut out the 'middle man' and find a venue and actors themselves. Many pubs, for example, have a performance space for music, comedy or drama. A pub audience has slightly different needs from a theatre audience; the performance has to cater for people sitting around tables, possibly with their view of the 'stage' obscured, and overcome background noise and distractions. For these reasons, at least, the audience concentration span is likely to be shorter.

If you plan your performance to be in a school/college context, for example for an end of year festival, you need to bear in mind possible limitations concerning content and language use, but you can assume a common understanding of local references.

You should also consider the fact that there are two audiences for words spoken in a drama: the fictional person addressed by the speaker and the actual group of spectators. In *The Caretaker*, for example, it was not clear who the man was speaking to – it was a sort of **soliloquy** (where a character alone on stage utters thoughts and feelings aloud, often directly to the audience). The audience, in this sense, has the characteristics of a sympathetic, but detached listener, someone who is does not know the speaker well, but is prepared to listen carefully to their story without commenting.

In other monologues, there is a separate character implied on the stage. For example, we understand that the character in 'Blots' (page 145) is talking to a psychiatrist. The audience, in this sense, may be in conflict with the main character, who is – in effect – ranting at them.

Writing your commentary

You should explain any decisions you made with a specific audience in mind. For example, about *The Caretaker* monologue: **I thought this monologue would be of particular interest to an audience familiar with a school situation – pupils, their parents, teachers. They would be able to identify with the various characters and understand about school politics.** If your main character is apparently speaking to an audience on the stage as well (another fictional character), as in 'Blots', explain how you created a sense of this person without them actually appearing or speaking, eg **The main audience will soon realise that they are 'overhearing' the character talking to another person, as some of their words are responses to questions or instructions. It is obviously a psychiatrist, as there are words from the semantic field of psychiatry.**

Key term

soliloquy

No, no ... not long at all. You said nine, so I thought I'd be here by 9:10 or so. Not that I wanted to keep you waiting! No, just thought that since you'd be coming from work, you might want to have a drink first and then I could join you. So, I got down here around 9:05. Yeah, what time is it?

5   9:38? Wow. (beat) Actually, I have this issue with lateness. I can't be late. It's not a compulsion, it's a disability. Like the Universe is set against it. See, I know it's Not Cool to be early, so I make a devoted effort to be late. Then, somehow, even though it's a weekend and I have to make a lot of transfers to get down here, the schedules seem to align just for me, and every time I get off one train to make a transfer, the one I need is waiting right 10 across the platform for me. It's a curse. Yeah, so when I got here, I noticed you weren't, so I just walked around the block a few times. Wow, this is embarrassing.

   Oh, ok. Sure, got it. How ... kitschy of you: strawberry margarita it is! Frozen. No salt. Thank you. (*Waits for him to speak.*) You know I saw a set of perfectly good golf clubs 15 tossed out on the curb while I was circling the neighbourhood deciding how long was just too pathetically long to wait for you? Perfectly good golf clubs! Why would someone throw them away? Have you ever noticed that the people who live in this neighbourhood think that once they become Lower East Siders they have to make a show of tossing off their privileged upbringing so that they can fully take on this Bohemian Lifestyle they feel 20 they've earned because they live on Ludlow and Delancey? (*beat*) I'm sorry, I never asked. Where do you live? (*Waits for him to speak.*) Upstairs? You live above this bar, and you were still 38 minutes late to meet me? (*Waits for him to speak.*) Ok. Ok. Why did you ask me out tonight? I'm serious. Why did you invite me on a date the day after we met? Because I thought that was a clear sign that you were actually interested in me. That you actually 25 thought I was a person worth investing some time and energy into. But it's fine. I'm sorry. I jumped to that conclusion all on my own.

   This is a pretty convenient location for you, huh? I don't mean to imply that you had ulterior motives for inviting me to The Bar Directly Below Your Apartment. Not at all. It just seems to me you could have spent a little more time considering the kind of place I 30 might enjoy. It certainly would have improved your chances of 'taking me upstairs.' So to speak.

   Why are people like this? Why, all these years after high school, is it still considered Awesome to pretend to be something you're not so you can hang out with a bunch of people as disingenuous as you are? You are just like every other newly-minted hipster 35 who thinks that the neighbourhood he lives in defines who he is. Who thinks that if he shaves his head and broods just enough to stay under the clinically depressed borderline, no one will know Mommy and Daddy up in Scarsdale are still paying his rent! But don't you get it? That's who you are! Metro North. Country Clubs. And here's the kicker: there's nothing WRONG with that! Why can't we all just be who 40 our mothers raised us to be? Golf clubs and all! (*beat*) I'm sorry. It's not you, it's this neighbourhood; it always gets to me.

   No. It is you. It is people like you who made this neighbourhood into the one place on this island in which people like me don't feel welcome. The one neighbourhood that makes me spend over an hour deciding what to wear because God-forbid I feel Not Cool 45 while sitting in a themed karaoke bar that looks like it was decorated by Don Hoe's puke. My God! I can't believe how much time I have spent feeling inferior because I am considerate. Feeling like a apple-polisher when I take the time to use capital letters and accurate punctuation in friendly emails. Letting people condescend when I don't laugh at the jokes made at the Ugly Girl's expense or when I cringe because you use the word 'retarded' to describe a thing that is not, in fact, mentally impaired. Being fashionably 50 late, and fashionably snide and fashionably ironic does not make you Cool. It makes you an idiot.

Read the monologue on page 152 and answer the questions below.

1 Comment on the audience (in both senses). Who is she speaking to? Do you think the writer had a particular audience (age group, social background, etc) for this monologue in mind?

2 Who is the speaker (main character) – their age, gender, occupation, social background, personality? Identify some features of idiolect that help to create this character.

3 What is the situation at the beginning? Where is she, what is she doing, why? How does the situation change by the end?

4 Which techniques are used? Is the opening an effective hook? Does it capture interest and leave questions unanswered? Is there dramatic irony? Does the audience realise some things before the speaker? Are there clues (foreshadowing) to indicate what will change by the end?

5 How would you redraft it? What changes would you suggest? Can any parts be cut without losing the main point? Could the setting be charged to make it easier for a UK audience to understand?

5 Writing your commentary

Your commentary should be about, but not more than, 500 words long. This means that you need to be concise and to the point. Your final commentary should include explanation of these three areas, although not necessarily in this order:

- how and why you chose the main character and situation
- how you crafted your final script to achieve your purposes for the stated audience
- what you learned about this genre – from studying examples of dramatic monologues and theories about drama and scriptwriting.

The main focus of your commentary is on your final script for a dramatic monologue, so this section should be the longest. Explain some significant language choices that you made in order to achieve particular effects for your intended audience and purpose. Try to comment on various levels of language as the mark scheme rewards this. You do not need to use the general terms (pragmatics, discourse, grammar, lexis, phonology) as long as you are making comments on these aspects. For example:

• **Discourse**	I decided to write the monologue as the character addressing another person, because I felt this added realism. The spectators and the fictional characters are all in a pub. The actual audience are then in the position of eavesdropping on a private row – which is usually irresistible.
• **Pragmatics**	The script is rather like a one-sided telephone conversation, with the other part of the adjacency pair [see Unit 1, page XX and below] missing. This sets up some dramatic tension, as the audience has to guess or assume the other character's contributions.
• **Grammar**	I began with a lot of negatives to establish the character's insecurity.
• **Lexis**	The vocabulary choice created a young, trendy voice, with references to specific cultural things, but I toned down the number of Americanisms to make the script appeal more to a UK audience.
• **Phonology/graphology**	I used capital letters to show the character using a different intonation, as if quoting another voice.

'Adjacency pair' is the technical term used in conversation analysis to refer to exchanges that usually occur in pairs, eg greeting + greeting; apology + acceptance; offer of help + thanks; question + response, and so on.

Assessment objectives

You can earn top marks for your commentary by:

- choosing a range of appropriate terminology to discuss your own language use (including grammar, discourse and pragmatics) (AO1)
- explaining and evaluating the impact of a range of linguistic choices in the stimulus texts and your own writing (AO2).

Assessing the commentary

Below are two examples of commentaries on the monologue on pages 152–153. Notice the points each writer makes to refer to context (genre, purpose, audience) and language features at various levels. Which do you think provides the better explanation of the process the writer went through, making thoughtful choices of style to suit their purposes? (Refer to AOs)

> ## Writing your commentary
>
> In these short versions of the commentary, there is no space for reference to style models, but you should include some in your final commentary.

Example A

In my monologue, I used features of spoken language to create a character. She uses slang (Yeah) to show she is a young person and some USA dialect (Wow, Awesome). She does not use any typically female language, such as tag questions, but she shows that she is more concerned than the man in behaving properly (I can't be late). She also uses formal lexis (disingenuous) to show she is well educated. I created a romantic situation by using a semantic field of dating (invite me on a date, 'taking me upstairs') and bars (strawberry margarita). This would be entertaining for a younger audience. The drama comes because she realises she does not want to go out with him. I show her anger by using capital letters and exclamatory sentences (there's nothing WRONG with that!). At the climax, I use the rhetorical devices of triples (fashionably late … fashionably snide … fashionably ironic) to increase the tension. I finish with a taboo word to show how much she dislikes him. This use of taboo language would make the monologue unsuitable for young children, and older people would probably disapprove. I think I have created a successful drama for people of both sexes aged between 17–25.

Example B

I intended to plunge the audience into the dramatic situation of 'girl meets boy for a first date in a bar'. I wanted the focus to be on the female character's feelings, so the audience only hear her side of the conversation. It is obvious that she is responding to another as there are the second halves of adjacency pairs (Oh, ok. Sure got it.) Her rather obsessive character is established in her discourse, with lexis connected to lateness, time and train travel, as well as critical comments about the consumer society (Perfectly good golf clubs!) and standards of writing (accurate punctuation). This impression is maintained by her choice of high-level lexis, but I also use USA slang (here's the kicker) to create a specific, youthful persona. The dramatic irony comes right at the beginning, where she is clearly accepting his apology for keeping her waiting. The audience should begin to suspect that this man cannot live up to her expectations. This becomes more obvious and is the turning point for the character when she repeats in amazement 'Upstairs?' I use capital letters to indicate her tone of sarcasm (The Bar Directly Below Your Apartment). From this point, she really does give a monologue. I use long, compl ex sentence structures (linked by conjunctions 'when … or … because') to indicate that she is ranting towards the final sentence, which is short and simple in contrast to emphasise her judgement of this type of person.

Glossary of key terms

abbreviation [page 43]
the shortened form of a word or phrase

abstract [page 113]
a brief summary of a story

acronym [page 44]
a means of word formation, by taking the initial letters of other words

active voice [page 29]
the form of verbs where the subject performs the action of the verb, and an object is often required

addresser-addressee relationship [page 27]
the term for the relationship between the speaker/writer and the listener(s)/reader(s)

adjacency pair [page 57]
the term in conversation analysis for the two halves of an interaction between speakers, the first turn and the response

adverbial [page 54]
a word or phrase modifying the verb or clause, typically indicating time, place or manner

agenda-setting [page 57]
the process of deciding what things need to be discussed

anachrony [page 117]
a literary term referring to the use of flashbacks and flash forwards when telling a story, not following the logical order

antonym [page 45]
a word that means the opposite to another

associative meaning [page 45]
the sense of a word that one connects with another concept

audience [page 27]
the receivers of a communication, written or verbal

authorial intervention [page 98]
the degree to which the writer shapes the original spoken words when they are written down

backchannel behaviour [page 17]
the noises the listener makes in the background as response to what the speaker is saying

Black Vernacular English (BVE) [page 79]
a variety of American or Caribbean English, also known as Ebonics (see also African-American Vernacular English, AAVE)

blend [page 41]
the term for the creation of new words by combining and abbreviating two already existing ones

borrowing/ed [page 41]
relating to the adoption of root words from other languages, in order to create new words

channel [page 129]
a medium for the communication of information

chronology [page 117]
the arrangement of narrative events in order, beginning with the earliest events and moving forward in time

clause [page 54]
a unit of grammar within a sentence, containing at least a verb

closed question [page 104]
a question that expects a simple 'yes' or 'no' answer

coda [page 117]
a final additional element to a story, providing a conclusion

collocation [page 45]
the term for words that are typically found, or expected to be found, together

colloquial [page 17]
informal language typically used in speaking

complicating action [page 117]
the events in a story that provide the conflict/drama

compounding [page 42]
the process of creating new words by joining together other, independent words

connotation [page 45]
an idea or feeling that a word creates in addition to its primary meaning

consonant [page 37]
technically, a speech sound where the breath is at least partially obstructed, and which can be added to a vowel to form a syllable

context [page 10]
the circumstances of the text

convergence [page 76]
an individual's adjustment of speech patterns to match people of another group or social identity, with the purpose of expressing a shared identity

conversation analysis [page 57]
the study of how conversations work

corpus [page 17]
a body of written texts (from the Latin, 'corpus', body)

covert prestige [page 38]
the term for pronunciation previously considered to be inferior, but which has now quietly taken on a form considered superior

declarative [page 25]
a grammatical form expressing a statement

deixis [page 15]
a term for words or expressions that rely on context to give them meaning

demotic [page 67]
relating to the language of the people

denotation [page 45]
what a word or phrase literally means or refers to

derivation [page 41]
taking a basic word unit and adding prefixes or suffixes to create new, related words

descriptive [page 49]
the type of approach that describes in a neutral way the grammar in use

direct speech (DS) [page 100]
the exact words uttered by a speaker, presented within quotation marks

discourse [page 11]
a word with several meanings – including the study of the whole text in context, the overall structure of written texts, and the way that texts transmit an underlying ideology

discourse marker [page 19]
words or phrases that mark the divisions between the parts of a communication

divergence [page 76]
an individual's adjustment of speech patterns to be distinct from people of another group or social identity, with the purpose of expressing a feeling of separation

dramatic irony [page 148]
the dramatic term for the mismatch between what the audience realises and what the character fails to understand

elision [page 37]
the joining together of words, leading to the omission of a syllable when spoken or written

ellipsis [page 19]
the omission of part of a sentence that can be understood from the context

estuary English [page 80]
a type of pronunciation increasingly being used, with some features of a 'Cockney' accent merged into a more standard RP, probably originating around the estuary of the River Thames

etymology [page 41]
the study of the origins of words

evaluation [page 117]
the element in a story that shows why the story is of interest to the reader

face [page 86]
the self-image that someone presents publicly

field [page 10]
the broader topic in which something is located

field-related jargon [page 22]
words or expressions specific to particular subjects – often precise, complex and difficult to understand

figurative [page 46]
the term for words that are not used literally, such as in metaphors or similes, often suggesting a comparison between two things

figurative meaning [page 45]
the sense of a word beyond its basic, literal usage

filler/filled pause [page 17]
sounds (er, um) or words (y'know) that are spoken to fill potential gaps in utterances

first person narrative [page 115]
a story that relates events from the point of view of one character, using the pronoun 'I'

first person pronoun [page 29]
I/me or we/us

footing [page 29]
a term referring to participants' stance towards each other in a communication

foreshadowing [page 148]
the hints and clues in a story about what is going to happen

formality [page 12]
the way people adjust the tone of their language to suit the situation they are in (see also register)

framing move [page 58]
words or phrases (see also discourse markers) indicating a change of direction in a conversation

free direct speech (FDS) [page 100]
the term used when the text shows only the words of the speakers, without any comments from the author

free indirect speech (FIS) [page 102]
the term used when the text mixes elements of the third person report of indirect speech with first person direct speech, allowing the author to be free with the phrasing and to create ambiguity or a colloquial feel for literary effect

function [page 10]
the purpose of something, beyond simply its structure

glottal stop [page 38]
a speech sound produced by a momentary closure of the glottis, followed by an explosive

grammar [page 11]
the structure or form of language within a sentence

grapheme [page 35]
the term for the basic unit in written language

graphology [page 11]
the study of the visual aspects of texts

greeting [page 56]
the way people acknowledge each other, indicating in the process the nature of their relationship

hedge [page 54]
a word or phrase that softens the force with which something is said

historic present [page 118]
the term for the use of the present tense in telling something that happened in the past, used for literary effect to create a sense of immediate drama

human limitation [page 115]
the literary term whereby the reader can know only what the narrator knows

idiolect [page 142]
the term for an individual's language or speech patterns

imperative [page 19]
a grammatical form conventionally expressing an order

implicature [page 85]
the term for what the speaker/writer is implying or suggesting beyond the literal sense

inciting moment [page 122]
the literary term for an event that creates disharmony, or destroys the previously existing balance

informality [page 15]
a manner of communication that is spontaneous, private and reliant on the context of the participants' relationship

indirect speech (IS) [page 102]
the communication of what someone else has said, with changes to verb tense and pronouns; also referred to as reported speech

inquit/quotative [page 76]
a verb that functions to introduce direct speech with quotation marks (from the Latin, inquit, 'he said')

intensifier [page 18]
an adverb used to strengthen or modify a verb

interrogative [page 19]
a grammatical form conventionally expressing a question

interruption [page 58]
stopping someone speaking by speaking oneself

intonation [page 40]
the rise and fall of the voice in pitch in speaking

jargon [page 22]
words or expressions specific to particular subjects, often precise, complex and difficult to understand

key constituent [page 31]
an essential part of something whole

lexical item [page 17]
a single word within the vocabulary of a language

lexis [page 11]
the total set of words in a language, often called the 'vocabulary' of a language

literal meaning [page 45]
the most basic sense of a word

marker of sympathetic circularity [page 19]
a word or phrase used in conversation whose purpose is to check that the receiver remains engaged with the conversation

metaphor [page 46]
a comparison between two seemingly unrelated things. Metaphors create a much stronger, more definite image than similes because the object is transformed into the other eg "she was my rock"

mitigated imperative [page 83]
a grammatical form expressing an order in a subtle manner

MLU [page 57]
mean length of utterance – a statistical term for assessing in a conversation how much each person speaks

modal auxiliary verb [page 51]
a verb that modifies the meaning of the main verb in a clause

modal expression [page 19]
a word or phrase indicating the attitude of the speaker towards the situation being described

mode [page 10]
the text type
the way that language is transmitted from person to person

monologue [page 142]
a discourse of one speaker, ranging from a person alone speaking to themselves, to one person addressing a large public audience

morpheme [page 41]
the smallest meaningful unit of language

morphology [page 11]
the study of word formation

narrative [page 113]
a construct describing a sequence of events, requiring a narrator to tell a story to an audience

narrative report of a speech act (NRSA) [page 102]
the written summary of someone's speech; 'they bickered for hours'

negative face [page 86]
someone's right, in interactions with others, not to be imposed upon

negative politeness [page 86]
the use of strategies, such as more formal lexis and grammar, to emphasise respect when there is a social distance between speakers

neologism [page 41]
the term for a new word or expression

nominalisation [page 29]
the process of transforming verbs into nouns

omniscient narrator [page 115]
a third-person narrator, telling a story from the outside and knowing both everything that occurs and the internal workings of all the characters

onomatopoeia [page 44]
the formation of a word reflecting the sound of the object or action to which it refers

open question [page 104]
a question that expects more than a simple 'yes' or 'no' answer

orientation [page 113]
the information that sets up a story and provides the context in which the narrative unfolds

overlapping speech [page 58]
where one speaker starts before the previous speaker has finished

passive voice [page 29]
indicates that the grammatical subject is the recipient (not the source) of the action denoted by the verb

past tense [page 51]
the form of a verb expressing something that occurred or existed previously

phatic [page 25]
referring to the social aspect of communication, rather than its message

phoneme [page 35]
the smallest sound in a language that is capable of conveying a distinction in meaning

phonology [page 11]
the study of speech sounds in a language

phrase [page 53]
a small group of words (or a single word) forming a grammatical unit within clauses and sentences

pitch [page 40]
the level of a voice, the highness or lowness of a tone

politeness [page 86]
the theory that participants pay attention to the other's face needs in order for a conversation to succeed

positive face [page 86]
someone's need, in interactions with others, to be liked and accepted

positive politeness [page 86]
the use of strategies, such as shared dialect, informal lexis, informal grammar and more direct requests, to emphasise solidarity with others

post-modification [page 53]
putting a word or words after a noun to build a phrase

pragmatics [page 12]
the study of how meanings are conveyed in the social contexts of language use

prefix [page 41]
a morpheme added to the beginning of a word to modify its meaning

premodification [page 53]
putting a word or words before a noun to build a phrase

prescriptive [page 49]
the type of approach that lays down the rules for 'correct grammar'

present tense [page 51]
the form of a verb typically expressing something occurring or existing now

prestige [page 38]
the term for pronunciation considered to be superior

real world narrative [page 117]
a story that relates events that actually happened, as opposed to fiction

Received Pronunciation (RP) [page 67]
the accent provided as the standard pronunciation of individual words in a dictionary, also recognised as a marker of social status

register/formality [page 12]
a form of language appropriate to a particular situation or context, including its mode, tenor and function

reported speech [page 102]
the communication of what someone else has said, with changes to verb tense and pronouns; also referred to as indirect speech

result/resolution [page 117]
how a story finishes, finding an ending/solution to the conflict the story sets out

root [page 41]
the morpheme, the basic unit, from which more complex words may be created by the addition of extra parts

salutation [page 56]
a greeting, for example at the beginning of a letter

schwa [page 39]
the most common phoneme in spoken English, represented by the symbol of an inverted 'e'; it occurs in nearly every polysyllabic word and is often called a 'weak vowel'

second person pronoun [page 29]
you (singular or plural), thee, thou in some forms of English

semantic field [page 22]
a group of words drawn from a particular area of experience, eg. Food or colours

semantics [page 12]
the study of the relationships between words and meanings

showing [page 115]
a narrative technique whereby a scene is described and it is left to the reader to draw conclusions

slang [page 42]
informal language, usually spoken, often short-lived

soliloquy [page 151]
the dramatic device whereby a character alone on stage utters his/her thoughts and feelings aloud

Standard English (SE) [page 43]
the conventional and accepted forms of words and usage in the English language (standard is sometimes written with a lower-case letter as a more neutral description)

stigmatised [page 38]
the term for language use considered to be inferior

stress [page 39]
place emphasis on a word or syllable, in speech often perceived as increased volume

structure [page 27]
the way that language is put together and given shape

sub-text [page 142]
the literary term for underlying ('pragmatic') meanings within a text

subject-specific lexis [page 22]
a group of words relating to a particular topic

suffix [page 41]
a morpheme added to the end of a word to modify its meaning

synonym [page 45]
a word that has the same, or similar, meaning, to another

taboo language [page 71]
language that is considered forbidden within a certain social circumstance because it is highly inappropriate

tag question [page 18]
a short interrogative structure attached to a declarative, eg. 'Nice day, isn't it?'

telling [page 115]
a narrative technique whereby explicit judgements are made on characters' motives and the like

tenor [page 10]
the nature of the relationship between the writer/speaker and the audience, reflecting their roles and status

terms of address [page 17]
the manner in which someone refers to another, reflecting the nature of their relationship

text [page 10]
a sequence of sentences or utterances in spoken, written, printed or electronic language

text structure/genre conventions [page 56]
the way that a text is put together and given shape, with reference to the styles that receivers expect according to subject matter

third person narrative [page 115]
a story that relates the events using 'he', 'she' and 'they' to refer to all the characters, though the story can still be told from the point of view of one character only

transactional [page 25]
referring to language used to pass on information

turntaking [page 85]
the ways speakers manage to exchange turns in a conversation without speaking at the same time or leaving awkward pauses

utterance [page 58]
the physical realisation of a sentence in its spoken or written form

verbatim [page 98]
reproducing a speech exactly – every word spoken, in order

voice [page 115]
an opinion or attitude uttered by someone that reflects that person's identity

vowel [page 37]
the nucleus of a syllable, technically a speech sound produced by comparatively open configuration of the vocal tract

word-class [page 44]
a category of words of similar function, such as a noun

Published by:
Pearson Education Limited
Edinburgh Gate
Harlow
Essex CM20 2JE

© Pearson Education 2008

First published 2008
10 9 8 7 6
ISBN 978-1-84690-242-0

Printed in Malaysia (CTP-PPSB)

Pearson Education Limited accepts no responsibility for the content on any third party Websites to which a link from this book is provided or for any use of personal data by the third party operating such a Website. The links are provided 'as is' with no warranty, express or implied, for the information provided within them.

Picture Credits
The publisher would like to thank the following for their kind permission to reproduce their photographs: Corbis: Bettmann 98; Kevin Cruff 46; © Crown Copyright 2002-2008: 32; Getty Images: AFP/Stringer 52; Cambridge Jones/contributor 78; Nat Travers/contributor 136; Scoopt/contributor 143; Time Life Pictures/Stringer 115; Ronald Grant Archive: British Screen Productions 69; Lebrecht Music and Arts Photo Library: 35t; Pearson Education Ltd: Professor Aitchison 131; TopFoto: 120. All other images © Pearson Education.

Picture Research by: Ann Thomson

We are grateful to the following for permission to reproduce copyright material:
10 Downing Street for the speech by Tony Blair on the Conference on Education on 4th September 1997, Crown copyright; AP Watt and Jon Ronson for an extract from *Think outside the box* by Jon Ronson originally published in *The Guardian* on 21st October 2006, used with permission of AP Watt on behalf of Jon Ronson Ltd; Lynn Barber for an extract from her interview with Graham Norton as published in *The Observer* 28th October 2001, used with permission; Julie Blake for an extract from her weblog 'E-Julie' on Thursday 19th January 2006, used with permission; Jean Binta Breeze for the poem 'Caribbean Woman' by Jean Binta Breeze published by Bloodaxe Books; Cambridge University Press for the table "CANCODE top 40" from Cambridge and Nottingham Corpus of Discourse in English copyright © Cambridge University Press 2008. This publication has made use of the Cambridge and Nottingham Corpus of Discourse in English (CANCODE). CANCODE was funded by Cambridge University Press and is a five-million word computerised corpus of spoken English, made up of recordings from a variety of settings in the countries of the United Kingdom and Ireland. The corpus is designed with conversational goals. CANCODE was built by Cambridge University Press and the University of Nottingham and it forms part of the CIC (Cambridge International Corpus). It provides insights into language use, and offers a resource to supplement what is already known about English from other, non-corpus-based research, thereby providing valuable and accurate information for researchers and those preparing teaching materials. Sole copyright of the corpus resides with Cambridge University Press from whom all permission to reproduce material must be obtained; Department of Transport for slogans from the THINK! Road Safety Campaign www.thinkroadsafety.gov.uk Crown Copyright © 2008; Development Hell Ltd for extracts adapted from the an interview with Paul McCartney by Sylvia Patterson published in *The Word*, July 2007 and an interview with Van Morrison by Barry McIlheney published in The Word, August 2007 copyright © 2007; The English and Media Centre for an interview with Malcolm Coulthard by Alison Ross, first published in emagazine 15, 2002 by kind permission of the English and Media Centre; Guardian News & Media Ltd for extracts from "How English lessons got lost in translation" by James Simpson published in *The Guardian* 19th June 2007; "'You can't say all strippers are abused': Dita Von Teese, the 'queen of burlesque', on fame, fortune and feminism" by Hannah Pol published in *The Guardian* 28th June 2007; and the Guardian Weekly advert published in *The Guardian Weekly* 20th July 2007 copyright © Guardian 2007; Duncan Haye's Office, United Agents for a transcript from *The Office* Episode 1 written by Ricky Gervais and Stephen Merchant reprinted with permission; Mirrorpix for an extract from "Football: King James too hot for the Saints" published in *The Sunday Mirror* 12th August 2007 copyright © Mirrorpix 2007; Professor John Mullam for an extract from "Word of the week: Innit" by Professor Mullam, published in *The Guardian* 31st July 2002 copyright © Professor John Mullam; News International Syndication for an extract from "Hey, Hey it's the Monkeys" by Craig McLean published in *The Times Magazine* 28th July 2007 copyright © NI Syndication Ltd 2007; Kate Oliver and the English and Media Centre for reproduction of an email, by kind permission of Kate Oliver and the English and Media Centre; Oxford University Press for an excerpt on text messages from *Concise Oxford Dictionary 11e*, 2004 reproduced by permission of Oxford University Press; PFD for the poem "Translate" by Benjamin Zephaniah copyright © Benjamin Zephaniah, reproduced by permission of PFD www.pfd.co.uk on behalf of Benjamin Zephaniah; The Random House Group Ltd for an extract from *Tricks of the Mind* by Derren Brown, published by Channel 4 Books/Transworld. Reprinted by permission of The Random House Group Ltd; Sheil Land Associates for an extract from *George Don't Do That....* by Joyce Grenfell published by Hodder and Stoughton copyright © 1977 by Joyce Grenfell, reproduced by permission of Sheil Land Associates; Simon & Schuster, Inc for an extract from "Raising children who think for themselves" by Elisa Medhus copyright © 2001 Elisa Medhus, reprinted with permission of Atria Books, a Division of Simon & Schuster, Inc for Beyond Words Publishing; Sound Advice (London) Ltd for an extract about 'Health & Safety' from the 2007 Cornbury Music Festival leaflet, used with permission; Writers House LLC for an extract from the speech "I Have a Dream" by Dr Martin Luther King Jr, reprinted by arrangement with The Heirs to the Estate of Martin Luther King Jr., c/o Writers House as agent for the proprietor New York, NY, copyright © 1963 Martin Luther King Jr, copyright renewed 1991 Coretta Scott King; and students Emily Hammerton-Barry, Kisa Charles, Declan Doyle, Neil Gaukwin, Paul Goldhawk, Alicia Gregory, Jonny Gregory, Lauren Nicholson, and Viv Ratcliffe for assistance and material.

Every effort has been made to trace the copyright holders and we apologise in advance for any unintentional omissions. We would be pleased to insert the appropriate acknowledgement in any subsequent edition of this publication.